Privacy
In The
Workplace

Privacy
In The
Workplace

A GUIDE
FOR
HUMAN RESOURCE
MANAGERS

Jon D. Bible
and
Darien A. McWhirter

Q

QUORUM BOOKS
NEW YORK • WESTPORT, CONNECTICUT • LONDON

This publication is designed to provide accurate and authoritative information in regard to the subject matter covered. It is sold with the understanding that the publisher is not engaged in rendering legal, accounting, or other professional advice. If legal advice or other expert assistance is required, the services of a competent professional person should be sought. *From A Declaration of Principles jointly adopted by a Committee of the American Bar Association and a Committee of Publishers.*

Library of Congress Cataloging-in-Publication Data

Bible, Jon D.
  Privacy in the workplace: A guide for human
resource managers/Jon D. Bible and Darien A. McWhirter
  Includes bibliographical references and index.
    1. Privacy, Right of—United States.   2. Employee
rights—United States.   I. McWhirter, Darien A. (Darien
Auburn)   II. Title.
KF1262.B52   1990   344.73'012596   90-9075
                         347.30412596
ISBN 0-89930-473-7 (lib. bdg. : alk. paper)

British Library Cataloguing in Publication Data is available.

Library of Congress Catalog Card Number: 90-9075
ISBN:0-89930-473-7

First published in 1990

Quorum Books, 88 Post Road West, Westport, CT 06881
An imprint of Greenwood Publishing Group, Inc.

Printed in the United States of America

The paper used in this book complies with the Permanent Paper Standard issued by the National Information Standards Organization (Z39.48-1984).

10 9 8 7 6 5 4 3 2 1

To the memory of
Justice Louis D. Brandeis
and
Samuel Warren
in commemoration of the publication
of their article, "The Right
to Privacy," by the *Harvard
Law Review* in 1890.

Contents

Preface

This is a book about *workplace privacy*. In a nutshell, this term has to do with the extent to which the law protects employees and job applicants from attempts by employers to learn information about them and to regulate their activities on and off the job. Just a few years ago this book would have required little time to write, for the law barely recognized the concept of job-related privacy. Under the legal doctrine of employment-at-will, most workers were deemed to hold their jobs at their bosses' pleasure, and this gave the latter almost carte blanche to dictate their conditions of employment. In the last two decades, however, great change has occurred in this area. While recent laws and court rulings have certainly not immunized employees and applicants against unwanted intrusions on their working lives, they have created some sturdy shields to use against invasive employer actions. In view of what has transpired, the word *privacy*—on this, the one hundredth anniversary of the birth of that legal concept—now has real meaning in the workplace setting.

Changes in job-related privacy law are occurring at such a breathtaking pace that it is hard for those affected to track new developments. At times it must seem to employers that as soon as they digest one new legal requirement, two more appear; as a result, even the most well-intentioned boss finds him or herself hard-pressed to know what is permissible. How should he or she balance, administratively and legally, the employees' privacy interests as well as business needs? What adjustments should be made in light of the prevalence of illicit drugs in the workplace and the advent of testing for these substances, the heightened ability of computers to monitor employees, and the trend toward employer liability for negligent hiring practices, to name but a few problems? To what extent should decisions be affected by these facts: the number of workplace privacy case jury verdicts against employers nationwide increased twentyfold between the periods 1981–84 and 1985–87; and whereas the average verdict in these cases was $0 in 1979–80, it was $316,000 in 1985–87?[1]

This book addresses these questions. In language stripped of as much legal jargon as possible, it discusses some basic aspects of our legal system and considers why employee screening attracts so much interest these days. It reviews factors impinging on the employers' right to screen, tracing both the evolution of the privacy concept from its recognition in an 1890 legal article to its current status as a constitutional, statutory and common law doctrine, and the growth of what is now known as the field of "employment law." Finally, it explores the privacy implications of specific employment screening devices such as drug, AIDS and polygraph tests. The book has two main goals: to help employers, managers and workers appreciate the nature and extent of each other's legal rights and duties, and to furnish these parties with practical suggestions for avoiding the myriad legal pitfalls which can arise in different work-related situations.

On July 26, 1990 President George Bush signed into law the Americans with Disabilities Act of 1990. The act outlaws discrimination by employers against handicapped individuals. The employment provisions of the act go into effect on July 26, 1992 for employers with 25 or more employees, and on July 26, 1994 for employers with 15 or more employees. The law makes it clear that it will not protect people who take illegal drugs. The act also ammended the Vocational Rehabilitation Act of 1973, discussed in the text, to make it clear that this law also does not protect those who take illegal drugs. The major effect of this new law will be to prevent employment discrimination by employers who are not currently covered either by the Vocational Rehabilitation Act or a state law outlawing handicap discrimination in employment. The vast majority of employers in the United States are already covered by state laws outlawing discrimination against the handicapped. The full text of this act is contained in the appendix.

One caveat: this is not a do-it-yourself book. Local law varies greatly, and the outcomes of legal cases turn largely on the facts involved. Although this book furnishes advice about many aspects of privacy law, specific legal problems should be entrusted to a competent attorney who can assess the situation in light of the law existing at that time and in that locale.

NOTE

1. THE BUREAU OF NATIONAL AFFAIRS, INC., WORKPLACE PRIVACY: EMPLOYEE TESTING, SURVEILLANCE, WRONGFUL DISCHARGE, AND OTHER AREAS OF VULNERABILITY (1987), 1–2.

PART I

SETTING THE STAGE: AN INTRODUCTION TO THE LEGAL SYSTEM

To appreciate the extent to which the law protects employee privacy, one needs a basic understanding of how our legal system works. One also needs some insight into why employers want and may even need to conduct background checks on employees and job applicants, test them for drugs and other substances, and engage in other types of screening to learn certain things about them. This section provides this background information. Chapter one explains where law originates, how the court system works, and how to classify employers as "public" or "private" for purposes of deciding if they are subject to federal constitutional constraints in dealing with workers and applicants. Chapter two traces the development of employment law during the last century, and chapter three looks at how "privacy" law has evolved as a legal concept during that time.

1

The American Legal System

SOURCES OF LAW

There are four sources of American law. Besides company policies and employment contracts, these sources may afford legal rights to employees. *Constitutional* law comes from the constitutions of the United States and the fifty states. *Statutory* law consists of Congressional and state legislation. City ordinances are also included in this category. *Administrative* law involves rules enacted by federal, state and local administrative boards and agencies. Last, and the oldest source, is the *common* law. This is a body of law with British roots which has been developed over the years by courts in each state to resolve legal disputes in areas in which no constitutional, statutory or administrative law exists.[1] Common law judges reach their decisions by considering how similar cases have been decided, how local custom suggests the dispute should be resolved, and what seems fair. Each ruling becomes a *precedent* to be examined by lawyers and judges in future cases. Contract and tort law, where so much recent legal activity affecting workers has occurred, are two examples of areas largely judge-made or common in nature.

With so many kinds of law—and often conflicting court cases construing that law—it is no wonder that keeping up with legal developments is so hard for employers. This problem is compounded by the fact that at times laws stemming from the various sources are contradictory. For example, a state may pass a statute allowing something barred by the U.S. Constitution, or an administrative agency may enact a rule which conflicts with a common law court case. Following is an oversimplified summary of how these conflicts are resolved: The federal Constitution prevails in the event of a conflict with federal, state or local statutes, agency rules and ordinances. State constitutions prevail over conflicting state statutes and rules, the common law, and local law, but must yield to the federal Constitution. Federal statutes supercede state and local statutes and ordinances and both federal and state agency rules; state statutes control state and local rules and local ordinances; and the common law is generally superceded by statutory, agency, and constitutional law.

CIVIL AND CRIMINAL LAW

Primary Differences

Law is either civil or criminal in nature. The civil law regulates the conduct of and disputes between private parties. Whether X breached a contract with Y, for example, is a civil matter involving only X's and Y's rights and duties with relation to each other; if a breach occurred it harms only Y. Criminal law, in contrast, deals with legal relations between people and society. Congress and the state legislatures decide what conduct to call criminal and what the penalties for it should be; when they pass laws criminalizing certain behavior, they are effectively saying that the behavior is bad enough that to engage in it is to commit an offense against society. One who murders, rapes or steals, for example, is deemed to have hurt not just the victim but society as a whole.

Procedures, Burden of Proof, and Remedies

The main civil remedy is damages, money which the court orders the wrongdoer (defendant) to pay to the victim (plaintiff). There are several kinds and they serve different purposes. *Compensatory* damages seek to reimburse the injured party for his out-of-pocket losses. This sum can be very large. In personal injury cases, for example, damages may compensate for medical bills, lost wages and earning capacity, and "pain and suffering," and thus be in the multimillion dollar range. *Punitive* damages may be awarded to the plaintiff if the defendant's conduct is especially outrageous; they are designed not to reimburse the plaintiff, but to punish the defendant and make an example of him to society to deter others from doing what he did. *Nominal* damages are a small sum, usually one dollar, which signify that a legal wrong occurred but caused the plaintiff little if any harm.

Another form of legal relief is the injunction, a court order forbidding or requiring the defendant to perform some act. Courts grant injunctions if damages would not give the victim meaningful relief. Assume, for example, that a family near a university fraternity which has loud parties files a nuisance suit seeking relief from the noise. For the court to order the fraternity to pay damages would mean little to the plaintiff, who wants peace and quiet. In this case the court might issue an injunction allowing the fraternity to have parties only at certain times and under certain conditions.

Criminal penalties include fines, which are paid to the government, and imprisonment. Occasionally a court may require a defendant to make restitution to a victim, but usually criminal victims are not compensated for their losses. Fines and jailings are based on the notion that because crimes theoretically involve offenses against society, any penalties imposed should benefit society; hence, society collects the fine and presumably profits from having the defendant jailed, in that he will be removed from the public's midst and hopefully dissuaded from erring again and others will be deterred from engaging in similar misconduct.

Besides the remedies involved, civil and criminal law differs in terms of who begins and pursues the case and the burden of proof. Criminal cases are prosecuted by the United States Department of Justice or by state district attorneys (depending on whether the crime is state or federal) who have complete discretion over whether to start and continue the case. The government pays the prosecution costs and has the burden of proof: to win, it must prove the defendant's guilt "beyond a reasonable doubt," meaning that if a juror has a "reasonable doubt" about guilt he is supposed to rule "not guilty." In civil cases, the victim (plaintiff) must pursue the case and pay his own attorney fees and court costs. Sometimes there will be a fee-shifting statute allowing the court to make the loser pay the costs for both sides, but the general rule in this country— unlike Britain, for example, where the loser pays both sides' costs—is that each party in a civil suit "pays his own freight." Plaintiffs have the burden of proof in civil cases, but it is less exacting than the criminal burden: to win, they must prove their case "by a preponderance of the evidence," which basically means that their evidence must be more persuasive than the defendant's.

In most cases an act will involve a crime but not a civil offense, or vice versa. Breach of contract, for instance, is a civil wrong, whereas speeding is a crime. An act may, however, involve both offenses. Every state has a law making assault a crime, for example, and a state could prosecute a defendant for violating that law, in which case it will control the case, pay prosecution costs, have to prove guilt beyond a reasonable doubt, and receive any fine imposed by the court. In addition, the victim could sue the defendant for civil assault, in which case he will control the lawsuit, pay the costs, have to prove the offense by a preponderance of the evidence, and receive any damages awarded. Given the differences in burdens of proof, criminal and civil litigation based on the same facts could result in a not guilty verdict in the criminal case and a guilty verdict in the civil case.

State of Mind

For the most part, both the civil and the criminal law operate on the premise that a person is not guilty of an offense unless, when he committed a harmful act, he had a "guilty state of mind." The law recognizes four types of guilty mind, or *mens rea*. The first involves *intent*. One acts intentionally when it is his conscious object to cause a result.[2] Thus, if X shoots at Y at such a distance that his chances of hitting him are small, but with the desire to kill him, X intends to kill Y; and if the bullet hits Y in a vital spot and Y dies, X is guilty of intentional murder.

The second type of guilty mind involves acts done *knowingly*. One acts knowingly when he does not mean to cause a particular result but is "aware that it is practically certain that his conduct will cause" that result.[3] The distinction between intentional and knowing conduct is subtle, and indeed some commentators take the position that the terms are synonymous or that the latter category is subsumed in the former. Assume, for example, that to kill his mother F for her life insurance, E places a bomb on a plane that he knows is carrying both F and G. If the bomb explodes and F and G perish, some jurisdictions would hold that E intentionally killed F, as he desired her death, but knowingly killed G, whose death E regarded as a regrettable necessity but was also one which E knew was practically certain to occur. Others, however, would hold that E intended to kill both F and G, on the theory that one is guilty of intent when, whatever his desire may be, one knows that a result is almost certain to follow from his conduct.

Recklessness exists if an actor neither meant for a result to occur nor knew it was almost certain to occur, but knew that his conduct *might* cause the result. Specifically, recklessness involves "consciously disregard[ing] a substantial and unjustifiable risk that a [certain result will occur]." The risk must be "of such a nature and degree that, considering the nature and purpose of the actor's conduct and the circumstances known to him, its disregard involves a gross deviation from the standard of conduct that a law-abiding person would observe in the actor's situation."[4] Thus, where a defendant, having previously suffered blackouts and been warned not to drive alone, was driving alone when his car went out of control and killed another motorist, he was found guilty of driving "in willful and wanton disregard for the rights or safety of others." The court stated that one is guilty of such disregard where, knowing of the existing conditions "and conscious from such knowledge that injury will likely or probably result from his conduct, and with reckless indifference to the consequences," he goes ahead with the conduct.[5]

The last of the guilty mental states is *negligence*. The civil law defines this as "conduct which falls below the standard established by law for the protection of others against unreasonable risk of harm," with this standard being that of "a reasonable man under like circumstances," and the term *conduct* including both an act and a failure to act where one has a duty to do so.[6] One negligently causes a result, therefore, when she fails to exercise the care that a reasonable person would have exercised under the circumstances. The criminal law standard is stricter. One "acts negligently with respect to a material element of [a criminal] offense when he should be aware of a substantial and unjustifiable risk that the material element exists or will result from his conduct." The risk must be such that the actor's failure to perceive it, "considering the nature and purpose of his conduct and the circumstances known to him, involves a gross deviation from the standard of care that a reasonable person would observe in the actor's situation."

At the heart of these mental states is the concept of *fault*. Simply put, except for a few instances in which one can be held strictly liable for the results of his acts,[7] one is liable for harm he commits only if he was at fault when he performed the act, and one is at fault only if he acted intentionally, knowingly, recklessly or negligently. This explains, for example, why if *X* is adjudged to have been insane when he shot and killed *Y*, he is not guilty of murder: to murder is to intentionally cause one's death, and *X* cannot have intended *Y*'s death if he was so impaired when he pulled the trigger that he could not comprehend the consequences of his act. The penalty for harmful conduct, moreover, depends upon the degree of fault. The law attaches the severest penalties to intentional misconduct, on the theory that one who harms another intentionally is the most blameworthy and deserving of punishment, and, on a sliding scale, lesser penalties to knowing, reckless and negligent acts.

CLASSIFICATIONS OF LAW

Law can be classified in many ways. Corporate, securities, agency and environmental law are examples. From the standpoint of employee privacy, two of the most important branches of law are contract and tort law. Many legal concepts which now protect workers originated there.

Contract law involves the issue of whether a legally binding agreement has been formed, and if so, the consequences of its breach by one or more of the parties. Contracts may be express, where the parties spell out orally or in writing the terms of their bargain, or implied, where an intent to contract is inferred from the parties' statements and actions. Contract law is part of civil law and has recently become an important weapon in the employees' battle for legal rights in the workplace.

For years courts held that employees worked at their employer's will—hence the term *employment-at-will*—and enjoyed only those rights (if any) that were explicitly created by company policy or by their employment contract. During the last few years, however, courts have increasingly found employee rights implied in employment relationships, and this trend has produced several contractually-based exceptions to the at-will doctrine. In *Pugh v. See's Candies, Inc.*,[8] for example, a company vice president with thirty-two years of service was fired. When he asked why, he was told, "Look deep within yourself." The court found that his length of service, a series of commendations and promotions, the lack of any criticism of his work, and the assurance by his superiors that if he did a good job his future with the company would be secure created an implied contract that was breached by his firing. In some states a "covenant of good faith and fair dealing" has also been found to be implied in employment contracts.[9]

Tort law, which derives from a French word which essentially means civil wrong, is a branch of civil law that deals with non-criminal and non-contractual injuries. Assault, battery, negligence, trespass and defamation are examples of torts. Recently this field of law has joined contract law as a source of important exceptions to the employment-at-will doctrine.

Courts in some states, for example, have recognized a wrongful discharge tort in cases involving employees fired for filing workers' compensation claims or for other reasons held to violate "public policy."[10] During the last one hundred years, moreover, the law has recognized at least four distinct torts in the area of privacy both on and off the job. The origins and current status of the privacy concept are discussed in Chapter three.

THE COURT SYSTEM

The federal government and each state has its own court system. The federal system and most state systems have three levels: trial courts, intermediate appeals courts, and a supreme court. There are various kinds of trial courts in the federal and state systems and they have different names and functions. Some states, for example, have county and district courts and special forums such as probate and divorce courts; whether a plaintiff must file a suit in one or the other depends on the nature of the dispute and relief sought. Other states have different names for courts which perform largely the same functions. For example, New York calls its trial courts *supreme* courts, and Pennsylvania uses the term *chancery* courts. Texas has two high courts: the Texas Supreme Court, which handles civil appeals, and the Court of Criminal Appeals, which deals with criminal cases. Other states have one supreme court for civil and criminal cases, although not all states use that name. New York, for example, calls its highest court the Court of Appeals.

The federal system has courts of general and limited jurisdiction. Tax courts are an example of the latter: as their name reveals, their jurisdiction is limited to tax controversies. One may have a dispute heard in the general jurisdiction or federal district courts only if the plaintiff(s) and defendant(s) are citizens of different states and the amount in controversy exceeds $50,000, or if the dispute involves a federal constitutional, statutory or treaty provision; otherwise the case must be filed in state court. Whether a suit is in state or federal court may make a real difference: among other things the rules of procedure and evidence are different, which could make it tactically advantageous to be in one court rather than the other. Federal judges also serve for life, which theoretically makes them less susceptible to the pressures of public opinion than state judges, who in some states are elected by the voters and in others are appointed but keep their offices only if they are later approved by the voters.

Litigation begins in the trial courts, in which the judge, or jury if it is a jury trial, decides what the facts are and their legal consequences. The loser may appeal to an intermediate appeals court, where the case will be heard by a panel of judges, usually three, who will not retry the facts but instead will decide if the trial court correctly applied the law. The loser at this level may appeal to the highest state court or, in the federal system, to the U.S. Supreme Court. Most high courts have by constitution or statute been given discretion to decide which cases to hear, so that most appeals do not result in a high court decision. The U.S. Supreme Court, for example, issues decisions only in cases deemed to be of major national importance, which account for a very small percentage of all the cases appealed to it. It disposes of the rest by a process known as denying *certiorari*,[11] which leaves the intermediate appeals court's ruling intact but expresses no opinion on the merits of that ruling, or by summarily affirming or reversing the appeals court based on the briefs and the lower court records which have been submitted to it.

Supreme Court decisions are binding throughout the country. Decisions of the thirteen intermediate federal appellate courts, called United States Circuit Courts of Appeal, are binding in the states in that circuit, and those of the hundreds of district courts must be followed in that district. A federal district embraces either a state or, if a state is large, a part of that state. State court rulings are generally binding only in that state. As readers encounter cases in this book, therefore, they must keep in mind that the law announced in these cases is not necessarily binding in their area; thus, an opinion by the Ninth Circuit Court of Appeals, which embraces the western states, is not mandatory authority in Texas, which is in the Fifth Circuit. At the same time, because courts regard decisions by other courts as persuasive authority, the Fifth Circuit would pay attention and tend to follow the Ninth Circuit ruling if it were faced with a similar case.

PUBLIC VERSUS PRIVATE EMPLOYMENT

The "State Action" Doctrine

When people think they have been treated illegally, they often protest that their constitutional rights have been violated. The National Football League Players' Association made this claim when the NFL instituted its drug testing program, as have many workers confronted by such tests. What many people fail to realize, however, is that the U.S. Constitution is actually quite limited in scope and does not apply to most employers. To appreciate the implications of the Constitution in terms of workplace privacy, one must first understand to whom it does apply.

The constitutional provisions usually invoked in attacks on employee screening programs are the Fourth Amendment, which bars unreasonable searches and seizures, and the constitutional right of privacy. Like the rest of the first ten amendments, called the Bill of Rights, the Fourth Amendment technically applies only to the federal government.[12] The due process clause of the Fourteenth Amendment applies to state governments, however, and through a process called incorporation courts have, during the last half century, held that the Bill of Rights applies to state and local governments by virtue of being "incorporated" in that clause.[13] Thus, federal, state and local employers are subject to the Fourth Amendment and to the constitutional right of privacy. By contrast, private employers are generally not subject to these provisions, meaning that regardless of whatever other laws may be violated by their employment policies, those policies cannot be said to violate their workers' constitutional rights.

The reason for the use of the word "generally" in the preceding sentence is that courts have expanded the concept of Fourteenth Amendment "state action" to include cases involving private actors. Several theories may make private acts state acts and thus trigger constitutional constraints. State action exists if (1) a state assists a private party in abridging a constitutional right;[14] (2) a private party exercises power traditionally reserved to the government;[15] (3) the extent of governmental involvement in private conduct so blurs the line between the private party and the government as to make the conduct state action;[16] (4) a private actor implements a program prescribed by a government entity;[17] or (5) state control of a private party's acts is sufficient to make the acts the state's responsibility.[18]

Under any of these theories a private employer could be held subject to the constitutional provisions invoked in attacks on job screening programs. If, for example, an employer becomes so intertwined with a government that the entity controls his workers, he might be deemed an arm of that government. If workers perform their tasks on government property or under government supervision, their employer could be a "state actor." The same is true of a private employer who implements a drug testing program prescribed by federal statute or administrative rule. It must be stressed, however, that the Supreme Court articulated the state action theories discussed above when it was far less sensitive about distinguishing between government and private action than it has been lately. Rather than expand or even preserve the state action concept, the Court under Chief Justices Warren Burger and William H. Rehnquist has narrowed it, holding, for example, that state action exists only if the private actor displaces the government.[19] Thus, although private employers with links to a government entity can never be entirely sure that constitutional prohibitions will not be applied to them, they should have little to fear if those links are relatively insubstantial.

NOTES

1. Early on there was no legal tradition in this country, so it was necessary to borrow our law from other countries. As we were under British rule, British law, much of which was common in nature, was the logical source of most of our law. As colonies and then states and the national government formed, they began writing constitutions and

legislation which altered this borrowed law in some respects. The law which came from Britain and became our common law was never entirely replaced, however, and to this day survives to some extent (as altered by the courts) in all states except Louisiana, which is governed by a civil code. Texas statutes, for example, provide that the common law is deemed to be in effect insofar as it has not been superceded by constitutional or statutory law. V.T.C.A., Civil Practice & Remedies Code §5.001.

Because the common law is state law, it differs from state to state. One should not infer, therefore, that a common law ruling in one state is binding in another; at best, such rulings are a persuasive authority to be considered by other states' courts faced with a similar legal question.

2. Model Penal Code §2.02(2)(a)(i). Most modern codes use a conscious objective formulation. Others define the matter in terms of the defendant's purpose to cause a result, his specific intention to do so, his specific design to do so, or by reference to the defendant's having "actively desired" the result.

3. Model Penal Code §2.02(2)(b)(ii).

4. Model Penal Code §2.02(2)(c).

5. State v. Gooze, 81 A.2d 811, 814 (N.J. App. 1951).

6. Restatement Torts (Second) §§282–284 (1965).

7. Examples of strict liability offenses include violations of liquor or narcotics, pure food, and traffic laws. One is guilty of speeding, for example, whether or not he sped intentionally, knowingly, recklessly or negligently.

8. 116 Cal. App. 3rd 311 (1981).

9. *E.g.*, Heshizer, *The Implied Contract Exception to At-Will Employment*, 35 Lab. L. J. 131 (1984).

10. *E.g.*, Love, *Retaliatory Discharge for Filing a Workers' Compensation Claim: The Development of a Modern Tort Action*, 37 Hastings L. J. 551 (1986); Rohwer, *Terminable-at-Will Employment: New Theories for Job Security*, 15 Pac. L. J. 759 (1984).

11. *Certiorari* is a Latin term for a writ from a higher court to a lower one, requesting the record of a case for review. One way to seek review of a case in the Supreme Court is to petition the Court to issue this writ, which the Court does in about 2 percent of the cases filed with it. The vote of at least four of the nine justices is required for a writ of *certiorari* to be granted, and the Court is not obliged to, and seldom does, explain why it grants or denies a writ.

12. Barron v. Baltimore, 32 U.S. (7 Pet.) 242 (1833).

13. *E.g.*, Tribe, American Constitutional Law §11–2 (1988). The

Fourteenth Amendment provides in relevant part that "[n]o state shall make or enforce any law which shall ... deprive any person of life, liberty, or property, without due process of law[.]"

14. *E.g.*, Shelley v. Kraemer, 334 U.S. 1 (1948) (state court cannot enforce a privately negotiated racially restrictive covenant). For a discussion of state action, *see* Tribe, *supra* note 13, §18–1 et seq.

15. This is the "public function" or "governmental function" theory. *E.g.*, Evans v. Newton, 382 U.S. 296 (1966) (alternate ground for holding private park subject to Fourteenth Amendment); Marsh v. Alabama, 326 U.S. 501 (1946) (owners of privately owned company town are state actors because they perform public function).

16. This entanglement theory holds that substantial contacts between a state and a private actor may make the private actions indistinguishable from those of the state. The Supreme Court has not developed a test to determine the level of involvement needed to attribute private acts to the state. "Only by sifting facts and weighing circumstances can the nonobvious involvement of the State in private conduct be attributed its true significance." Burton v. Wilmington Parking Auth., 365 U.S. 715, 722 (1961) (private restaurant leasing space in state parking lot involved in state action).

17. *E.g.*, Skinner v. Railway Labor Executive's Ass'n., 109 S. Ct. 1402 (1989) (state action involved when private railroad company implemented drug testing program prescribed by federal administrative agency).

18. This state control theory is similar to the entanglement theory in that in both instances courts look at the facts of each case to determine whether the involvement in control is substantial enough to attribute the private acts to the state. *E.g.*, Parish v. NCAA, 506 F.2d 1028 (5th Cir. 1975) (state control theory used to find National Collegiate Athletic Association subject to Fourteenth Amendment to U. S. Constitution).

19. Flagg Bros., Inc. v. Brooks, 436 U.S. 149 (1978).

2

A History of Employment Law

The law of employer-employee relations has changed dramatically in this century. Whereas employees and applicants once were almost entirely at the mercy of employers in terms of their conditions of employment, they now enjoy a stronger bargaining position, better benefits, a safer working climate, and enhanced job security. An appreciation of the nature of these changes and of the current legal relationship between these parties is vital to an understanding of workplace privacy law. This chapter reviews some of the highlights in this area.

THE EARLY TWENTIETH CENTURY: EMPLOYERS IN COMMAND

At the dawn of this century, the common law governed nearly all aspects of the employer-employee relationship. This reflected the desire of that era's Congresses to keep job-related matters out of the federal arena and of state legislators to give employers a free hand in controlling workers. Given the laissez-faire attitude of lawmakers and the fact that courts were notoriously protective of property rights and unsympathetic to labor, what common law rights employees did have were quite limited in scope. Apart from occasionally letting injured workers sue for negligence and fired ones to recover for breach of contract, judges generally intervened in employment matters only to stop labor union activity.

The common law in most states required employers to furnish a safe workplace and competent co-workers, create and enforce safety rules, and warn workers of known dangers. The nineteenth century, however, saw the development of legal doctrines which prevented most employees from suing if harm resulted from the nonfulfillment of these duties. Even if a worker proved that his employer was negligent, for example, he received no damages if his own negligence contributed to his injury. And regardless of the condition of the workplace, damages were precluded if the injury was attributable to a co-worker's negligence. With such doctrines as these, the promise of relief from a system which all too often left employees dead or maimed proved to be nearly empty in practice.

Contract law was equally unfruitful for most employees. The common law recognized three kinds of contracts: written, oral and implied. Then, as now, most employment contracts were neither oral nor written, but were inferred from the parties' statements and actions. If an employee accepted a job offer, it was said that an employment contract had been created which implicitly entitled him to a reasonable wage in exchange for his implied agreement to do the work as well as he could.

The difficulty with these contracts involved their length. English courts assumed that if the time of employment was not specifically addressed, the employee was implicitly hired for one year. This made sense when people were farm workers, household servants or teachers: spring was the hiring season, and it was thought to be unfair to hire someone to work only until fall when they might not find work again until the following spring. But American judges faced a different situation. Most people toiled in factories and might be hired at any time depending on the need for particular products; in addition, their employers might need to lay them off if product demand dropped. If employers here had to hire people for a set length of time when there were no orders to fill, they could go broke. Accordingly, American judges invented the "at-will" employment concept, which held that workers could quit their job at any time, with or without reason, and that employers were similarly unconstrained in terms of discharging employees.

Although in theory the at-will doctrine benefitted both employees and employers by leaving each free to leave the other at his pleasure, in practice it was a curse for workers. If employers could fire for no reason, they could do so arbitrarily, and the employee would have no recourse. They could also impose any working conditions they wanted, no matter how unfair, and the employee's only remedy would be to seek a new job. In an era of high unemployment, this was not an attractive prospect.

In sum, in the early 1900's employers had virtually unlimited control over employees. Given the hands-off attitude of legislators, workers with complaints could look only to the common law for relief, and in practice that avenue was usually foreclosed as well. Numerous defenses available to employers made tort suits a waste of time for workers injured on the job, and both fired employees and those upset over working conditions typically found that the same was true if they tried to sue for breach of contract.

THE NEW DEAL: THE FEDS GETS INVOLVED

As the industrial revolution heated up, workers demanded relief from starvation wages, deplorable working conditions, long hours and child labor. Occasionally they banded together and went on strike to improve their lot. During the Progressive Era (roughly 1900 to 1917), some states responded by regulating child labor, wages and hours. The usual response of the laissez-faire, business-oriented courts, however, was to void these laws under the Due Process Clause of the Fourteenth Amendment to the Constitution, which prevents states from denying citizens life, liberty or property without due process of law. Courts reasoned that corporations were "citizens" under this amendment, and that in legislating for workers states deprived both master and servant of liberty within the meaning of the Due Process Clause by restricting their "freedom ... to contract with each other in relation to their employment."[1] In an amazing feat of legerdemain, courts also turned on its head the Sherman Antitrust Act of 1890, designed to bar anticompetitive business activity, using it to enjoin labor strikes on the ground that they were illegal restraints of trade.

One law that had managed to gain a foothold by this time was the workers' compensation law. England passed the first such law in 1897 and American states soon followed suit. Today all states have workers' compensation systems, which give employees injured on the job a small but certain sum of money to pay medical bills and living costs while disabled in return for preventing them from suing their employer. Because these laws allow payments to workers hurt in accidents, they usually do not cover harm caused by an employer's intentional wrongdoing. Thus, an employee suffering an invasion of his privacy on the job would not need to resort to these laws but instead could sue in court, since most invasions of privacy are intentional. Because the main injury in privacy cases is emotional and most worker's compensation systems cover physical injuries, these systems would not afford an appropriate forum to resolve a privacy claim in any event.

Employer-employee relations continued to be a state law matter until the 1930's. That decade, however, saw the federal government assume an increasingly dominant role in this area. The largescale shift of policymaking power from local to federal authorities that occurred at this time was caused largely by the confluence of three events: the Depression, the election of Franklin D. Roosevelt as President in 1932, and the change in the composition of the Supreme Court. Although some of this power was returned to the states in the 1980's during the Reagan presidency, most of the law that prevails in the workplace still emanates from "the feds."

As the Depression deepened in the early 1930's, it became clear that President Hoover's plan to let the private sector handle the problem was not working and that government intervention was needed. After Roosevelt's election and at his insistence, Congress began legislating to boost production of and demand for goods and services, reduce unemployment, and improve working conditions for the nation's laborforce. The vast bulk of the worker-oriented legislation was enacted during the middle and late 1930's, a period often referred to as the "Second New Deal" to distinguish it from the first three years after FDR's election, in which the primary goal of Congress and the new Democratic administration was to get business back on its feet. Among the most important of these laws were the National Labor Relations (Wagner) Act,[2] which required employers to negotiate in good faith with employees bargaining collectively, listed unfair labor practices and regulated unions; the Social Security Act,[3] which spawned social security and unemployment compensation; and the Fair Labor Standards Act,[4] which regulated wages, hours and child labor. In enacting these laws, the federal government, for the first time in our history, demonstrated a strong commitment to bettering the lot of workers.

How these laws would fare in the Supreme Court, however, was anyone's guess. Since the 1880's the Court had been dominated by conservative, pro-business justices who favored states' rights and a limited role for the federal government. In the mid 1930's they invalidated many laws enacted during the 1932–35 period, often on the basis that Congress either lacked authority to enact such laws or in passing them had delegated too much authority to the President. Earlier a majority of these justices had held that states generally could not legislate on behalf of workers, creating a no-man's land in which neither federal nor state authorities could operate. In 1937, however, these justices began retiring and were replaced with New Deal men with a different ideological slant. By the latter part of the decade, when the constitutionality of the laws referred to above was tested, the Court majority consisted of justices far more sympathetic towards workers and government efforts to aid them. They believed that lawmakers should have wide leeway in terms of social and economic engineering, and they routinely upheld legislative efforts in this area. The more willing the Court was to affirm such laws, the more eager to enact them lawmakers proved to be. Indeed, the extent of government involvement in employer-employee relations today, especially at the federal level, is largely attributable to the dramatic shift in the Court's philosophy which occurred at this time.

One effect of the Wagner Act was to modify the at-will employment doctrine by barring some reasons for dismissing employees. Workers, for example, could no longer be fired for unionizing or engaging in "concerted activity for their mutual aid and protection." But they also could not sue if they felt that an unfair labor practice had occurred; instead, they had to convince the general counsel of the National Labor Relations Board to bring a case to the Board on their behalf. Often, this was not easy to do. The Board, moreover, was limited in terms of the relief it could award: generally, it could (and still can) only award back pay and order the reinstatement of the employee to his former job.

Employees lost some of the act's protection during the anti-labor climate of the late 1940's. In 1947 Congress passed the Taft-Hartley amendments, which outlawed the closed shop and secondary boycotts, made unions liable for breach of contract and damages due to jurisdictional strikes between rival unions vying to represent workers, legalized injunctions against strikes that endangered the national health and safety, empowered the President to order striking workers to cool off for 60 days, and required union leaders to take a non-Communist oath. The framework of the act remained intact, however, and subsequent Congresses and rulings of the courts and the National Labor Relations Board restored and even bolstered its protections.

THE 1960's: THE DISCRIMINATION PROBLEM

In the 1930's Congress thought that if employees could unionize and if employers had to bargain with them in good faith, the two sides could resolve any problem that might arise. But by the 1960's it was clear that collective bargaining could not solve one major problem: discrimination by both employers and unions. Thus, in 1964 Congress passed the Civil Rights Act, Title VII of which bars discrimination based on "race, color, religion, sex or national origin."[5] The Equal Employment Opportunity Commission (EEOC) was set up to enforce this statute, but this time employees were also allowed to sue in federal court. While they could only receive two years' back pay and be reinstated to their job, the losing employer also had to pay their legal fees. During the next quarter century nearly every state passed civil rights laws, often adding to the federal list other bases for suit, so that federal, state and/or local laws now bar discrimination based on everything from marital status and age to sexual orientation. Although the federal law calls for a court hearing, many state civil rights statutes permit employees to have a jury and to receive full damages, including punitive damages.

Title VII encompasses two types of discrimination: disparate treatment and disparate impact. The former is more blatant and is what most people have in mind when they think of discrimination: one is denied a job or is treated adversely on the job because of gender, national origin or the like. To win a disparate treatment suit a plaintiff must prove several things. A rejected job-seeker claiming racial discrimination, for example, must prove that he is in a racial minority, that he applied and was qualified for the job, that despite his qualifications he was rejected, and that afterwards the position remained open and the employer continued to seek applicants with his qualifications. If this is done, the employer may attempt to prove that he had a legitimate, nondiscriminatory reason for not hiring the plaintiff. The plaintiff then may try to prove that the reason given by the defendant is merely a pretext for illegal discrimination on his part.[6]

Proof of an employer's intent to discriminate is required in a disparate treatment case. Disparate impact claims, on the other hand, assert that discrimination is accomplished subtly, through facially neutral employment practices that harm a disportionately high percentage of a protected group. Evidence of intent to discriminate is not needed under this theory: to make out a *prima facie* case of disparate impact discrimination, a plaintiff must show that there are statistical disparities in the employer's work force and identify the employment practice(s) allegedly responsible for the disparities. If this is done, the employer must offer evidence of a business justification for the practice, although the plaintiff continues to bear the burden of persuasion and thus must disprove the employer's assertion that the practice serves valid employment goals. Plaintiffs may also try to show that other practices without a discriminatory effect would serve those goals equally well and thus should be adopted instead.[7]

In 1973, Congress enacted the Rehabilitation Act.[8] This law bars discrimination in hiring, retaining or assigning employees based on real or perceived physical or emotional handicaps. It also requires employers reasonably to accommodate handicapped employees, such as by eliminating physical barriers in the workplace or altering work schedules or duties. Although the law applies only to employers receiving federal funds and thus does not reach a great deal of discrimination based on handicaps, many state and local governments have enacted more comprehensive laws. On July 26, 1990, President George Bush signed into law the Americans with Disabilities Act of 1990. The employment provisions of the act do not begin to go into effect until July 26, 1992. It is clear that the act will protect the victims of AIDS from job discrimination. At the same time it requires the Secretary of Health and Human Services to write regulations dealing with food handlers.

THE 1980's: WORKPLACE SAFETY AND RELATED CONCERNS

Safety Versus Privacy

After years of grappling with discrimination, job security, wages, hours and benefits, Congress began focusing on the problem of deaths and injuries caused by industrial accidents. In 1970 it enacted the Occupational Safety and Health Act,[9] which created workplace safety standards, set up a system of inspections and fines, and let workers fired for revealing unsafe practices complain to the Secretary of Labor, who could seek reinstatement and back pay. Although most states have not responded to this invitation, the act also allows states to develop similar systems if the Secretary of Labor finds them as effective as that prescribed by the federal act. As a result of this law, dangerous conditions at the job site have been, if far from eliminated, at least substantially reduced.

But this law has also raised troubling questions. In 1981, for example, the Occupational Safety and Health Administration charged the Nazar Rubber Company with failing to protect its employees from unreasonable exposure to chemical substances used in making its products.[10] The agency required Nazar to conduct yearly physical examinations of employees and to establish genetic benchmarks to determine if its employees' health was deteriorating because of the exposure. While at first glance this order seems desirable, the requirement that employees undergo such examinations raises a privacy issue which the agency did not address. To what extent must an employee's privacy yield to the need to protect the health of co-workers? Should the answer depend on how obvious or direct the health threat is? What type of examination may be given?

Another safety issue involves the effect of smoking on co-workers and customers. Given the health risk involved, courts have allowed workers to sue employers who refuse to stop co-workers from smoking or to segregate those who do.[11] The Surgeon General, however, has said that smokers are drug addicts. Are they thus shielded by laws barring discrimination against the handicapped? What of the privacy interests at stake in this context: do employers illegally invade their employees' privacy if they try to keep them from smoking? If they do not make this effort, are they potentially liable for harm suffered by co-workers and customers as a result of the smoke?

Workers are not the only ones with safety concerns. For many reasons, including the risk of litigation resulting from accidents and faulty products and concern for worker health, employers have begun trying to determine if workers are fit for particular jobs. Screening methods now being used on employees and applicants include polygraph tests to enable employers to form an opinion about their honesty, urinalysis to ferret out substance use, psychiatric evaluations to determine if they are emotionally suited for the job, and genetic tests to see if they have an increased risk of disease and thus may not be as productive as would ordinarily be expected or may be unduly costly in terms of insurance or health benefits. In 1979, the U.S. Supreme Court approved these efforts, holding that the New York City Transit Authority could bar workers on methadone maintenance.[12]

Safety Concerns in Court

Unfit employees threaten the safety of co-workers and the public, and ways to identify them are needed. But just as privacy interests are implicated when employers prevent workers from smoking or test them for exposure to chemicals, they are also raised when employees are subjected to drug tests or psychological exams. How should the competing interests of job safety and employee privacy be reconciled? On the one hand, a court recently required a teacher to be evaluated psychiatrically before returning to her job,[13] reasoning that the need to provide a safe climate for students outweighed any privacy right of the teacher. But courts have also held that the random use of drug tests on teachers is not a justified invasion of privacy absent reason to suspect a given teacher of drug use.[14] Future court battles will continue to pit those who feel that job safety is paramount against those alarmed by the Orwellian implications of employee surveillance. To make matters worse, if an employee is found to be, for example, on drugs or psychologically unfit for his job, he may be legally handicapped and thus not subject to discharge if the handicap can be reasonably accommodated.

As noted, at the turn of the century the at-will employment doctrine, the many employer defenses to tort and contract suits, the dearth of worker-oriented legislation, and the unsympathetic attitude of courts deprived most workers of a meaningful remedy for unfair treatment on the job. Although employees began acquiring constitutional and statutory rights in the 1930's, their status under the common law changed little. In the 1970's, however, state courts began reexamining some of the common law doctrines that had hampered employees for so long. Increasingly these doctrines, which were created during the industrial revolution, have been found inapplicable to a service-oriented, white-collar workforce, and many have been altered or abolished as a result.

The attack has proceeded on both the contract and tort law fronts. For example, to bypass state workers' compensations laws, which bar workers from suing employers for harm caused by negligence, employees have begun claiming fraud, defamation, and infliction of emotional distress. Because these tort theories are based on intentional wrongdoing and require no proof of physical injury, they do not relegate employees to workers' compensation systems but instead allow them to sue in court for relief.

Fraud suits have been brought by workers to whom bosses have lied. In one case, an employer induced a job candidate to join his company by saying he was licensed to sell insurance and securities, when he could sell only insurance. The court awarded damages to the plaintiff.[15] Fraud may also occur if an employer has vital information that he withholds from his employees, as DuPont learned when its doctors withheld from employees the fact that they had diseases caused by exposure to asbestos. The New Jersey Supreme Court ruled that DuPont had a duty to disclose this information and that its failure to do so warranted a $1,200,000 punitive damage award.[16] One inference to be drawn from this case is that if an employer invades a worker's privacy and in so doing learns certain facts, that employer may have a duty—the failure of which to carry out could result in liability being imposed—to reveal those facts to other employees.

Employees have also filed defamation suits based on unfounded charges of job-related misconduct. In Texas, an employee won $200,000 in damages when he was fired after a drug test suggested that he was using methadone, although he presented evidence from a doctor that he was taking medicine similar to methadone in chemical composition.[17] Under the circumstances, the court found the employer's charge both false and defamatory.

"Intentional infliction of mental distress" is another basis of recovery. Like invasion of privacy, this tort has gained recognition only in this century. To win, an employee must prove that his employer acted outrageously and that this caused severe emotional distress. In one case, a supervisor knew an employee was under a doctor's care for depression. When he saw the employee take a drink, the supervisor told the employee that he must enter the company drug treatment program or lose his job. When the employee requested time to mull this over, he was fired. In a subsequent suit, the jury awarded the employee both compensatory and punitive damages.[18]

During the 1980's courts also expanded the "wrongful discharge" theory. The federal government invented this tort concept in the 1930's to prevent the firing of union members; basically, it means that while employers in an at-will relation with their employees are generally free to fire them for any or no reason, if they dismiss wrongfully, and the reason is deemed impermissible by the courts, the employer may be held liable for damages and/or ordered to reinstate the employee. Wrongful discharge typically is found to have occurred where an employee was fired either for exercising a right protected by a statute or constitutional provision, or for a reason deemed unacceptable on public policy grounds. With the advent of civil rights laws in the recent years, courts have expanded the list of constitutionally- and statutorily-based reasons why workers may not be fired, so that dismissals are now wrongful if they stem from, among other things, union membership; the receipt of retirement or other benefits under the 1974 Employee Retirement Income Security Act (ERISA);[19] the reporting of workplace safety violations to OSHA; race, religion, sex, age or handicap; or, in the government employment context, the exercise of constitutional rights, such as the First Amendment right of free speech.

To these reasons why employees cannot be fired courts have added a lengthening list of common law or public policy reasons. These exceptions to at-will employment, which vary widely among the states, now include firing for refusing to perform an illegal act, performing a legal duty such as serving on a jury, reporting to the authorities illegal conduct by one's employer, and exercising a legal right such as filing a workers' compensation claim.[20] Before there was a law on the subject in West Virginia, its supreme court ruled that state public policy was violated when an employee was fired for refusing to take a polygraph test.[21] Courts are now being asked whether this principle applies to employees fired (or to applicants not hired) for refusing to take drug, personality and genetic tests.

Besides tort law, contract law is increasingly affording new avenues for overturning firings.[22] In several states, courts have ruled that employment contracts impliedly contain a "covenant of good faith and fair dealing" which is violated if a discharge is based on an impermissible reason. Statements made in employee handbooks or policy manuals have also been held to form implied contracts. In one case, for example, the court said that where a company manual stated that an employee could be fired only for "just cause" and the employee was told that he "could work until 65 as long as he did his job," binding assurances had been made.[23] Statements made to candidates by company recruiters, such as suggestions that a certain opportunity exists or that certain benefits will be afforded, may have the same effect.

CONCLUSION

A century ago, when producing the most goods and services at the least cost was society's goal, the law of employer-employee relations was simple: employees could be fired at any time, and those hurt on the job had to look to workers' compensation law for relief. Gradually, however, other societal goals were recognized, so that today, while the quality of goods and services remains important, protecting worker safety and privacy and ensuring some threshold level of job security and benefits are also deemed vital. These goals have found expression in an expanding array of constitutional, common law and statutory protections for employees.

If the employees' situation has changed dramatically in recent years, however, so has the employers'. Now, besides trying to stay competitive, employers must cope with, among other things, a proliferation of consumer protection laws and lawsuits with million-dollar verdicts. Since employee fitness significantly affects an employer's ability to handle these problems successfully, employers understandably are always on the lookout for new ways to assess fitness. As they find these ways, conflicts with the new legal protections for workers inevitably occur. These collisions are the stuff of both litigation and lawmaking, in which courts and legislators are asked to find a viable middle ground between the competing interests—to balance these interests, in other words, so that the needs of each group and the public are adequately protected but businesses can still run efficiently. How well this balance is achieved in the future will play a large role in America's ability to maintain harmonious and productive workforces and, in turn, to compete effectively in the world market.

NOTES

1. *E.g.*, Lochner v. New York, 198 U.S. 45 (1905). Given the disparity in bargaining power it was hardly true that employers and workers enjoyed the freedom to contract on equal terms, but this theory nonetheless prevailed from the late 1800's through the middle 1930's and was often invoked by courts to invalidate laws which sought to improve the social or economic position of employees.

2. 29 U.S.C. §151 *et seq.*

3. 42 U.S.C. §301 *et seq.*

4. 29 U.S.C. §701 *et seq.*

5. 42 U.S.C. §2000e *et seq.*

6. *E.g.*, Griggs v. Duke Power Co., 401 U.S. 424 (1971); McDonnell Douglas Corp. v. Green, 411 U.S. 792 (1973).

7. Wards Cove Packing Co., Inc. v. Atonio, 109 S. Ct. 2115 (1989). Since the Court's decision in *Griggs, supra* note 6, it had been widely assumed by lawyers and courts that the employer had the burden to prove as well as offer evidence on the business justification claim and that the plaintiff did not have to identify the specific employment practice that allegedly caused whatever disparate impact he could show. In this regard, *Ward's Cove* seems to have substantially rewritten Title VII law *sub silentio*. Only time and more litigation will clarify whether, as some commentators have suggested, *Ward's Cove* has made it almost impossible for disparate impact claims to succeed in the future. It should be noted, however, that at the time of this writing (early 1990), Congress is considering legislation that would overturn *Ward's Cove*.

8. 29 U.S.C. §794 *et seq.*

9. 29 U.S.C. §651 *et seq.*

10. Sec. of Labor v. Nazar Rubber Co., OSHRC Docket No. 79–4005 (1981).

11. *E.g.*, Shrimp v. New Jersey Bell Tel. Co., 368 A.2d 408 (N.J. Dist. 1976); McCarthy v. Dept. of Health, 759 P.2d 351 (Wash. 1988).

12. New York Transit Authority v. Beazer, 440 U.S. 568 (1979).

13. Daury v. Smith, 842 F.2d 9 (1st Cir. 1988).

14. Patchogue-Medford Congress v. Bd. of Educ., 505 N.Y.S.2d 888 (N.Y. App. 1986).

15. Conder v. A. L. Williams & Assoc., 739 P.2d 634 (Utah App. 1987).

16. Millison v. DuPont, 501 A.2d 505 (N.J. 1985), *on appeal after trial*, 545 A.2d 213 (N.J. App. 1988).

17. Houston Belt & Terminal Railway Co. v. Wherry, 548 S.W.2d 743 (Tex. Civ. App. – Houston [1st Dist.] 1976), *writ ref'd n.r.e.*

18. Wanger v. Knudson, 428 N.W.2d 242 (S.D. 1988).

19. 29 U.S.C. §1001 *et seq.*

20. *E.g.*, MCWHIRTER, YOUR RIGHTS AT WORK, Ch. 6 (1989).

21. Cordle v. Gen. Hugh Mercer Corp., 325 S.E.2d 111 (W. Va. 1984).

22. *E.g.*, SOVEREIGN, PERSONNEL LAW (1989) at 178–184.

23. Toussant v. Blue Cross and Blue Shield of Michigan, 292 N.W.2d 880 (Mich. 1980).

3

A Century of Privacy Law

Few legal concepts are as misunderstood as the right of privacy. This became clear in 1987, when Robert Bork was nominated to the U.S. Supreme Court. Asked during his confirmation hearings about his views on privacy law, Bork essentially replied that the federal constitutional right of privacy developed in recent Court cases was created out of thin air. The Constitution, he stressed, says nothing about privacy; if Americans are to enjoy any rights in this area, therefore, it can properly be only by virtue of laws enacted by their elected representatives.[1]

What Bork was criticizing was not the *idea* of privacy, but the way in which courts have by fiat given privacy the status of a constitutional right. But the storm of criticism that met his remarks showed that this distinction was lost on his audience. To laymen and legal scholars, Bork wanted not just to transfer control over privacy law from the judicial to the legislative arena, but to dismantle that law, and they perceived this as an assault on a fundamental right. These perceptions—that privacy is a natural right and that Bork meant to abolish that right—were key factors underlying the public's opposition to the Bork nomination and the Senate's rejection of it.

From a legal standpoint, Bork suffered a bum rap. For although most people would endorse former Supreme Court Justice Hugo Black's remark that, "I like my privacy as well as the next one,"[2] privacy is neither a natural nor an inalienable right. Indeed, it was first argued that privacy should be made a part of the common law only one hundred years ago. Only in 1965 did the Supreme Court endorse the concept of a constitutional right of privacy. And only in the last few years have lawmakers begun enacting privacy statutes. The right of privacy, therefore, is of relatively recent vintage; like any other legal right, moreover, it can be expanded, applied selectively or even eliminated by its creators. A brief history of its evolution follows.

THE FIRST QUARTER CENTURY: THE RIGHT OF PUBLICITY

In 1890 the *Harvard Law Review* published an article called "The Right to Privacy." In it, Boston attorneys Samuel Warren and Louis D. Brandeis (later a Supreme Court justice) argued that the law should recognize a right to an "inviolate personality" that would protect "thoughts, emotions, and sensations ... whether expressed in writing, or in conduct, in conversation, in attitudes, or in facial expression."[3] Noting that the common law responded well to societal needs, they also argued that courts should create this new right rather than wait for legislators to act. "The intensity and complexity of life" and "modern enterprise and invention," they said, made the time ripe for judges to redefine the nature of personal rights to protect "appearance, sayings, acts, and ... personal relation[s], domestic or otherwise."[4]

This redefinition, they argued, would not require much rewriting of the law, for recent court cases had already come close to recognizing a legally enforceable privacy right. In the 1880's, for example, professional photographers who sold their customers' pictures without their consent were held liable for breaching an implied agreement that the prints would be "appropriated to the use of the customer only."[5] Courts were using nuisance and defamation law to shield people from, respectively, "offensive noises and odors ... dust and smoke, and excessive vibration" and harm to reputation.[6] And the concept of "intangible property" guarded "the products and processes of the mind, such as works of literature and art, goodwill, trade secrets, and trademarks."[7] Believing that what these cases really protected was privacy, the authors argued that courts should simply recognize this right rather than try to force new cases into old legal categories. This would further the common law trend toward acknowledging both nonphysical injuries, such as harm to reputation, and intangible property, such as goodwill and copyright, by recognizing the nonphysical injury of emotional distress and the intangible property rights inherent in one's private life. It would also fill the void left by the implied contract theory, which logically could not apply when the parties involved were strangers.

The crux of the authors' argument was that everyone should own the "facts relating to his private life." While they argued for a general privacy right, however, Warren and Brandeis had a specific problem in mind: the press was "overstepping in every direction the obvious bounds of propriety and of decency," and "idle gossip" was crowding out real news. This caused great "mental pain and distress" to innocent people who found the "sacred precincts of [their] private and domestic life" invaded as intimate personal facts were splashed across the pages of newspapers. The right sought by the authors would combat this problem by giving people a legal remedy for unwanted and unjustified public exposure.

In exchange for the recognition of two principles, Warren and Brandeis said they would accept four limitations on the right of privacy. The principles were that truth should not be a defense in an action for privacy invasion, as it is in defamation law, and that what motivates someone who publishes intimate personal facts should be irrelevant. Only what is printed, the justification for printing it, and the impact of publication on the plaintiff should matter. The limits were: (1) one can consent expressly or impliedly to a privacy invasion; (2) oral publications should not be actionable unless special damages are proven; (3) some communications should be privileged, as in defamation cases, such as those made in court or before legislatures; and (4) the press can publish what is of general interest, with this right applying expansively to public figures, such as politicians, who in putting themselves in the public eye automatically renounce some of their privacy. As an example of proper versus improper publication, the authors offered a man with a lisp: if he seeks public office people have a right to know about his impediment, but not otherwise.[8]

Four years after "The Right to Privacy" appeared, Herbert S. Hadley published an article by the same title.[9] He argued that the limitations on privacy that Warren and Brandeis were willing to accept would mean that "the small class who would thus be entitled to enjoy the privilege of privacy and seclusion would probably find that their habits of life and appearance would be of as little importance to the general public as would the right to privacy itself." He also insisted that the common law should not recognize mental anguish as a basis for damages "except where a physical condition results [from] the act producing the anguish," and that, "when an individual goes among people, when he walks along the streets in the sight of all who care to look upon him, he has waived his right to the privacy of his personality."

To illustrate how courts were handling privacy claims, Hadley discussed cases which had arisen before and after the publication of the Warren and Brandeis article. One was *Pollard v. Photographic Co.*, noted above,[10] where a British Court enjoined the unauthorized commercial use of pictures taken for a woman by a photographer. But in 1893 the heirs of a Mr. Corliss failed to persuade a court to halt the publication of an unauthorized biography of him with his picture on the cover.[11] There was no claim of libel, only that publication would harm the heirs' feelings. Saying that people should be free to publish what they wish if there is no "offense against public morals or private reputation," the court held that whether Corliss was a public figure, or for that matter was dead or alive, was irrelevant. The picture had been obtained legitimately, and the judge did not feel that its use on a biography cover, authorized or not, warranted damages or an injunction against publication.

Both ends of the spectrum of judicial attitudes toward privacy can be seen in these cases. On the one hand, while it stopped short of recognizing a right to privacy, the *Pollard* court was plainly concerned about the effect on the plaintiff's sensibilities of the unauthorized use of her picture, and it ruled in her favor. It held that in accepting employment the photographer had formed a confidential relationship with the plaintiff, and that his use of her picture without her consent violated both an implied part of their contract and her faith in him, as such use was not within the parties' contemplation when they bargained. In so doing, the court rejected the claim that "a person has no property in his own features" and that "short of doing what is libellous or otherwise illegal, there is no restriction on the photographer's using his negative." On the other hand, the *Corliss* court did not speak of property rights in one's likeness, implied agreements or confidences, and it seemed unconcerned with sensibilities. In its view the issues were clearcut: the photo had been legitimately bought, its use involved free speech and would not harm public morals or anyone's reputation, and no law shielded the heirs' feelings from the effects of publication.

With the publication of these articles, the points of contention regarding the right of privacy became explicit. Warren, Brandeis and Hadley agreed that the law should recognize this right but differed over who should create it and what shape it should take. Noting that the common law adapted well to the needs of a changing society, Warren and Brandeis argued that judges should develop the right case-by-case, whereas Hadley felt that this task was better left to lawmakers. Warren and Brandeis thought that mental anguish should be compensated in invasion of privacy cases, while Hadley would require a physical manifestation of harm. Finally, responding to Warren and Brandeis' claim that privacy should be a broad right protecting against unwanted exposure and intrusions, Hadley asserted that much of what they would put under the privacy umbrella should be left to the realm of ethics and morals and not be made part of the legal system.

A few years later, a Ms. Roberson sought relief in the New York courts when she found her picture used to advertise flour without her consent. In a 4–3 vote, the Court of Appeals turned her down.[12] Outraged at the court's refusal to recognize her right of privacy, the press vilified the court, prompting one judge to defend the ruling in an article.[13] The decision and the article appeared in 1902; a year later, the New York legislature barred the "unauthorized use of the name or picture of any person for the purposes of trade" and permitted injured parties to recover damages and to stop further unsanctioned use.[14] In so doing, they plainly responded to commentators who had condemned the court for refusing to endorse the emerging common law notion of intangible property rights inherent in one's private life. These writers argued that the commercial use of one's name or picture should be protected and that this would not raise the free speech issues that might arise in other applications of the privacy theory.

In 1912 Wilbur Larremore reviewed the privacy cases reported since 1890—all twelve of them.[15] Like Warren, Brandeis and Hadley, he sought the recognition of a right to control the commercial use of one's name and image, and he surveyed the cases which found this right in the common law. The Georgia Supreme Court did this in 1905, when a Mr. Pavesich found his picture being used without his consent to advertise an insurance company.[16] Missouri soon followed suit, with its high court saying: "Property is not necessarily a taxable thing any more than it is always a tangible thing. It may consist of things incorporeal, and things incorporeal may consist of rights common in every man."[17] Larremore noted that some courts refused to recognize this right absent a statute expressly creating it, but argued that the trend was toward acceptance of the concept and that other courts should follow those in Georgia and Missouri and adjust their common law accordingly.

Two cases reviewed by Larremore dealt with another concept discussed by Warren and Brandeis: the right to protect intimate facts. One was the case involving Mr. Corliss' heirs. The other involved a Ms. Hillman, who sued a newspaper after finding her picture in an article about her father's arrest for fraud.[18] There, the court refused to recognize a privacy right absent legislation creating it and ruled against Hillman. Larremore disagreed with the outcome of the case but conceded the need to distinguish between the "right to keep private facts private" at stake in that case and the "right of publicity," which he felt was more deserving of recognition. He also endorsed Warren and Brandeis' view that damages should be awarded for mental anguish even if there is no physical manifestation of injury; specifically, he backed a 1904 court ruling which let a railroad passenger sue for mental distress because a conductor had used abusive language toward her, even though she had suffered no physical harm as a result.[19]

In sum, twenty-five years after the appearance of the Warren and Brandeis article, the "right of publicity" was well on its way to becoming rooted in the common law. While courts still used the breach of faith and breach of contract theories seen in cases like *Pollard*, they had begun to accept the idea that people have rights in their name and image and that recognizing a theory which protects these rights is preferable to forcing cases into old legal pigeonholes. As the idea of a right to publicity gained ground, the issues became: (1) how does one decide if the use of a name or image is legitimate? and (2) does the right of publicity survive death? On the other hand, it was also clear that the "right to keep private facts private" was not faring well. With just one case involving a live person decided, and with it lost, it seemed that Herbert Hadley may have been right when he speculated that the class of people actually covered by this right was too small to worry about.

THE SECOND QUARTER CENTURY: THE RIGHT OF SECLUSION

Through the 1930's scholars continued to debate whether legislatures or courts should create a right of privacy and what its contours should be. While the academicians argued, however, the courts went about fine-tuning this right. By 1936 things had evolved to the point that Gerald Dickler could say that the privacy concept really embraced three distinct rights: a "right of publicity," which barred the unauthorized appropriation of one's name or image; a "right of seclusion," which shielded people from unwanted intrusions; and a "right to keep private facts private."[20]

The right of publicity was the most widely accepted. While courts and commentators still found it hard to delineate between proper and improper use, they agreed that the commercial use of one's name or image should be controlled by the individual as other property is. Dickler also felt that a second set of cases stood for the principle that people have a right to avoid unwanted intrusions on their lives. In perhaps the first case involving this theory, a woman won damages in 1881 for the distress she suffered when she found that a man brought to her childbirth by a doctor was not a medical assistant.[21] In 1929 courts refused to let a "crusading law enforcer" examine the bank accounts of city police to "assist him in some investigation" he was making.[22] And in 1931, a man recovered for anguish caused by the tapping of his phone.[23] None of these cases involved proof of physical harm.

The private facts right, on the other hand, continued to lag far behind. When it was asserted against newspapers which published personal facts, courts often conceded that the publication implicated privacy interests but ruled for the defendants under the Warren and Brandeis "public figure" and "news of general interest" exceptions. The Kentucky Supreme Court, for example, refused to let a plaintiff recover for the publication of his picture in a paper even though the story falsely attributed statements to him. The Court said that at times one "whether willingly or not, becomes an actor in an occurrence of public or general interest. When this takes place, he emerges from seclusion, and it is not an invasion of his right of privacy to publish his photograph with an account of such occurrence."[24] Dickler disagreed with the case, not because it recognized a press privilege, which he favored, but because it extended the privilege to the "false recording of news."

Only if the outrageousness of a publication was extreme could plaintiffs expect to win. In 1930, for example, a family recovered damages when a paper printed a picture of their "abnormal deceased child" without their consent.[25] The child was born with its heart outside its body and died soon after birth. And in Kentucky, a doctor successfully sued a creditor who posted a five-by-eight foot sign proclaiming that the doctor owed him $49.67. Interestingly, the defendant was not permitted to claim truth as a defense, although truth was then an absolute defense to defamation actions in Kentucky.[26]

The close of the second quarter century after the Warren and Brandeis article thus saw the right of publicity become even more firmly entrenched and a right of seclusion gaining a foothold in the law. At best, however, judges remained lukewarm towards the right to keep private facts private.

THE THIRD QUARTER CENTURY: THE RIGHT OF FREE SPEECH

In 1941, Louis Nizer argued that in focusing so much on privacy, courts had paid too little attention to the right of free speech.[27] This right, he claimed, is implicated in privacy suits against the media. After citing with approval cases recognizing a privilege to report whatever might remotely be deemed news, Nizer examined cases involving the depiction of newsworthy events. For example, in *Binns v. Vitagraph Co. of America*[28] which involved a film dramatization of a rescue at sea, the court distinguished between "news" and "commercialization" so that dramatizations fell on the commercial side of the line and allowed the real hero to win damages for invasion of privacy. Nizer objected, saying this line should be moved so that dramatizations would be included with news reports. In his view, press freedom should be broad enough for the media to be able to truthfully dramatize newsworthy events without fearing lawsuits.

Two other dramatization cases had been decided by 1941, both for the plaintiffs. One writer summarized the facts of *Melvin v. Reid* as follows:

The fact situation rivals the English problem play of the nineties: Gabrielle Darley, erstwhile prostitute and defendant in a murder trial in which she was acquitted, marries into respectable society. She reforms, gaining many friends who are unaware of her early transgressions. Then appears, on the local screens, and in the moving picture cathedrals of the country, a film entitled "The Red Kimono," based on the true history of her past life, and employing her maiden name as that of the principal character; and billboards and fences are plastered with smug announcements that the production was plotted around the true story of her life.[29]

The California courts let Darley sue for invasion of privacy because her married name had been used in advertising the film. This use, said the court, violated a state constitutional provision guaranteeing citizens the right to pursue happiness. That Darley's new name was a matter of public record for anyone to look up seemed to make no difference to this court.

Mau v. Rio Grande Oil Co.[30] involved the radio show "Calling All Cars," which dramatized real crime stories. The plaintiff claimed that he suffered anguish when he heard a broadcast of a reinactment of an incident in which he was robbed and shot. His distress, he said, was so acute that he could not work the next day, which caused him to be fired. Relying on state statutes and on the *Melvin* case, the court ruled for the plaintiff, thus joining the *Melvin* court in finding that dramatizations are not news shielded by a broad publication privilege.

In 1960 Dean William Prosser published a seminal article on privacy.[31] Prosser agreed with Dickler that privacy involves three rights, but he went further and said that the "private facts" right had two parts. In one line of disclosure cases, he observed, the facts were private but the plaintiff's reputation was unharmed; in the other, the information revealed was misleading and put the plaintiff in a false light, but its disclosure did not rise to the level of defamation. Plaintiffs usually won false light cases, he said, but not the others. Unlike other commentators such as Larremore and Dickler, Prosser did not single out this category of cases with an eye toward stimulating their growth; on the contrary, he worried that false light privacy might swallow up defamation law. He asked, "What of the numerous restrictions and limitations which have hedged defamation about for many years, in the interest of freedom of the press and the discouragement of trivial and extortionate claims? Are they of so little consequence that they may be circumvented in so casual and cavalier a fashion?"[32]

Prosser's article spawned debates over whether privacy rights should be recognized at all and whether privacy is one right or several smaller ones. His four-part analysis has been accepted by nearly all courts, however, and was incorporated in the 1977 *Restatement (Second) of Torts*. Several states have adopted his description of privacy, summarized below, and each privacy tort has been applied in the workplace.

In 1963 Marc Franklin revived concern over the free speech/ privacy conflict on which Louis Nizer had focused in 1941.[33] He began with *Hubbard v. Journal Pub. Co.*,[34] where a newspaper was sued for revealing that a girl had been sexually assaulted by her brother: The newspaper had gotten the facts from court records. The New Mexico Supreme Court held for the paper on three grounds: it was privileged to publish information in public records; the information was newsworthy; and the plaintiff was, albeit involuntarily, a public figure.

Rather than base its ruling on the common law concepts of privilege, public figure and newsworthiness, Franklin thought the court should have found the publication protected by the First Amendment. He was appalled that in most privacy cases against the media the defendants did not even invoke the amendment, and he especially feared a case then on appeal to the Supreme Court. In that case, *New York Times v. Sullivan*,[35] Alabama courts had awarded $500,000 in libel damages against the paper. Franklin thought this was government censorship of the press.

At issue was a *Times* advertisement which was critical of the behavior of Birmingham, Alabama's police during civil rights protests. Sullivan, a city commissioner, sued for libel, arguing that while the ad did not mention him by name, its criticism reflected adversely on him in his capacity as police commissioner. But the U.S. Supreme Court said that the press must have "breathing room" if free speech is to survive, and that a rule requiring a "critic of official conduct to guarantee the truth of all his factual assertions" would lead to self-censorship which would inhibit the free exchange of ideas. It held that public figures suing the media for defamation must prove not only that a publication was false and had hurt their reputation, but also that the media acted with "malice," that is, knew what they were saying was false or acted with reckless disregard of its truth.

In *Time Inc. v. Hill*,[36] escaped convicts held the Hill family hostage for nineteen hours. The incident attracted widespread publicity and led to a novel, play and movie. When the play opened, *Life Magazine* published an article entitled "True Crime Inspires Tense Play," which noted similarities between the fictional work and the real event and indicated incorrectly that the play depicted the true facts. The Hills sued in New York under the 1903 law that had overturned the *Roberson* case. The jury awarded $30,000 in damages, and the New York Court of Appeals affirmed based on the inaccuracies in the story. The Supreme Court reversed, however, holding that these plaintiffs had to prove malice just as public figures must do in defamation actions.

In 1974, the Court held that private figures who prove damages and fault need not prove malice in libel suits against the media.[37] Law review commentators argued that the test should be the same in privacy suits—if private parties need not prove malice to win libel cases, in other words, they should not have to do so in false light privacy cases. In 1890 Warren and Brandeis had said that neither truth nor malice should be issues in privacy cases, but in the 1960's the U.S. Supreme Court found that in view of the constitutional right of free speech they were major issues. Thus, in false light privacy suits, truth would be a defense, absent a showing of malice.

By the 1980's false light privacy law was in disarray, and scholars were calling for its abandonment. One writer claimed that cases in this area were really trying both to protect reputation and to punish people who cause emotional distress, and he observed that other branches of tort law already did this.[38] The law of defamation protects reputations, and the "intentional infliction of mental distress" tort, which affords relief to those who suffer mental distress at the hands of people who should have known that their acts might cause such distress, protects peace of mind. In 1984 the North Carolina Supreme Court heeded the advice of these commentators, refusing to recognize a false light privacy tort in that state.[39]

How would courts react to infliction of mental distress suits against the media? In 1988, the Supreme Court gave a partial answer in *Hustler Magazine v. Falwell*,[40] the facts of which were summarized by the Court as follows:

Gertz vs Robert

Welch

The inside front cover of the November 1983 issue of Hustler Magazine featured a "parody" of an advertisement for Campari Liquer that contained the name and picture of respondent and was entitled "Jerry Falwell talks about his first time." This parody was modeled after actual Campari ads that included interviews with various celebrities about their "first times." Although it was apparent by the end of each interview that this meant the first time they sampled Campari, the ads clearly played on the sexual double entendre of the general subject of "first times." Copying the form and layout of these Campari ads, Hustler's editors chose respondent as the featured celebrity and drafted an alleged "interview" with him in which he states that his "first time" was during a drunken incestuous rendezvous with his mother in an outhouse. The Hustler parody portrays respondent and his mother as drunk and immoral, and suggests that respondent is a hypocrite who preaches only when he is drunk. In small print at the bottom of the page, the ad contains the disclaimer, "ad parody—not to be taken seriously." The magazine's table of contents also lists the ad as "Fiction: Ad and Personality Parody."[41]

Falwell sued for false light invasion of privacy, libel and infliction of mental distress. The district court directed a verdict for *Hustler* on the libel claim, ruling that no one could have reasonably thought that the ad described true facts about Falwell. But the jury accepted the mental distress claim and awarded Falwell $150,000 in damages.

The Supreme Court reversed. Although the case involved intentional infliction of mental distress and not libel, Chief Justice Rehnquist said for a unanimous Court, Falwell was a "public figure" who must meet the "malice" test set out in *Sullivan* and *Hill*. That test requires public figures to prove that a publication contains a false statement of fact and that the authors knew the statement was false or acted with reckless disregard of its truth. Because Falwell had not claimed that *Hustler* had printed a "statement of fact," false or not, the test had not been met. As a result of this case, public figures in both libel and emotional distress suits against the media now face quite imposing obstacles to recovery.

So do private figures. In *The Florida Star v. B. J. F.*,[42] the Supreme Court overturned a damage award against a newspaper which printed the name of a rape victim which it had obtained from police records. Although state law made it unlawful to "print ... in any instrument of mass communication" the name of the victim of a sexual offense, the Court found that under the facts of this case, prosecuting the newspaper violated the First Amendment. The Court conceded that there were important privacy interests at stake, but it also stressed that the newspaper had simply published truthful information contained in records which the police department had placed in a press room accessible to the public. If fault lay anywhere, it was with the department, which itself violated the statute noted above in including the victim's name in records made available to the public, or with the state, which could have taken several stringent protective measures to guard against the release of this information to the media. The newspaper, the Court held, should not be blamed for printing newsworthy information that was essentially handed to it on a platter, especially in view of the vital free speech interests involved.

The Florida Star was not a libel case, because what the paper printed was true; instead, the plaintiff claimed, as Falwell had, that the release of the information at issue caused her severe emotional distress and violated her privacy rights. Before trial, the plaintiff settled with the police department, leaving only the newspaper as a defendant, and in view of the Court's ruling that proved to be a poor choice: if the plaintiff had a valid complaint against anyone, it was the department. The upshot of this case is that in a conflict between privacy and First Amendment rights, the latter will generally prevail. Put another way, *The Florida Star* case should make it as hard for private plaintiffs to prevail in privacy and infliction of emotional distress suits against the news media as *Hustler* makes it for public figures.

One hundred years of privacy law thus finds all states having incorporated in their constitutional, statutory, or common law some variation of the privacy rights identified by Dean Prosser in 1960. Federal law also embraces some of these rights, which are summarized below.

Appropriation of Name or Likeness. This right prohibits the appropriation for commercial use of one's name or likeness without his consent. Often called the right of publicity, it has, for example, been cited by employees whose companies have used their photographs to advertise products without their consent. It is the most firmly established and the least controversial of the four privacy rights.

Intrusion in Intimate Areas. This theory imposes liability for intrusions on one's seclusion or private affairs if the intrusion would be highly offensive to a reasonable person and no valid reason for it exists. The intrusion may be physical, such as breaking into a home or examining a wallet or purse, or non-physical, such as wiretapping a conversation. To be protected, the area invaded must truly be private; no privacy right, for example, prevents someone from watching a person on a street.

The tort is based on the psychological distress caused by the intrusion; whether the defendant learned anything private or embarrassing about the plaintiff or disclosed such data is irrelevant. Workplace intrusion suits have resulted from the surveillance of employees, searches of their belongings, and their dismissals for socializing with a competitor's employees.[43]

Public Disclosure of Private Facts. This tort prohibits the public disclosure of private facts if the publicity would be highly offensive to a reasonable person and the facts are not of valid public concern. Liability may result whether or not the information is true or the plaintiff could sue for defamation. For information to be protected it must be truly private, such as facts about sexual relations, personal illnesses with negative connotations, and other intimate details of one's private life. In the workplace, for example, workers have sued supervisors for disclosing, without their consent, that they have AIDS.

False Light Privacy. This tort involves publicity which puts the plaintiff in a false light in the public eye. The portrayal must be highly offensive to a reasonable person, but the plaintiff need not be defamed. It has been relied upon by workers claiming to have been wrongfully accused of dishonesty or other misconduct.

As noted, the status of false light privacy is unclear. Recent cases raise doubts about how much is left of this tort where public figures sue the media, since public figure is now defined broadly and these plaintiffs must prove falsity, harm to reputation, and malice. As for private parties, it can be argued that they should have to prove the same things, for otherwise the media would always have to worry about how to classify those about whom they report, and this could chill free speech. But it can also be said that by now the definition of public figure is fairly clear and the media need only refrain from putting purely private individuals in a false light, and that this is not too onerous a burden given our common interest in privacy.

THE FOURTH QUARTER CENTURY: CONSTITUTIONAL PRIVACY

Besides privacy rights granted by other laws, some employees are also protected by the federal Constitution. This is because of a series of Supreme Court cases dating back to the 1960's. The justices most responsible for the development of "constitutional privacy" were Louis Brandeis, who cowrote the 1890 *Harvard Law Review* article and sat on the Court from 1916 to 1939, and William O. Douglas, who replaced Brandeis and sat until 1975.

First tapped as a source of constitutional privacy rights was the Fourth Amendment, which protects people "in their persons, houses, papers, and effects, against unreasonable searches and seizures." In 1932 the Court said that this amendment should be "construed liberally to safeguard the right of privacy."[44] But other cases of that era showed that what the Court had in mind was *physical* trespass. In *Olmstead v. United States*,[45] for example, it held that because a police wiretap involved no physical intrusion on the property or person of the man whose conversations were monitored, its use did not trigger the amendment. In dissent, Justice Brandeis argued that the amendment is not so confined in scope, but his plea fell on deaf ears.

The idea that the amendment reaches only physical trespass survived until the 1960's, when the Court took a different tack. In 1961 it held that evidence obtained illegally by police may not be used in state courts, for this violates the "right of privacy" protected by the amendment.[46] Six years later it decided *Katz v. United States*,[47] which involved a listening device attached by police to a phone booth often used by Katz. There, the Court abandoned the physical trespass concept, holding that the amendment protects any "subjective expectation of privacy" that society deems reasonable. In finding for Katz because of his reasonable expectation that his conversations would not be overheard, although he did not own the booth and the FBI did not trespass on his property, the Court took Brandeis' approach in *Olmstead* and overruled that case. By 1968 the Court was speaking simply about the "reasonable expectation of privacy" test in Fourth Amendment cases.[48]

The Court has recently retreated somewhat from its stance of the 1960's. Although it has neither readopted the view that only physical intrusions invoke the Fourth Amendment nor abandoned the "reasonable expectation of privacy" test, the Court has, in the last few years, tended to find privacy expectations "reasonable" less often than in the past, and it has also begun applying less exacting criteria in judging the reasonableness of searches. For example, it has held that while people have a reasonable privacy expectation in the area immediately around their houses, they have no such expectation in an open field, despite the fact that for police to walk in a private field technically involves a trespass.[49] And because people cannot reasonably expect the contents of garbage placed on a curb to be private, police can inspect that garbage at will.[50] On the other hand, people do have reasonable privacy expectations in the contents of their pockets, briefcases and bodies.[51]

In 1987 the Supreme Court ruled for the first time on the propriety of workplace searches. *O'Connor v. Ortega*[52] is a good news-bad news case from the employees' perspective. On the one hand, the Court held that public employees may have a reasonable privacy expectation in their desks and lockers and may sue under the Fourth Amendment if their bosses invade those areas. But the Court also held that the government, in its role of employer, may search workers under laxer standards than those governing searches of citizens. It need only have a reasonable suspicion that the area in question contains something illegal, and it may take away an employee's expectation of privacy in his desk or locker simply by giving notice that these areas are subject to inspection.

But the concept of constitutional privacy involves more than freedom from unreasonable searches. In 1949, for example, the Court upheld a law banning the use of loudspeakers on the streets.[53] Holding that the user's right to speak freely had to be weighed against the right of people in their homes to be free from unwanted intrusions, the Court said that legislatures could strike the balance in favor of privacy. The Court recently reaffirmed this view in *Ward v. Rock Against Racism*,[54] which held that to ensure the tranquillity of a quiet area near Central Park used for reclining and walking, New York could regulate the volume of amplified music emanating from the Naumberg Acoustic Bandshell, an amphitheater and stage structure located nearby. In 1951 the Court balanced speech and privacy rights in upholding a law controlling solicitors on private property.[55] And in 1960 it voided a statute requiring teachers to disclose organizations to which they belonged,[56] saying that this compromised their freedom of association.

The Court issued its most important and controversial privacy ruling in 1965. *Griswold v. Connecticut*[57] involved an 1879 law making it a crime to use contraceptives or to counsel people about them. After the Director of Planned Parenthood was convicted for giving facts about contraception to a married woman,[58] six justices found that the law violated the "constitutional right of privacy." Speaking for a plurality of the Court, Justice Douglas said that although the word *privacy* appears nowhere in the Constitution and a constitutional right of privacy had not heretofore been explicitly recognized in any judicial opinion, the intent of the Bill of Rights, read as a whole, was to protect people from unwanted governmental invasions. Lurking in the "emanations" and "penumbras" of the amendments in the Bill of Rights, Douglas went on, is a privacy right which Connecticut violated when it barred married couples from using birth control and doctors from disseminating facts about it.

The notion that constitutional amendments which say nothing about privacy have "penumbras" and "emanations" containing a privacy right has been endlessly praised and ridiculed by courts and legal commentators.[59] *Griswold* is still good law, however, and it established something which had been implicit in Court rulings for some time. Because it involved married people, it recognized a privacy right only in that context; in 1972, however, the Court held that single people have this right,[60] and in 1973 it held that the right is broad enough to embrace the decision whether to bear a child.[61] Today the concept has evolved to the point that it is regarded as having two aspects: an interest in personal autonomy, involving the right to make decisions free from the interference of others on such topics as marriage, procreation, contraception, family relationships, and child rearing; and an interest in avoiding public disclosure of intimate facts.[62] It must be stressed, however, that the Court has made it clear that there are limits beyond which it will not go in the constitutional privacy area. For example, despite Justice Blackmun's protest that the case really involved autonomy, the Court held in *Bowers v. Hardwick*[63] that adults have no "privacy" right to engage in homosexual acts which precludes states from criminalizing such acts. And in *Webster v. Reproductive Services,*[64] it hinted that it may, possibly in the near future, rule that women have no constitutional right to an abortion. In view of how firmly entrenched the concept of constitutional privacy has become, it is hard to believe that the Court would ever jettison the concept entirely, but recent cases do suggest that we ought not be surprised to see the right expanded no further, and perhaps even curtailed, in future cases.

CONCLUSION

The last one hundred years have witnessed the plea of two lawyers for the law to protect personal privacy find a response in federal, state and local court cases, statutes and ordinances, constitutional provisions, and agency rules. Although the substance of these laws and rulings differs significantly, all protect to some extent the right of people to make certain decisions about their lives without interference from others, to not have publicly disclosed intimate personal information, to not be characterized in a false light in the public eye, and to not have their name or likeness taken for commercial use without their permission. The extent to which these protections available in society at large have been implemented in specific workplace contexts is the subject of the remaining parts of this book.

NOTES

1. *E.g.*, BORK, THE TEMPTING OF AMERICA 95–100 (1990).
2. Griswold v. Connecticut, 381 U.S. 479, 510 (1965) (Black, J. dissenting).
3. 4 HARV. L. REV. 193 (1890).
4. *Id.* at 196, 206 and 213.
5. Pollard v. Photographic Co., 40 Ch. Div. 345, 350 (1888); Tuck v. Priester, 19 Q.B.D. 639 (1887).
6. Warren and Brandeis, *supra* note 3, at 194.
7. *Id.* at 194–95.
8. *Id.* at 213–220.
9. Hadley, *The Right to Privacy*, 3 Nw. U.L. REV. 1 (1894).
10. *See supra* text accompanying note 5.
11. Corliss v. E. W. Walker Co., 57 Fed. Rep. 434 (Cir. Mass. 1893).
12. Roberson v. Rochester Folding Box Co., 64 N.E. 442 (1902).
13. O'Brien, *The Right of Privacy*, 2 COLUM. L. REV. 437 (1902).
14. New York Cons. Laws, Civil Rights Law, Art. 5.
15. Larremore, *The Law of Privacy*, 12 COLUM. L. REV. 693 (1912).
16. Pavesich v. New England Life Ins. Co., 50 S.E. 68 (1905).
17. Larremore, *supra* note 15, at 695.
18. Hillman v. Star Pub. Co., 117 P. 594 (1911).
19. Gillespie v. Brooklyn Heights R.R. Co., 70 N.E. 857 (1904). This right to sue common carriers for abusive language is alive and well today. *See* Ricci v. American Airlines, 544 A.2d 428 (N.J. App. 1988), where a man recovered damages for the unkind treatment he received from a flight attendant.
20. Dickler, *The Right of Privacy: A Proposed Redefinition*, 70 U.S.L. Rev. 435 (1936).
21. DeMay v. Roberts, 46 Mich. 160, 9 N.W. 146 (1881).
22. Brex v. Smith, 146 A. 34 (1929).
23. Rhodes v. Graham, 37 S.W.2d 46 (1931).
24. Jones v. Herald Post Co., 18 S.W.2d 972 (1929).
25. Bazemore v. Savannah Hospital, 155 S.E. 194 (1930).
26. Brents v. Morgan, 299 S.W. 967 (1927).

27. Nizer, *The Right of Privacy: A Half Century's Development*, 39 MICH. L. REV. 526 (1941).

28. 103 N.E. 1108 (1913).

29. 112 Cal. App. 285 (1931). The facts are summarized in Dickler, *supra* note 20, at 446.

30. 28 F. Supp. 845 (D.C. Cal. 1939).

31. Prosser, *Privacy*, 48 CALIF. L. REV. 383 (1960).

32. *Id.* at 401.

33. Franklin, *A Constitutional Problem in Privacy Protection: Legal Inhibitions on Reporting of Fact*, 16 STAN. L. REV. 107 (1963).

34. 69 N. M. 473, 368 P.2d 147 (1962).

35. 376 U.S. 254 (1964).

36. 385 U.S. 374 (1967).

37. Gertz v. Robert Welch, Inc., 418 U.S. 323 (1974).

38. Note, *False Light Invasion of Privacy: False Tort?*, 17 Sw. U.L.J. 135 (1987).

39. Renwick v. News & Observer Pub. Co., 310 N.C. 312, 312 S.E.2d 405 (1984).

40. 108 S. Ct. 876 (1988).

41. *Id.* at 878.

42. 109 S. Ct. 2603 (1989).

43. *E.g.*, K-Mart Corp. Store No. 7441 v. Trotti, 677 S.W.2d 632 (Tex. App. - Houstin [1st Dist.] 1984), *writ ref'd n.r.e.*; Rulon-Miller v. International Business Machine Corp., 162 Cal. App.3d 241 (1984).

44. United States v. Lefkowitz, 285 U.S. 452, 464 (1932).

45. 277 U.S. 438 (1928).

46. Mapp v. Ohio, 367 U.S. 643, 655 (1961).

47. 389 U.S. 347 (1967).

48. Terry v. Ohio, 392 U.S. 1 (1968).

49. Oliver v. United States, 466 U.S. 170 (1984).

50. California v. Greenwood, 108 S. Ct. 1625 (1988).

51. Winston v. Lee, 470 U.S. 753 (1985); Ybarra v. Illinois, 444 U.S. 85 (1970); Schmerber v. California, 384 U.S. 757 (1966).

52. 107 S. Ct. 1492 (1987).

53. Kovacs v. Cooper, 336 U.S. 77 (1949).

54. 109 S. Ct. 2746 (1989).

55. Bread v. Alexandria, 341 U.S. 622 (1951).

56. Shelton v. Tucker, 364 U.S. 479 (1960); Note, *Constitutional Right of Privacy*, 40 N.C.L. REV. 788 (1962).

57. 381 U.S. 479 (1965).

58. Since its passage, the Connecticut law had not been enforced. While it remained unenforced, its constitutionality could not be re-

solved, as courts usually decline to decide cases that do not involve a genuine legal dispute. To create such a dispute, some Yale professors finally convinced local prosecutors to have the Director of Planned Parenthood fined for violating it. Thus, all parties in the controversy, including the prosecutors and the defendant, were obliging participants in a set-up case arranged to meet the requirement that only actual cases and controversies come before the courts.

59. *E.g.*, BORK, THE TEMPTING OF AMERICA, 95–100 (1990).

60. Eisenstadt v. Baird, 405 U.S. 438 (1972).

61. Roe v. Wade, 410 U.S. 113 (1973).

62. Whalen v. Roe, 429 U.S. 589 (1977); Paul v. Davis, 424 U.S. 693 (1976).

63. 106 S. Ct. 2841 (1986).

64. 109 S. Ct. 3040 (1989).

PART II

EMPLOYER SCREENING PRACTICES: RECRUITING AND ASSESSING JOB CANDIDATES

In view of the considerations discussed previously, it is imperative that employers try to learn as much as possible about the backgrounds and qualifications of their workforces. In some occupations, there may even be a duty to try to identify certain risk factors to lessen the potential of harm to others. Efforts to obtain such information will, however, inevitably clash with the privacy interests of the people being studied. How has the law struck the balance in this area? What legal constraints apply to employers in recruiting and assessing the capabilities of prospective employees?

Unfortunately, there is no uniform set of rules to which employers may look for guidance. On the contrary, employers must become familiar with a patchwork of often overlapping federal, state and local constitutional and statutory provisions, agency rules and case law. It is similarly difficult for labor to know the extent of its rights, as this depends on the same factors facing the employer as well as on whether the job sought is in the public or private sector. In this part of the book, major federal and a representative sample of state laws and court rulings affecting the recruiting of employees will be discussed.

4

Why Employers Screen

Although there seems to be a tendency to think otherwise, employment screening is not a 1980's innovation. On the contrary, it has gone on nearly as long as there has been employment. In the 1940's, employers began requiring employees and applicants to take psychological and aptitude tests. Honesty testing via polygraphs, which originated in the area of criminal science in the 1920's, became a fairly common assessment tool of employers a couple of decades ago. At about the same time, toxicological advances made urinalysis a viable response to the spreading use of illicit drugs in the workplace. And as futuristic as it sounds, genetic screening of employees began being carried out by chemical companies in the early 1970's.

Despite the long history of job screening, it did not cause much of a stir until fairly recently. One reason is that until then labor had few meaningful legal rights. As long as employers basically had a free hand to impose employment standards and to fire or not hire if those conditions were not met, it made little sense to question the legality of screening practices. In recent years, however, employees and applicants have acquired significant legal protection in the form of labor, privacy, and anti-discrimination laws and court rulings. One result has been that some brakes have been applied to workplace screening practices.

In the 1970's, for example, courts began construing federal civil rights laws as barring aptitude and similar employment tests which had a racially discriminatory impact if employers could not prove a valid, job-related need for them. Later, concerns about employee privacy and about the accuracy of the tests caused courts and lawmakers to limit the use of polygraph, urine, genetic and psychological testing. At the same time, the Equal Employment Opportunity Commission (EEOC) began issuing restrictive employee selection guidelines which undermined the rationale for and efficacy of many job tests and screening devices. In light of events such as these, many employers simply jettisoned these tools rather than undertake the rigorous and often futile process of trying to validate their use.

Why do employers resort to employment screening, especially when it raises so many legal problems and is so controversial? Are they that worried in principle about the purity of their workforce? Have they simply assumed, in Orwellian fashion, the right to monitor their workers 24 hours a day so as to weed out those with any defects, real or perceived? Or do they have more pressing and legitimate concerns?

Employers clearly have sound reasons for wanting only qualified and reliable personnel. Not only is the quality of its workforce at the heart of a company's competitive position, but that quality may have a direct bearing on the extent to which litigation against the company for accidents traceable to its employees or for defective products succeeds or is even attempted. An employer cannot expect to acquire such personnel without looking past the credentials voluntarily brought forth by employees and job applicants, because in these days of diploma mills, cocaine and crime, one cannot just assume that everyone will be honest about their background and abilities. Insofar as employment tests and other screening devices help employers to conduct more searching background and qualifications checks, employers will understandably want and even be eager to use them.

One legitimate way to use these devices is to gauge ability. Above all, employers want workers who can do the job. Often competency assessment will be simple, as with a typing test for a job requiring that skill. But other qualifications are not as easily measured. Most would say, for example, that to be a good courtroom lawyer one must at least be assertive, well organized, and capable of handling pressure and thinking quickly on her feet. While the experience, education and references of someone seeking this job will tell the prospective employer much about the candidate's potential in these areas, there may be no substitute for a psychological, stress or similar examination. And some would say that only a urine test will reveal whether an airline pilot is impaired by drugs and thus is not "competent" to fly his plane.

Besides competency, screening can be used to assess character. Hiring a qualified person to be an accountant, for example, means little if he juggles the books and absconds with the firm's money. If an in-depth investigation of the credentials offered by an applicant reveals distortions or lies, the employer can reasonably reach negative conclusions about his character and thus his suitability for the job. Indications that the applicant has often left prior jobs, and the reasons for leaving, may warrant the conclusion that the candidate is a job-hopper unlikely to stay around for long. Tests may also assist in assessing whether other traits, such as motivation, thoroughness, conscientiousness and laziness, exist. Finally, while there are many legal restrictions on credit checking and on wage garnishments and the like, proper screening in these areas could speak volumes about a person's reliability or the extent to which an employer should fear having to deal with theft or other legal problems caused by that person.

A third reason to screen involves the need for a healthy workforce. Not only do health and productivity go together, but poor physical or mental health causes excessive absenteeism, high insurance costs, workplace safety problems, and even disability and death. If a task entails particular mental or physical stress, it is appropriate to see if workers are fit for that task. Finally, some occupations, such as transit worker or airline pilot, affect the public safety and thus present other valid reasons for fitness screening.

Health screening of employees and applicants has long been a common practice. Recently, however, exclusions from the workforce of people with health problems have been successfully attacked on the basis of federal and state age, privacy and handicap discrimination laws, among other things. A special set of problems is created by alcohol and drug testing of workers and applicants, as this area is being increasingly regulated by federal and state laws and court rulings. The same is true of employer actions affecting AIDS victims. Thus, while employers have a plain interest in fitness screening, they have nowhere near the leeway in this area that they once had.

Apart from these justifications for screening, there are compelling legal reasons for it. The *negligent hiring* and *negligent retention* doctrines are two reasons. That an employer can, under the legal doctrine of *respondeat superior*, be held legally liable for injuries caused by an employee's wrongdoing is another.

Most jurisdictions now recognize a cause of action for negligent hiring or retention. Under these doctrines, an employer can be held liable for hiring or retaining a worker whom he knew or should have known had dangerous propensities. To win this suit, a plaintiff must prove that the employer hired or retained someone unfit for employment and knew or should have known of the lack of fitness, that the plaintiff was injured by a tortious act of the employee, that the employer owed a duty of care to the plaintiff, and that hiring or retaining the employee was the proximate cause of his injury.[1] These cases often arise when an employee harms an employer's customer or another with whom the employer deals in the course of his business. Liability may result because the employer knew of the employee's unsuitability at the time of the hiring, because a careful background check would have disclosed the problem and it can thus be said that if the employer had acted prudently he would have found the problem, or because information is acquired after the employee is hired which should have prompted the employer not to retain the worker. Conditions that could render an applicant unsuitable for employment include a prior criminal record or psychiatric treatment, a violent temper or alcoholism.[2]

In *Kendall v. Gore Properties*,[3] a woman was murdered by a man hired by her landlord to paint her apartment. The landlord hired the man with no reference check and gave him a key to the apartment. After the murder, it was found that the man had been in a mental institution. The Court held the landlord-employer liable, ruling that tenants may reasonably expect that their landlords will not let dangerous strangers have access to their homes. The case establishes that innocent people have a right to be protected from exposure to dangerous employees and that employers have a duty to use reasonable care in hiring. In *Wilson N. Jones Memorial Hosp. v. Davis*,[4] a hospital with a screening procedure requiring four employment and three personal references and a check of at least one of each before hiring an applicant was held liable when an orderly hurt the plaintiff while removing a catheter. The jury found that the hospital had made no pre-hiring reference check and only one post-hiring check to verify employment dates and jobs held. Had the hospital followed its own procedure, it would have learned that the orderly had a criminal record and had falsely claimed eight months' training at the Navy Medical Corps School.

The employer's duty of reasonable care does not end at the hiring stage. Under the doctrine of negligent retention, an employer may be liable for keeping a worker with dangerous traits if the employer learned of the traits after hiring the employee. The difference between this tort and the negligent hiring tort is that in the latter case, liability results if the employer should have known of the worker's dangerous tendencies, whereas in the former he must actually have known of those traits after the hiring. Because imposing liability for what an employer should have known is a far cry from doing so for what he knew, the negligent hiring doctrine plainly is the more onerous from the employer's standpoint.

Negligent entrustment can also be a problem for employers. This tort imposes liability for harm to third parties caused by incompetent workers using company property. It requires proof that an owner entrusted property to an employee who the employer knew or should have known was unlicensed, incompetent or reckless; that the employee was negligent; and that the negligence proximately caused the plaintiff's injury.[5] Most cases involve entrusting company trucks to unqualified drivers, and in them the employer's investigation of the driving record and experience of the driver will be significant. Negligence has been found, for example, where employers did not try to verify the employee's driving record or inspect his license or continued to let the driver operate company vehicles after obtaining information pointing to the driver's incompetence.[6]

In addition to these theories, the respondeat superior doctrine may impose liability on employers, not for their wrongful acts, but for those of an employee. This theory has been stated as follows: "A master is responsible for want of care on [his] servant's part toward those to whom [the] master owes [a] duty of care, provided failure of [the] servant to use such care occurred in the course of his employment."[7] Under this theory an employer could, for example, be liable for harm to a consumer caused by a product or service improperly made or performed by an employee impaired by drugs. The theory could also be relied on as an alternate basis for liability in cases alleging negligent hiring or retention by an employer. To illustrate, if an employee commits a tortious act during the scope of employment and in furtherance of his employer's business—elements that must be present for respondeat superior to apply—and that act harms a customer, and it is later found that the boss knew or had reason to know of the worker's dangerous propensities when he was hired, the plaintiff could try to hold the employer directly liable under the negligent hiring doctrine for his own misconduct in improperly hiring the worker, and vicariously liable under the respondeat superior doctrine for the wrong done by the employee during the course and scope of his employment.

NOTES

1. *E.g.*, PROSSER, HANDBOOK OF THE LAW OF TORTS, 143–44 (4th ed. West 1971); 5 PERSONAL INJURY: ACTIONS, DEFENSES, DAMAGES, "NEGLIGENCE" (Matthew Bender 1986).
2. *E.g.*, Bennett v. United States, 803 F.2d 1502 (9th Cir. 1986); Pittard v. Four Seasons Motor Inn, Inc., 688 P.2d 333 (N.M. App. 1984); Stone v. Hurst Lumber Co., 386 P.2d 910 (Utah 1963).
3. 236 F.2d 673 (D.C. Cir. 1956).
4. 553 S.W.2d 180 (Tex. Civ. App. Waco 1977), writ ref'd n.r.e.
5. *E.g.*, Williams v. Steves Ind., Inc., 699 S.W.2d 570 (Tex. 1985).
6. *E.g.*, Horth Houston Pole Line Corp. v. McAllister, 667 S.W.2d 829 (Tex. App. Houston [14th Dist.] 1984), no writ.
7. BLACK'S LAW DICTIONARY 1179 (5th ed. 1979).

5

Employment Discrimination Laws

In assessing the legality of employer screening methods, it is important to distinguish between actions taken to obtain information and actions taken as a result of information. Information that an applicant uses drugs, for example, could come from a urine test, background check, or answer to a questionnaire, or it might be offered voluntarily. Once the fact of drug use is established, however, there arises the issue of employment consequences. These could include rejection in the case of applicants; discharge, suspension, or compulsory participation in a rehabilitation program for employees; or no consequences at all.

Legal results may flow from both the negative employment action and the data-gathering process. To illustrate, there must generally be adverse employment action for Title VII of the 1964 Civil Rights Act to be violated. It is unlawful, for example, to refuse to hire someone because of her religion, but it is usually permissible to take steps to learn what religion an applicant practices—in fact, the latter may be necessary to enable the employer to reasonably accommodate the person's religious beliefs, as Title VII requires. In contrast, even a properly administered drug test may violate privacy rights even if nothing is done with the information obtained. Employers must thus be conscious of existing legal parameters both in gathering and in using information about candidates. Because federal and state employment discrimination laws affect both of these functions, an appreciation of the general requirements and impact of these laws is essential.

TITLE VII

The major federal law pertaining to employment discrimination is Title VII of the Civil Rights Act of 1964.[1] This law provides that it is an unlawful employment practice for an employer to refuse to hire because of race, color, religion, sex, or national origin; or to limit, segregate, or classify employees or applicants so as to deny job opportunities on one of these bases. There are some exceptions. Employers engaged in work involving national security, for example, may dismiss or not hire anyone who cannot meet the demands of a national security program, if such is required for the position at issue.[2] Employment actions taken against members of the United States Communist Party or organizations required to register as a Communist front group by the Subversive Activities Control Board are also lawful.[3] Otherwise, Title VII limits an employer's freedom to investigate and base employment decisions on an applicant's background.

Title VII does not ban pre-employment inquiries *per se*. Inquiries about race, religion and the like, however, have traditionally been disfavored under civil rights laws. Unless it is clear why an employer needs this data, such inquiries are suspected of forming the basis for discrimination. What is not asked, moreover, may be as important as what is. In *EEOC v. Spokane Concrete Prods.*,[4] for example, a woman applied to be a truck driver, which required working with concrete pipe. She had a license and experience in carrying heavy items. During the interview, she was only asked if she had transportation and child care, told that weights of up to 300 pounds were involved, and asked "Do you get my message?" by the interviewer. The court held that the company's failure to ask about the woman's qualifications for the job created an inference of discrimination. As there was no evidence that a woman could not do the job, she should have been asked all questions usually asked of a male applicant regarding experience, health, and so on.

Pre-employment inquiries, it should be noted, seldom prompt litigation because the Equal Employment Opportunity Commission requires extensive recordkeeping on the demographics of workforces, including information on applicants.[5] In addition, the EEOC and the courts have endorsed voluntary affirmative action programs by private employers. These factors undercut the presumption that inquiries as to minority status are necessarily suspect.

EEOC guidelines afford some guidance as to the permissibility of questions about religion and sex. For example, they allow inquiries about gender if made in good faith for a nondiscriminatory purpose.[6] But a caveat accompanies this provision: "Any pre-employment inquiry in connection with prospective employment which expresses directly or indirectly any limitation, specification, or discrimination as to sex shall be unlawful unless based upon a bona fide occupational qualification." If a female applicant is not hired after an interview in which she is questioned about pregnancy or possible child care problems, and male candidates are not asked the same questions, it can be inferred that the refusal to hire was discriminatory. In *Anderson v. City of Bessemer*,[7] the Supreme Court upheld a lower court finding of sex discrimination based on this kind of disparity in questioning. The plaintiff, a woman applicant for the job of Recreation Director, was asked if she would do night work and travel as part of the job. In *King v. Trans World Airlines*,[8] the plaintiff was denied a job after an interview in which she was asked about her pregnancy during a prior job, marital status, child care arrangements, and childbearing plans. The court of appeals held that she had established sex discrimination in the hiring process by showing that the questions about her family duties were not asked of other candidates.

As to religion, the guidelines say that "the use of pre-selection inquiries which determine an applicant's availability has an exclusionary effect on the employment opportunities of persons with certain religious practices. The use of such inquiries will, therefore, be considered to violate Title VII."[9] An inquiry about availability is allowed only if the employer can show that it did not have the effect of excluding employees needing accommodation for religious practices, or if it was otherwise justified by business necessity. An employer with a legitimate interest in knowing the availability of applicants prior to selection must consider procedures that would serve this interest only and have a less drastic exclusionary effect on persons whose religious practices need accommodation.

Title VII does not expressly bar discrimination based on prior arrests or convictions, credit history, or drug usage. But plaintiffs have challenged employment decisions based on such factors as having a disparate impact on a protected group. In *Green v. Missouri Pac. R. R. Co.*,[10] for example, the court voided as racially discriminatory policies banning the employment of anyone with an arrest or conviction record. As will be discussed, the case law also suggests a limitation, based on its racial impact, on adverse employment action based on poor credit history.

STATE LAWS

Most states have fair employment practices laws which limit or prohibit pre-employment inquiries about an applicant's gender. Twenty-four states expressly ban inquiries which discriminate because an applicant is in a protected class.[11] There, the general ban on discrimination in employment extends to pre-employment inquiries, including applications and interviews. The remaining laws do not address pre-employment inquiries *per se*, but even in these states certain inquiries should be avoided because they can constitute potent evidence that some other action, such as a refusal to hire, was taken with discriminatory intent.

States which have fair employment practices laws often publish pre-employment inquiry guides. These are booklets designed to aid interviewers in avoiding questions deemed impermissible under federal or that state's law. Twenty-three states[12] and the District of Columbia have such guides, and unlawful pre-employment inquiries are directly prohibited by statute in several of these jurisdictions. Generally, the guidelines themselves are not statutes, though they occasionally take the form of administrative rules. They are most often published by the agency responsible for enforcing the fair employment practices laws in that state.

Questions about an applicant's race, gender, or status as a member of another protected class are usually deemed suspect, although most guides acknowledge that such queries may be required by law or for recordkeeping purposes. California's Pre-employment Inquiry Guidelines, for instance, states that employers may "collect applicant-flow and other recordkeeping data for statistical purposes," and it encourages employers to "solicit this information on a voluntary basis in order to comply with federal and state requirements and for affirmative action efforts." And questions considered objectionable by guidelines typically range beyond inquiries about race and gender. Common examples are questions about height and weight, arrests, credit or economic status, pregnancy, child care, and birth control. The only exception is when the condition inquired about is a "bona fide occupational qualification" (BFOQ). Arizona's Guide to Pre-employment Inquiries, for example, allows queries about an applicant's gender if gender is a BFOQ for the position; if a relationship to the job or a compelling business reason is shown, inquiries about height and weight, type of military discharge, arrests, and economic status are also permitted.

MISCELLANEOUS LAWS

Union Membership Status

The National Labor Relations Act prohibits employers from discharging or refusing to hire based on membership in a labor organization.[13] Similarly, state right-to-work laws, which prohibit the denial of employment because of membership in a labor organization, indirectly limit an employer's ability to inquire about union status. Such laws exist in sixteen states.[14]

Other Laws

In addition to the categories discussed above, a miscellany of laws affect background checks. The Omnibus Crime Control and Safe Streets Act of 1968,[15] for example, limits an employer's ability to intercept or monitor the phone conversations of employees. Federal law also prohibits the denial of civilian federal employment solely because of prior drug or alcohol abuse.[16] A Florida law, apparently intended to reserve to the state the exclusive right to enact such laws, prohibits local governments from enacting ordinances requiring the background screening of individuals engaged in specific types of employment.[17] In New York, it is unlawful to discriminate in employment because an applicant is disabled and has a guide, hearing, or other service dog.[18] In Virginia, all application forms used by private employers must ask applicants if they are legally eligible for employment in the United States.[19]

CONCLUSION

Federal and most state laws ban employment discrimination based on race, color, religion, sex, national origin, and, in many instances, handicap. The discrimination may be overt, or it may be accomplished through subtle means, such as questions ostensibly designed to learn about the capabilities of applicants. Either way, it is impermissible. The rule of thumb in this area is simple: unless they obviously relate to a valid business purpose, employer inquiries touching on the protected categories noted above should be avoided at all costs.

NOTES

1. 42 U.S.C. §2000e et seq. The act applies to private employers who have at least fifteen employees on each working day in at least twenty weeks in the current or preceding year and are in an industry affecting interstate commerce. 42 U.S.C. §§2000e(b). State and local government employees are covered. §§2000a(b), 2000e-2(a). Finally, the act applies to labor organizations representing employees in industries affecting interstate commerce, §§2000e(e), 2000e-2(c), and to

employment agencies that supply employees to covered employers. §§2000e(c), 2000e-2(b).

2. 42 U.S.C. §2000e-2(g).

3. 42 U.S.C. §2000e-2(f).

4. 534 F. Supp. 518 (E.D. Wash. 1982).

5. *E.g.*, 29 C.F.R. §§1602 (recordkeeping and reporting requirements), 1607.4 (requiring recordkeeping on the impact of job selection procedures).

6. 29 C.F.R. §1604.7.

7. 470 U.S. 564 (1985).

8. 738 F.2d 255 (8th Cir. 1984).

9. 29 C.F.R. §1605.3.

10. 523 F.2d 1290 (8th Cir. 1975). In contrast, the U. S. Supreme Court has upheld a city transit system's rule prohibiting the employment of methadone users against claims of racial or national origin discrimination. New York City Transit Auth. v. Beazer, 440 U.S. 568 (1979).

11. Alaska, Arizona, California, Colorado, Hawaii, Illinois, Kansas, Maine, Massachusetts, Michigan, Minnesota, Missouri, New Hampshire, New Jersey, New Mexico, New York, Ohio, Oregon, Pennsylvania, Rhode Island, Utah, Washington, West Virginia, and Wisconsin.

12. Arizona, California, Colorado, Delaware, Hawaii, Idaho, Illinois, Indiana, Maine, Michigan, Missouri, Nevada, New Hampshire, New Jersey, New York, Ohio, Pennsylvania, Rhode Island, South Dakota, Utah, Washington, West Virginia, Wisconsin.

13. 29 U.S.C. §158.

14. Arizona, Arkansas, Georgia, Louisiana, Massachusetts, Michigan, Minnesota, Nebraska, Nevada, New Hampshire, North Dakota, South Carolina, South Dakota, Tennessee, Utah, and Virginia.

15. 18 U.S.C.A. §2510. The act does not bar interception through an extension line or by a party to the conversation. 18 U.S.C.A. §2511(2)(d).

16. 42 U.S.C. §§290dd–1(b)(1); 290ee–1(b)(1).

17. Fla. Stat. Ann. §166.0443.

18. N. Y. Civ. Rights Law § 47-a.

19. Va. Code Ann. § 40.1–11.1

6

Recruiting and Assessing Candidates

ADVERTISING FOR EMPLOYEES

Advertising is often the first step in employee screening. A major law firm, for example, may send its recruiters only to certain prestigious schools. An employer wanting only youthful employees may advertise in magazines geared to youth. A construction company may hire only by word-of-mouth, perhaps to avoid hiring minority workers. As one might guess from the last example, federal and state antidiscrimination laws have rendered certain advertising and recruiting practices illegal or at least questionable because of their tendency to screen out blacks, women, or members of other protected groups. Conversely, special efforts to attract women and minorities have, despite their potential for reverse discrimination, become an accepted part of both voluntary and court-imposed affirmative action programs.

Title VII of the 1964 Civil Rights Act prohibits covered employers and others, including labor unions and employment agencies, from causing to be printed or published any notice for employment indicating a preference, limitation, specification, or discrimination based on race, color, religion, sex, or national origin. An exception is made in the case of jobs for which such a restriction is a bona fide occupational qualification (BFOQ). The U.S. Supreme Court has upheld the validity of applying this kind of ban to a newspaper as against a constitutional challenge based on freedom of the press.[1]

A once-prominent example of discriminatory advertising invalidated by Title VII is the listing of job openings in newspaper classifieds under the headings of "Help Wanted—Male" and "Help Wanted—Female." Even without sex-labeled columns, advertisements such as "Wanted—men who want to be truck operators" and the use of a feminine designation such as "stewardess" have been found to be discriminatory.[2] But it is also possible to go too far the other way. An employment agency, for example, was found to have violated Title VII when it placed an advertisement stating that one qualification for a position was that applicants be members of a minority. That the agency was trying to serve a federal contractor with an affirmative action program did not justify its action.[3]

Age discrimination laws have prompted their own collection of "trigger words" deemed unacceptable by regulatory agencies and courts because they indicate age preference. EEOC regulations give these examples of terms considered to violate the Age Discrimination in Employment Act of 1967 (ADEA)[4] if they appear in help wanted notices: "age 25 to 35," "young," "college student," "recent college graduate," "boy," "girl," "age 40 to 50," "age over 65," "retired person," and "supplement your pension."[5] Courts have also banned the term "career girl."[6]

The main issue arising in litigation has been under what circumstances word-of-mouth recruiting involves unlawful discrimination. This practice is not *per se* unlawful, and challenges to it have been rejected, especially if the result of the hiring process shows no discriminatory impact.[7] But when word-of-mouth recruiting is done by a virtually all-white workforce and results in almost all-white hiring, discrimination has occurred. The same principles apply to nepotistic hiring and to "hiring at the gate."[8]

As for the use of employment agencies, Title VII applies to the agencies themselves and to their employment, recruiting, and advertising practices. There is little litigation involving employment agencies, and much of it has to do with what entities are within the definition of "employment agency."[9] EEOC guidelines declare it illegal for an employment agency to deal, for most jobs, with persons of only one sex.[10] They also state that the agency shares the employer's guilt if a job order contains a discriminatory specification or if the agency otherwise has reason to doubt an employer's assertion that gender is a bona fide occupational qualification.[11]

WRITTEN APPLICATIONS AND QUESTIONNAIRES

The function of employment applications is to assemble an initial body of information about applicants and their qualifications for the position in question. Applications routinely solicit information about prior education and job experience. They also often request personal and/or employment references and the applicant's consent to a medical examination or a background check. Applications run into trouble, however, when they ask questions which are personal or have no bearing on job performance. For instance, the question "Are you currently using illegal drugs?" may be quite clearly job-related, but the question "Have you ever used illegal drugs?" may cross the line of unacceptability and invade privacy.

The main restraints on pre-employment inquiries come from state and federal antidiscrimination statutes, chiefly Title VII of the Civil Rights Act of 1964. Inquiries about pregnancy, child care or childbearing plans, for example, implicate these laws. As chapter 5 observed, pre-employment inquiry guidelines accompany fair employment practices laws in many states, and they set forth what are considered unacceptable areas of inquiry.

Sometimes an inquiry itself may be illegal. More commonly, a question is not illegal *per se*, but, absent other explanations of a negative employment decision, can constitute persuasive evidence that the decision was made with discriminatory intent. In one case, for example, the U.S. Supreme Court upheld a finding of discriminatory failure to hire based in part on questions regarding child care duties and the female applicant's willingness to travel.[12] In this connection, questions may reflect the existence of an employer rule that is itself illegal. To illustrate, minimum height requirements have been held invalid for most jobs because they screen out disproportionate numbers of females, Hispanics, and others.[13] Accordingly, asking an applicant's height on a job application would be at least suspect.

In light of fair employment practices laws and court rulings, employers should avoid inquiries about the following: (1) race, sex, religion, national origin, or age, unless required for a valid purpose, such as recordkeeping, which is made clear in the application; (2) marital status, child care duties, intentions as to pregnancy, and birth control; (3) height, weight, type of military discharge, and arrest or conviction records, unless it is made clear that the employer does not have a flat rule against hiring persons with such records; (4) economic status, including credit information, prior bankruptcy or garnishments; (5) political or religious views or associations; and (6) personal matters such as sexual preference. Such inquiries are permitted if the subject of inquiry is a bona fide occupational qualification for the particular job; the female sex, for example, would be a BFOQ for the position of ladies' room attendant. As chapter five discussed, however, the BFOQ exception is very narrow. It must also be stressed that the above list is not intended to be complete, but merely reflective of federal and most states' laws. State laws may declare other types of questions to be out-of-bounds.

INTERVIEWS

The oral interview is but an extension of the data-seeking process that begins with the application. Thus, questions asked during an interview can raise the same problems that inquiries on application forms do. In several respects, moreover, oral interviews have even more potential for creating difficulty. First, the employer does not have the firm control over what goes on in an interview that she has over what appears on a written application form. What occurs will depend on the idiosyncracies and biases of the individual hiring officer. There may also be problems in proving what was or was not said. Because of this, interviewing personnel should be carefully trained and receive written guidelines for conducting interviews according to existing legal requirements.

EMPLOYMENT REFERENCES

References can be among the most valuable tools for assessing potential employees, but they are not without risks. It is, however, the employer who gives the reference who typically runs into trouble rather than the employer who seeks it. To illustrate: Employer A fires a worker because of suspected theft. Employer B, who is considering hiring the employee, calls or writes A for a reference. If A tells the truth, the worker may sue for defamation, and even if A wins he will incur the legal expenses, loss of time, aggravation, and bad publicity that attend lawsuits. If A falsely gives a favorable reference, he may be exposed to liability if the employee steals from B. And this problem is not limited to theft, but can also arise if an employee is fired for almost any negative reason that cannot be solidly proved, including breach of company confidentiality, dishonesty, or insubordination.

The general rule is that employers are protected by a qualified privilege when giving references to another employer, if the communication is made in good faith. The litigation that has occurred, however, demonstrates the foolhardiness of relying too heavily on this privilege. The problem is especially acute if the information makes its way beyond the persons having a legitimate business reason to have it.

Some companies, as a matter of policy, have stopped giving references, beyond simply affirming that the person worked there. But even this may not solve the problem. Contrary to the usual rule that an employer's communication solely to an employee is not a publication, which must occur for a statement to be defamatory,[14] some courts have found publication when it is forseeable that the employee will be compelled to publish the reason for his discharge.[15] Self-publication can occur as follows: An employee is fired for insubordination and is told that this is the reason. When applying for a new job, he may be validly required to state the reason for leaving the other one. He cannot be expected to lie, so his truthful response is the vehicle for publication of the former employer's defamatory communication.

Along with defamation, employees receiving bad references often assert intentional interference with a contract, although employers are not liable for this tort if they act on the basis of a valid business justification.[16] Other theories of liability may include invasion of privacy and intentional infliction of mental distress, which require unreasonable and outrageous conduct by the employer, but, unlike defamation, do not demand that the statements be false. Employers who promise a good reference and give a bad one may be liable for fraud.[17] The bottom line of this is that employers cannot rely on getting accurate information from a reference, as the referring employer may convey either no information or only facts that would be fully demonstrable should a lawsuit occur.

Some states have service letter statutes. They require employers to furnish, upon request of an employee leaving their service, a letter stating the period of employment and the nature of service.[18] The law may require the employer to state the true reason for the worker's voluntary leaving or discharge.[19] Laws mandating employee access to their personnel records may contain an exemption prohibiting the disclosure of references, at least if the identity of the person giving the information would be disclosed.[20]

ARREST AND CONVICTION RECORDS

Title VII Limitations

Because an arrest carries no connotation of guilt, employers have found it difficult to defend the disqualification of applicants based on prior arrests. Under Title VII, the blanket rejection of applicants on this ground has been attacked as having a disparate impact on minorities. In *Gregory v. Litton Systems, Inc.*,[21] a black man accepted employment before completing the employer's standard security form, which required the disclosure of arrests. When he noted that he had been arrested fourteen times, the company withdrew its job offer pursuant to a policy of not hiring anyone with a history of non-traffic arrests. The court found that the policy was enforced objectively and revealed no intent to discriminate; nonetheless, it held that Title VII was violated, noting the overwhelming evidence that blacks are arrested more often than whites. Anticipating the U.S. Supreme Court's decision in *Griggs v. Duke Power Co.*,[22] it then found no business necessity for the policy. *Gregory* has generally been followed in cases dealing with arrest records under Title VII.

The use of convictions to justify adverse personnel decisions has had mixed success. In *Green v. Missouri Pac. R. R. Co.*,[23] the plaintiff admitted in his application that he had been convicted for refusing military induction. Under its policy of rejecting anyone convicted of non-traffic offenses, the company rejected Green because of his criminal record. The court, however, held that this use of convictions violated Title VII because of its disparate impact on blacks. Not only did Green show through the use of statistics that blacks are convicted of crime at a much higher rate than whites, but an examination of company records showed that black applicants were, under the policy, more than twice as likely to be rejected at Missouri Pacific than whites. The court held that this created a *prima facie* case of discrimination. Considering the claim that there was a business need for the policy, the court also said that it could not conceive of any need that "would automatically place every individual convicted of any offense, except a minor traffic offense, in the permanent ranks of the unemployed."[24]

When faced with similar facts, other courts have followed *Green*. They have, however, distinguished cases in which convictions are only one factor in the hiring decision or the job involves a special degree of trust. In *Heatherington v. State Personnel Bd.*,[25] for example, the plaintiff alleged that a California law prohibiting the employment of an ex-felon as a peace officer had a disparate impact on minorities. Distinguishing *Green*, the court held that the employer successfully showed that past criminal conduct bore a significant relationship to the duties of peace officer.

State Laws

Most states regulate the use of arrest or conviction records in making employment decisions. There are two types of statutes: those authorizing or requiring the employer's use of criminal record data, and those limiting or prohibiting the use of such material. While these categories may appear to be mutually exclusive, several states have enacted both types of statute.

Statutes forbidding the use of criminal record information are based on a legislative policy to encourage the rehabilitation of people with a criminal past. Some laws apply only to arrest or conviction records, and some apply to both. The policy is most compelling in the case of arrest records, since arrests carry no connotation of guilt; for this reason, several states prohibit employers from inquiring about arrests that did not lead to conviction.[26] Other states include discrimination based on arrests in their fair employment practices laws.[27] Still others provide for the sealing of arrest records without creating an express bar on the use of such information.[28]

The rehabilitative aspect of the policy is stronger in the case of criminal convictions, as a greater stigma attaches when the commission of a crime has been proved. This policy, however, is offset by safety concerns prompted by the need for trustworthy and stable employees in certain jobs. Many states have solved this conflict by enacting a general prohibitive statute and then excepting specific occupations. The California Penal Code, for example, bars employers from inquiring about prior conviction records, but another statute authorizes banks to fingerprint applicants so as to conduct a criminal records check.[29] Fingerprinting is also a prerequisite for employment and licensure in a wide range of other occupations.

These California statutes are typical of the state laws which authorize or require a criminal record check, and most states have such laws. In contrast to the broad language of statutes limiting such checks, laws requiring checks usually focus on and are linked to a policy that flows from particular occupations. The fiduciary nature of bank employment, for example, creates a public interest in ensuring that banks hire trust-worthy people; likewise, some laws restrict the employment of people in positions where they will be in contact with children or carry weapons. Many states require or authorize criminal record checks and/or fingerprinting for private detectives or their employees. A smaller number require a check for such jobs as peace officer, Alcoholic Beverage Control employee, and private security agent.

FINGERPRINTING

Many states authorize or require the use of fingerprints in the hiring or licensing process for specific occupations. As with criminal records checks, fingerprinting is a common prerequisite to employment in jobs involving a high degree of trust. Among the occupations for which fingerprinting may be required are attorney, bail bondsman, mortgage broker, private detective, teacher, day care personnel, jobs involving work with the handicapped or the elderly, and jobs linked to sporting events or to gambling.

In contrast to the large number of laws authorizing the pre-employment use of fingerprints, two states, California and New York, limit their use. The New York law provides that, unless otherwise permitted, no person may be required to be finger-printed as a condition of employment.[30] The New York legis-lature, however, has singled out several jobs for which fingerprinting is deemed advisable. The California law does not bar fingerprinting *per se*; but rather provides that no one may require, as a condition of employment, that a person be photographed or fingerprinted by anyone who desires that the results be given to anyone else if they could be used to the detriment of the individual. This law is virtually the only direct statutory ban on the use of photographs in the hiring process. Requiring an applicant's photograph prior to a hiring decision, however, could be evidence that discrimination in violation of state or federal law has occurred. For this reason, such use is barred by the pre-employment guides in many states.

FINANCIAL STATUS

Title VII Limitations

The pre-employment investigation of credit records or financial status has been challenged as having a disparate impact on minorities. In most cases, the employer has been a bank or a financial institution, and the courts have found a business reason for the employer's inquiry into the financial acumen of the plaintiff. In *Paxton v. Union National Bank*,[31] for example, a bank employee was fired after a background check revealed inaccuracies in his application. Although the employee had disclosed a bankruptcy, he had falsely stated that his debts had been discharged, and he had also failed to reveal his default on another debt. A memorandum regarding the discharge revealed that the employer was disturbed by the large debts that it seemed the employee could not repay; based on this evidence, the court found that the discharge was motivated by the employee's financial status. Finding that this represented a justifiable concern, the court held that a bank "has a legitimate interest in the credit history of its employees" which is based on the desire to have honest, responsible employees, the fact that an employee with a poor credit history has a greater motivation to commit theft, and the perception that bank customers will not wish to entrust their money to such employees.[32] Other cases have echoed this sentiment with regard to financial institutions.[33]

What remains unsettled is whether courts would be so lenient with an employer whose business is not closely tied to financial matters. Guidance can be obtained from cases dealing with wage garnishments and bankruptcy under Title VII; in the majority, the courts have sided with the employer.[34] An exception is *Keenan v. American Cast Iron Pipe Co.*[35] There, the plaintiff was fired pursuant to a policy under which employees were reprimanded for the first and second wage attachments and discharged for the third. On appeal from a grant of summary judgment for the company, the court held that both reprimands and discharges are subject to Title VII coverage, and it remanded the case to the trial court to consider whether the policy had a discriminatory effect on the defendant's employees. In *Johnson v. Pike Corp. of Am.*,[36] the court voided a policy of firing employees after they received "several" wage attachments, holding that "[t]he sole permissible reason for discrimination against actual or prospective employees involves the individual's capability to perform the job effectively."[37]

Taken together, these decisions reveal a reluctance on the part of courts to find illegal discrimination in a policy of basing personnel decisions on an investigation of an applicant's financial status. Despite the dissenting voices of *Johnson* and *Keenan*, most courts have accepted the employer's argument that its economic interests create a valid justification for such policies.

Fair Credit Reporting Act

The federal Fair Credit Reporting Act[38] regulates businesses that furnish consumer or credit reports to others. The act allows reports to be provided for employment purposes, but if a report given to an employer contains data that likely will affect adversely the subject's ability to obtain employment, the agency must notify the subject of this information and of the name and address to which it has been reported. If employment is denied because of the report, its user must inform the subject of this fact and of the name and address of the agency which supplied the report.

State Laws

Four states[39] have laws regulating consumer reporting agencies. The Montana statute defines an investigative consumer report as containing data "on a consumer's character, general reputation, personal characteristics or mode of living... obtained through personal interviews with neighbors, friends [or others]."[40] These reports may also include credit information and information from public records, such as judgments, tax liens, and arrest and conviction data. Consumer reporting agencies, which are in the business of collecting and distributing this data, are frequently used by those seeking to investigate the background of a job applicant.

The states that regulate these agencies vary in terms of how extensively they do so. California, for example, requires only that the person seeking a report notify the subject that "an investigative consumer report regarding the consumer's character, general reputation, personal characteristics, and mode of living will be made."[41] In Connecticut, information agencies must keep a record of all data "open at reasonable times to the inspection of the person to whom [it] relates or . . . his authorized agent or attorney."[42] Maine also requires notice to the subject of the report, but it allows agencies to waive the notice requirement if "strict procedures" are maintained to ensure that the information is accurate.[43] Finally, although it allows the use of reports for employment purposes, the Montana law limits the information which can be distributed.[44]

In ten states[45] an employer may not refuse to hire an applicant because he is subject to a court order withholding income for child support. While these laws do not directly bar questions about child support obligations, such a question, followed by a refusal to hire, could be evidence that the statute was violated. An additional three states[46] bar the refusal to hire because of any income withholding order. Louisiana provides that employment may not be denied because of voluntary wage assignments or one garnishment.[47] A large number of states prohibit a discharge based on garnishment orders.

MEDICAL STATUS

Several states limit an employer's use of an applicant's medical record. The majority of these, however, allow employers to condition employment on a medical examination, limiting the employer only by mandating that the cost of any examination not be paid by the applicant. Florida, Louisiana, and North Carolina bar employers from requiring a test for the sickle-cell trait as a condition of employment.[48] North Carolina extends this prohibition to the blood trait for hemoglobin C. By the end of the 1980's most states prohibited discrimination in hiring on the basis of prior claims of workers' compensation, either through specific statutory provisions or judicial interpretation of common law discharge doctrines.[49]

Three states limit inquiries into mental illness. Alaska does not allow employers to use treatment for mental illness as a basis for discrimination in employment, licensing, or resumption of professional practice.[50] Maryland bars employers from asking applicants about psychological, psychiatric, or physical illness, disability, handicap, or any treatment which does not relate directly to the applicant's capacity to perform the work in question.[51] In Massachusetts, it is unlawful to refuse to hire an applicant solely because she refuses to answer questions about treatment for mental illness, provided that she has a certificate of mental competence from a psychiatrist.[52]

CONCLUSION

Title VII of the 1964 Civil Rights Act bars employment advertisements that discriminate on the basis of race, color, religion, sex, or national origin. Most litigation involving recruiting methods has concerned the circumstances under which word-of-mouth recruiting has involved discrimination. Any recruiting technique which tends to screen out women, blacks, or members of other protected groups should be avoided. The same is true of techniques which may result in age discrimination in violation of the Age Discrimination in Employment Act of 1967.

Employers who give a reference for a former employee are vulnerable to legal complications. If they provide an honest, adverse reference, the worker may sue for defamation. If they give a false, favorable one, they risk being held responsible for the negative performance of the employee in the new job. Despite the usual rule that an employer is protected by a qualified privilege when giving references, if the communication is made in good faith, the situation has spawned vexatious litigation. The problem is compounded when the information reaches people with no valid reason to possess it.

Inquiries into an applicant's conviction or arrest records are generally permissible if the position is sensitive and there is a greater than average need for trustworthy employees. Otherwise, such inquiries, especially into records of arrests, which carry no connotation of guilt, are problematic. As a rule, fingerprinting by employers is permissible prior to hiring and in some instances is a prerequisite for the job. Only two states, California and New York, have restricted the use of fingerprinting in employment.

Inquiries as to an applicant's financial status and credit worthiness are generally permitted when the position sought involves trust. Some states limit employers' rights to fire employees because wage executions have been filed against them. Most states permit some inquiry by employers into the medical history of prospective employees.

NOTES

1. 42 U.S.C. §2000e-3(b). The Supreme Court case is Pittsburgh Press Co. v. Comm'n. on Human Relations, 413 U.S. 376 (1973), *reh'g denied*, 414 U.S. 881 (1973). Most state fair employment practices laws also ban discriminatory advertising practices. *E.g.*, Nebraska (Neb. Rev. Stat. §48–1104(2)); New York (N. Y. Exec. Law §296 3a(b)).

2. *E.g.*, Hailes v. United Air Lines, 464 F.2d 1006 (5th Cir. 1972).

3. EEOC Dec. No. 79–63, 26 Fair Empl. Prac. Cas. 1778 (June 14, 1979).

4. 29 U.S.C. §§621–634.

5. 29 C.F.R. §1625.4(a).

6. Hodgson v. Approved Personnel Serv., Inc., 529 F.2d 760 (4th Cir. 1975).

7. *E.g.*, Wilkins v. Univ. of Houston, 654 F.2d 388 (5th Cir. 1981), *cert. denied*, 459 U.S. 822 (1982); Causey v. Ford Motor Co., 516 F.2d 416 (5th Cir. 1975).

8. *E.g.*, Waters v. Olinkraft, Inc., 475 F. Supp. 743 (W.D. Ark. 1979).

9. *E.g.*, Dumas v. Town of Mt. Vernon, 612 F.2d 974 (5th Cir. 1980) (county personnel board held to be an employment agency subject to Title VII).

10. 29 C.F.R. §1604.6(a).

11. 29 C.F.R. §1604.6(b).

12. Anderson v. City of Bessemer City, 470 U.S. 564 (1985).

13. Dothard v. Rawlinson, 433 U.S. 321 (1977). Sometimes, however, height limitations have been upheld when separate standards apply to males and females so as not to be overly burdensome on one

sex or the other. *E.g.*, Smith v. Eastern Airlines, 651 F. Supp. 214 (S.D. Tex. 1986).

14. *E.g.*, Montgomery v. Big B, Inc., 460 So.2d 1286 (Ala. 1984).

15. *E.g.*, Lewis v. Equitable Life Ins. Co., 389 N.W. 2d 876 (Minn. 1986).

16. *E.g.*, Turner v. Halliburton, 722 P.2d 1106 (Kan. 1986).

17. *E.g.*, Silver v. Mohasco Corp., 462 N.Y.S.2d 917 (N.Y. App. 1983), *aff'd*, 465 N.E.2d 361 (N.Y. 1984).

18. *E.g.*, Cal. Lab. Code §1055.

19. *E.g.*, Ind. Code §22–6–3–1.

20. *E.g.*, Mich. Comp. Laws Ann. §423.501(2)(c)(i).

21. 316 F. Supp. 401 (C.D. Cal. 1970), *modified on other grounds*, 472 F.2d 631 (9th Cir. 1972).

22. 401 U.S. 424 (1971). See the discussion of *Griggs* in Chapter 2, *supra*.

23. 523 F.2d 1290 (8th Cir. 1975).

24. *Id.* at 1298.

25. 82 Cal. App. 3d 582 (1978).

26. *E.g.*, California, Michigan, New Mexico and New York.

27. *E.g.*, Hawaii, Illinois, Massachusetts, Wisconsin.

28. *E.g.*, Georgia, Massachusetts, Pennsylvania.

29. Cal. Penal Code §13326; Cal. Fin. Code §777.5.

30. N. Y. Lab. Law §201–1.

31. 519 F. Supp. 136 (E.D. Ark. 1981), *aff'd in part, rev'd in part on other grounds*, 688 F.2d 552 (8th Cir. 1982), *cert. denied*, 460 U.S. 1083 (1983).

32. *Id.* at 168.

33. *E.g.*, EEOC v. United Va. Bank/Seaboard Nat'l., 21 Fair Empl. Prac. Cas. 1392, 1402 (E.D. Va. 1977): "It is not improper for a bank to check into the financial background of anyone they are considering hiring."

34. *E.g.*, Friend v. Leidinger, 588 F.2d 61 (4th Cir. 1978) (firefighters offered insufficient proof that policy of reprimanding employees whose wages were subject to garnishment had disparate impact on minorities; policy was also justified by business need, as garnishments increase paperwork and thus are inconvenient and expensive to employer).

35. 707 F.2d 1274 (11th Cir. 1983).

36. 332 F. Supp. 490 (C.D. Cal. 1971).

37. *Id.* at 495.

38. 15 U.S.C. §1681 *et seq.*

39. California, Connecticut, Maine, and Montana.

40. Mont. Code Ann. §31–3-102(7).

41. Cal. Civ. Code §1786.16.

42. Conn. Gen. Stat. §31–134.

43. Me. Rev. Stat. Ann. tit. 10, § 1318.

44. Mont. Code Ann. §31–3-112.

45. Alabama, Arizona, Arkansas, the District of Columbia, Kentucky, Michigan, South Carolina, Utah, Washington, and Wyoming.

46. Mississippi, Montana, and New Mexico.

47. La. Rev. Stat. Ann. §23:731(c).

48. Fla. Stat. §448.076; La. Rev. Stat. Ann. §§23:1001–1004; N.C. Gen. Stat. §95–28.1.

49. Ark. Stat. Ann. §81–1335.

50. Alaska Stat. §47.30.865.

51. Md. Ann. Code art. 100, §95A. This section does not forbid a medical examination needed to assess an applicant's ability to perform the job.

52. Mass. Gen. Laws Ann. ch. 151B, §4(9A). No employment application may contain questions about this subject.

7

Common Law Limitations on Background Checks

In some cases, applicants subjected to an intrusive investigation may be able to establish invasion of privacy, defamation, or intentional infliction of emotional distress. As a practical matter, however, such actions are rarely brought. Candidates are usually unaware that a background investigation has been conducted. If they know of the investigation, it is usually because the employer has sought their cooperation in some way, and this may allow the employer to raise the defense of consent in a subsequent legal action. Finally, information obtained in an investigation is usually not disseminated beyond the confines of the employer's offices, making it hard to establish the element of publication required for the torts of defamation and false light privacy invasion. If, however, a plaintiff can surmount these difficulties, a tort action could be a viable remedy for an overly intrusive background investigation.

Courts have allowed tort actions in the analogous situation of employer intrusion on employee privacy. In *Phillips v. Smalley Maintenance Services, Inc.*,[1] an employer was held liable for invasion of privacy under Alabama law when he repeatedly asked an employee about her sexual practices. Another action for invasion of privacy in Massachusetts failed on technical grounds.[2] The plaintiffs were salesmen fired for refusing to complete an employment questionnaire which they found too personal. The court held that since the employer had never obtained the requested information, the plaintiffs could not prove any invasion of privacy.

LAWS IMPOSING A DUTY TO INVESTIGATE

In certain positions requiring a high degree of trustworthiness on the part of employees, employers have not only the right but possibly the duty of fully investigating applicants. In addition, the practice of some occupations requires a license which may be issued only after the applicant has been screened by the licensing authority. Statutes authorizing or requiring such investigations are generally limited to occupations in which people are entrusted to the employee's care or the employee may have the opportunity to harm the public. Underlying these laws is a legislative decision to protect persons external to the employment relationship, even if this burdens the employer and is done at the expense of the privacy rights of the applicants.

Most states, for example, require some form of inquiry into the background of people seeking work in child care facilities.[3] At a minimum, the investigation involves an inquiry into the applicant's criminal conviction record, with an emphasis on identifying convictions of specified crimes, for example, those of a sexual or violent nature. The extent of the inquiry varies widely, ranging from a nationwide criminal records check to a statement signed by the applicant affirming that he has not been convicted. To aid in locating conviction records, some states require the fingerprinting of applicants. Some require a check of child abuse registries or an inquiry into the applicant's moral character, while others demand an investigation of health or financial records. Often the statute forbids the employment of persons convicted of specified crimes.

Most state licensing statutes also require a criminal records check or fingerprinting. For some occupations, a more extensive check is needed. Nebraska, for example, demands that applicants for a detective license have their "character and reputation" examined.[4] An investigation is required for licensing in professions in which public trust will be placed in the practitioner, for example, an attorney, insurance agent, or private security guard, or the practitioner may be in a position to harm the public, as in emergency medical service. Courts have uniformly approved investigations in these instances; in fact, the state's power to examine license applicants is usually uncontested in these cases, with the inquiry focusing instead on whether the specific statutory requirement bears a rational relationship to the applicant's fitness for employment.[5] As might be expected, most suits challenging licensing investigations have been brought by applicants to the various state bars. These cases have upheld the state's right to conduct a wide-ranging check of aspiring lawyers.[6]

CONCLUSION

Intrusive background checks may afford a theoretical basis for lawsuits alleging the common law torts of intentional infliction of emotional distress, defamation, or invasion of privacy. In practice, however, such suits are rarely brought. The examinee may be unaware of the examination or may have consented to it. Statutes may also shield employers from suits of this nature or impose on them a duty to conduct the investigation.

NOTES

1. 711 F.2d 1524 (11th Cir. 1983).
2. Cort v. Bristol-Myers Co., 431 N.E.2d 908 (Mass. 1982).
3. Twenty-nine states have laws affecting child care employees: Alabama, Arkansas, California, Connecticut, Florida, Georgia, Hawaii, Idaho, Indiana, Iowa, Kentucky, Louisiana, Maine, Minnesota, Nebraska, Nevada, New Hampshire, New Mexico, New York, North Carolina, Ohio, Oregon, Rhode Island, South Carolina, Tennessee, Virginia, and Washington.
4. Neb. Rev. Stat. §71–3205.
5. *E.g.*, Schware v. Bd. of Bar Examiners, 353 U.S. 232 (1957) (occupational license qualifications need only bear a rational connection with applicant's fitness for employment); Dixon v. McMullen, 527 F.

Supp. 711, 723 (N.D. Tex. 1981) (holding, citing *Schware*, that a "state can require high standards of qualification for a profession such as good moral character, as long as it has a rational connection to the applicant's fitness or capacity ...").

6. *E.g.*, Martin-Trigona v. Underwood, 529 F.2d 33 (7th Cir. 1975) (selective service records of bar applicant could be examined); Florida Bd. of Bar Examiners Re: Applicant, 443 So.2d 71 (Fla. 1983) (applicant must answer questions about mental health).

PART III

EMPLOYER SCREENING PRACTICES: BODY AND MIND TESTS

The first two parts of this book discussed reasons why employers may want to learn about their employees' and applicants' health, aptitude and character, as well as factors affecting their ability legally to do so. This part will examine some of the testing devices available to employers and the possible legal implications of their use. It will be seen that there are nearly as many of these devices as there are reasons to test.

The most widespread form of testing is that designed to ferret out illicit substance use in the workplace. The magnitude of the problem and of the potential for harm in this area is hard to overstate. The National Institute on Drug Abuse has estimated that twenty million Americans use marijuana and four million use cocaine—indeed, it has been said that one of every six working-age Americans uses illicit drugs—and a House of Representatives subcommittee has claimed that drug use costs industry $26 billion per year in lost productivity. Employees who use drugs are 3.6 times more likely to be involved in on-the-job accidents, 2.5 times more likely to miss work for at least eight days, and 5 times more likely to file workers' compensation claims. They also receive 3 times the health benefits and work at 67 percent of the potential of unimpaired employees.[1]

Acquired immune deficiency syndrome (AIDS) is also an alarming problem. While there is no evidence that AIDS can be transmitted by the kind of contact that usually occurs in the work setting—touching, sneezing, or sharing an office or water fountain, for instance—employees with AIDS or AIDS-related complex (ARC) may suffer fever, weight loss, lethargy, coughs, diarrhea and other debilitating conditions that leave them unable to function for long periods of time. These workers are likely to be less productive and to pose greater liability risks to their employers because of accidents or shoddily-made products. They may also be "handicapped" under, and thus entitled to the protections of, state and federal law.

Genetic considerations are becoming more worrisome to employers. Because various substances in the workplace may cause or exacerbate blood diseases and respiratory infections, among other things, employers are eager to know if anyone in their employ is predisposed to certain illnesses and thus risky in terms of benefits, absenteeism, and similar costs. Emotional disorders may also raise these concerns as well as disrupt the workplace.

Finally, businesses may incur loss through such things as incompetency, mismanagement, and employee crimes such as theft. Employers are thus interested in their workers' honesty and in the reliability of data in resumes and applications. As the previous sections stressed, apart from any vicarious liability which employers may suffer if their employees make products or provide services which harm co-workers or third parties, judgment errors in the areas of hiring and retention may result in employers being held directly liable for such harm.

Given these problems, employers are constantly seeking ways to find the prospective bad apples in their workforce. Biochemical testing for drug use, AIDS, and genetic problems is one answer, as is honesty testing via lie detectors. Many of those affected are protesting, however, claiming invasion of privacy and violation of the principle of innocent until proven guilty. Even if they do not oppose screening in principle, some object to the kinds of tests being used or to testing conditions and accuracy. If litigation ensues, how should the competing interests be accommodated? Indeed, what interests are even at stake? These issues are the focus of this section.

NOTE

1. *Survey of the Law on Employee Drug Testing*, 42 MIAMI L. REV. 553, 557–58 (1988).

8

Drug Testing

Testing for drug use is done chiefly through urinalysis, which involves taking urine samples from employees or applicants and analyzing them to see if traces of illicit substances are present. This process is popular for several reasons. The collection of urine is easily accomplished, and is less invasive than blood or tissue sampling. Due to the concentrating action of the kidney, drugs and their metabolites[1] usually are more highly concentrated in urine than in other body fluids or tissues. Because it lacks the protein and cellular constituents found in blood or tissue, urine is easier to analyze. Finally, the long-term storage of samples is possible because of the stability of drugs and their metabolites in frozen urine. Advocates of urinalysis stress its effectiveness in identifying impaired individuals and thus lessening business costs for employers. Opponents grant the need for a drug-free work setting but insist that urinalysis is an unreliable and unduly intrusive means of obtaining one.

The number of testing programs has mushroomed in recent years,[2] and this has generated many lawsuits. Public sector employment cases involve claims that tests violate the ban on unreasonable searches and seizures in the Fourth Amendment

to the U.S. Constitution, the Fourteenth Amendment requirement of due process of law, and the constitutional right of
privacy.[3] Private sector cases raise wrongful discharge, breach
of contract, or invasion of state constitutional, statutory or
common law privacy claims. After discussing how tests operate
and some concerns about them, this chapter examines legal
issues raised by urine testing.

HOW URINE TESTS OPERATE

The most popular test is the enzyme multiplied immmu-
noassay (EMIT), which comes in inexpensive, portable kits and
can be given by non-technical personnel.[4] It uses a process
called competitive displacement and binding, in which urine
is added to a substance containing an "antibody" and an "indicator." If, for example, marijuana is the drug sought, it has
an element called a THC metabolite, which will displace the
indicator and bind itself to the antibody. Displacement occurs
because the metabolite's competitive displacement and binding
properties are stronger than those of the indicator. After separating from the antibody, the indicator is measured to assess
the concentration of the metabolite in the sample.

The flaw is that the displacement and binding properties of
unknown compounds in the urine tested may be stronger than
those of the elements in the drug sought. With marijuana,
compounds with these properties may interact with the indicator and antibody as the THC metabolite does, causing these
compounds to be mistaken for the metabolite. Compounds that
interact in this manner are said to "cross-react" with the metabolite. Cross-reactive displacement yields a "false-positive"—
a mistaken conclusion that marijuana is in the sample being
tested.

Cross-reaction may occur for many reasons. Ingredients in
nonprescription medicine such as Dristan and Midol may produce false-positives. Urine also contains polar acids, whose displacement and binding properties vary with the body chemistry
of the person tested, and they may cross-react. A pigment in
dark-skinned people may separate into chemical fragments
similar to those in the drug sought. Given the individualized

nature of urine composition, the probability that an unidentified compound will cross-react in an EMIT test cannot be accurately predicted. Cross-reaction is the main reason that this test is not deemed conclusive in confirming the presence of illicit substances in the person being tested.

Another test is the gas chromatography/mass spectrometer (GC/MS). It measures drug molecules by separating urine into individual ions. Unknown compounds which may cross-react in an EMIT test may also cause inaccurate results in GC/MS tests; of the available tests, however, this one is considered the most reliable, thus it is often used to confirm results of other tests. Because it requires a laboratory with special equipment and technicians, it is expensive, costing up to $50 per test.

Besides the deficiencies inherent in urine tests, critics of testing point to external problems. Carry-over from a preceding sample may yield a positive reaction, and problems may also occur as a sample is passed among handlers or because of improper test administration. These problems are a special concern in on-site tests using untrained personnel. Another limitation is that tests can prove only past marijuana use, not present intoxication. The THC metabolite which marijuana tests seek, for example, may remain in the body for weeks; since biochemical tests try to determine if this metabolite is in a urine sample, they cannot confirm whether the subject was impaired when tested. That one may test positive by passively inhaling marijuana smoke exacerbates the problem. Finally, results may be skewed by factors affecting the rate at which people process and excrete drugs, such as body weight and stress. Differences in excretion rates may cause the number of metabolites in the urine of a person who smoked marijuana just before being tested to be the same as that of one who smoked much earlier; thus, a person with X metabolites in his system may be impaired while another with that number is not, and tests cannot distinguish between these people.

URINE TESTING AND THE CONSTITUTION

The first chapter of this book discussed the issue of which

employers are subject to the Bill of Rights in the U.S. Constitution. It will be recalled that these constraints affect only federal, state and local government employers and private employers engaged in enough "state action" to trigger the Fourteenth Amendment. Other private employers will be governed by a number of other federal and state laws, but the Bill of Rights provisions will not be among them. Readers must keep this in mind as they work through the following discussion of the legality of urinalysis under the Fourth and Fourteenth Amendments and the constitutional right of privacy.

The Fourth Amendment

The most often-litigated issue raised by urinalysis concerns its status under the Fourth Amendment, which provides:

> The right of the people to be secure in their persons, houses, papers, and effects, against unreasonable searches and seizures, shall not be violated, and no warrants shall issue, but upon probable cause, supported by oath or affirmation, and particularly describing the place to be searched, and the person or things to be seized.

Whether a governmental investigation is a "search" is the initial issue in a Fourth Amendment analysis. If it is, whether the investigation required a warrant and was "reasonable" must be determined.

In 1989, the U.S. Supreme Court considered the "search" implications of workplace drug testing in *Skinner v. Railway Labor Executives' Ass'n.*[5] and *National Treasury Employees Union v. Von Raab.*[6] In doing so, the Court did not write on a clean slate, as scores of lower court precedents existed. These precedents agreed on many issues regarding drug testing but disagreed in some critical respects. To appreciate the impact of *Skinner* and *Von Raab*, it is important to understand something of what the lower court cases had said.

The cases agreed that a urinalysis involves a search because it invades reasonable privacy expectations. Courts compared compulsory testing to a government taking of blood, which entails a search,[7] and noted that tests intrude on privacy and dignity and allow both the discovery of medical data unrelated to drug use and the observation of off-duty employee activity. Second, that drug levels fall over time requires that tests be given promptly, and this obviates the need for a warrant. Third, because employees cannot, as a condition of employment, be forced to agree to an illegal drug test, an unconstitutional test will not be redeemed by an employee's "consent" to it, although advance consent may lessen the privacy expectation regarding it. Fourth, because a urinalysis is a "search," it must be conducted "reasonably." Reasonableness is assessed by balancing the extent of the test's intrusion on privacy against the degree to which it promotes valid government interests, taking into account the manner, place and justification of the intrusion.

The cases differed sharply over when a test is justified and is conducted reasonably. The split centered on these issues: (1) How significant is one's job, for example, whether it affects the public welfare, in terms of privacy interests and the justification for testing? (2) Does it matter if there is a history of drug use in the industry or evidence of a current problem? (3) May tests be given randomly or only with reason to believe a certain worker is impaired, and if the latter, what level of suspicion is needed? (4) How important are testing mechanics and accuracy?

Likening urinalysis to an administrative premises inspection, which needs little suspicion of wrongdoing, some courts held that individualized suspicion of impairment is not needed to test if the industry has a history of intense state regulation and privacy rights are protected. In *Shoemaker v. Handel*,[8] for example, New Jersey was allowed to randomly test horse racing jockeys. The court stressed the need to preserve public confidence in racing, in which wagering is heavy and corruption is a threat; New Jersey's intense regulation of the racing industry since 1939; the reduction of the jockeys' privacy expectations through their advance knowledge of the tests, and the testing plan's safeguards, which protected privacy and limited the testers' discretion. Finding the police industry the most intensely regulated in New Jersey, the court in *Policeman's Benevolent Ass'n., Local 318 v. Township of Washington*[9] used the same rationale in upholding random testing of police.

Other cases upheld random testing plans deemed "reasonable" upon an assessment of the relevant facts. In *Transportation Workers Local 234 v. SEPTA*,[10] the court held that a plan to test transportation workers randomly was reasonable in light of the interest in insuring public safety; documented cases of accidents involving workers impaired by and applicants testing positive for drugs; the fact that the plan applied only to jobs affecting the public safety; and the safeguards in the plan, including confidentiality and verification of results, chain-of-custody procedures, and a careful random selection mechanism. *Rushton v. Nebraska Public Power District*[11] upheld a nuclear power plant's plan, stressing that it does not require the act of urination to be witnessed, that test results are used to determine job fitness, and that the industry affects the public safety. *McDonell v. Hunter*[12] held that individualized suspicion is not needed if workers in sensitive jobs—prison guards, in that case—are tested uniformly, in routine physical examinations or by systematic random selection, but that other tests require a suspicion of drug use within twenty-four hours.

Many courts, however, required individualized suspicion to test. In *Copeland v. Philadelphia Police Department*,[13] a city was allowed to test a policeman accused by a former girlfriend of using drugs only on the basis of a "reasonable suspicion" that he had done so. Relevant factors included the nature of the tip, the informant's reliability, and the degree of corroboration, and the court found enough suspicion in Copeland's having been off his beat with a drug seller and not reporting this in his patrol log, coupled with the girlfriend's claim. *Lovvorn v. City of Chattanooga*[14] used the same standard in voiding a random testing plan for firefighters. While it acknowledged the interests at stake, the court held that the plan required samples to be given under observation, and it stressed the privacy interest involved. It then said that whether random testing is permissible depends not on whether an industry is heavily regulated, but on the nature of that industry and the harm to society that would likely result if mandatory tests were forbidden. Finding the likelihood of enormous societal losses because of an impaired firefighter to be relatively low, the court held that for random testing to be reasonable, there must be either evidence of a department-wide drug problem or individualized suspicion of impairment.

When *Skinner* and *Von Raab* appeared, therefore, the main question regarding urinalysis and the Fourth Amendment was whether tests require individualized suspicion of drug impairment. There, the Court answered in the negative. The outcomes of these cases seem to have been so tied to the particular facts involved, however, that it is too much to conclude that across-the-board random testing is now permissible. The most that can be said is that random testing is now legal with respect to certain employees in certain instances and under certain conditions.

Skinner involved federal rules requiring railroads to test their workers' blood and urine in the event of accidents involving death, serious injury or property damage. Specimens are obtained at a medical facility and sent to a laboratory for analysis, and employees are notified of the results and given a chance to respond before a final report is prepared. The rules also allow testing after certain rules violations or accidents if a supervisor reasonably suspects either impairment or that an employee's acts were a contributing factor. If results will be used to discipline, the employee must be allowed to have blood analyzed independently. The rules also seek to prevent sample tainting through chain-of-custody problems.

A 7–2 majority of the Supreme Court held that tests given in reliance on federal authority involve enough government action to trigger the Fourth Amendment, that the tests involve "searches," that neither a warrant nor "probable cause" is required to conduct them, and that their reasonableness depends on all the circumstances. But it declined to hold, as had the Ninth Circuit, that individualized suspicion is needed to insure that tests will detect current impairment. Where the privacy interests implicated by a search are minimal and vital governmental interests would be harmed by an individual suspicion rule, the Court said, the search may be reasonable despite its absence. Conceding that requiring the performance of an excretory function traditionally deemed private is not a minimal concern, the Court noted that the rules do not require urine to be given under observation and call for it to be analyzed in a laboratory; thus, the testing process is like that used in regular physical exams. Finally, the Court found that the workers' privacy expectations were lessened by their being involved in an industry regulated pervasively to ensure the public safety.

The Court also stressed that on-the-job intoxication is a major problem in the railroad industry and that workers, who discharge duties fraught with such risks that even a momentary lapse can be disastrous, can cause great loss before signs of impairment will be noticeable. History also shows that even the threat of discharge for working while impaired is not an effective deterrent unless violators know they will likely be detected; by tying testing to a triggering event, the timing of which cannot be predicted, the rule increases the deterrent effect of its penalties. And given the chaos at accident sites, it would be hard for investigators to find evidence creating a suspicion of impairment in a particular employee. An individual suspicion rule would thus bar testing in many cases, which could prevent the obtaining of clues as to the cause of an accident. Finally, the Court ruled that the inability of a test to measure drug intoxication is no basis for voiding it: to be relevant evidence need not conclusively prove the fact at issue, but only tend to make its existence more or less likely than it would otherwise be. Even if a test disclosed only recent drug use, the Court said, this would justify further investigation to determine if the employee used drugs at the relevant times.

In *Von Raab*, a 5–4 Court upheld testing rules of the Customs Service, which enforces customs laws and seizes contraband. Tests are a condition in jobs involving drug interdiction and classified material. Because the plan might serve as a guide to employers wanting to structure a legal urinalysis program, the lower court's detailed description of it is set out here:

> After an employee qualifies for a position covered by the Customs testing program, the Service advises him by letter that his final selection is contingent upon successful completion of drug screening. An independent contractor contacts the employee to fix the time and place for collecting the sample. On reporting for the test, the employee must produce photographic identifi-

cation and remove any outer garments, such as a coat or jacket, and personal belongings. The employee may produce the sample behind a partition, or in the privacy of a bathroom stall if he so chooses. To ensure against adulteration of the specimen, or substitution of a sample from another person, a monitor of the same sex as the employee remains close at hand to listen for the normal sounds of urination. Dye is added to the toilet water to prevent the employee from using the water to adulterate the sample.

Upon receiving the specimen, the monitor inspects it to ensure its proper temperature and color, places a tamper-proof custody seal over the container, and affixes an identification label indicating the date and the individual's specimen number. The employee signs a chain-of-custody form, which is initialed by the monitor, and the urine sample is placed in a plastic bag, sealed, and submitted to a laboratory.

The laboratory tests the sample for the presence of marijuana, cocaine, opiates, amphetamines, and phencyclidine. Two tests are used. An initial screening test uses the [EMIT]. Any specimen that is identified as positive on this initial test must then be confirmed using gas chromatography/mass spectrometry (GC/MS). Confirmed positive results are reported to a 'Medical Review Officer,' [a] licensed physician... who has knowledge of substance abuse disorders and has appropriate medical training to interpret and evaluate the individual's positive test result together with his or her medical history and any other relevant biomedical information.... After verifying the positive result, the Medical Review Officer transmits it to the agency.

Customs employees who test positive for drugs and who can offer no satisfactory explanation are subject to dismissal from the Service. Test results may not, however, be turned over to any other agency, including criminal prosecutors, without the employee's written consent.[15]

As in *Skinner*, the Court held that the tests involve a search and must be reasonable. It also ruled out warrants, noting that requiring one for each job-related intrusion would make it difficult for offices to function. It then turned to the individualized suspicion issue. Analogizing this search to building code inspections, which seek not to enforce the criminal law but to prevent conditions hazardous to the public, and to suspicionless searches of airline passengers, the Court said that sometimes the government's need to prevent latent harmful conditions justifies suspicionless searches. Searches of Customs workers are in this realm: their safety is continually threatened by drug traffickers, and this, coupled with their access to contraband and the chance of bribes, necessitates their unimpeachable integrity.

Also relevant in a "reasonableness" inquiry, the Court said, is the degree of interference with personal liberty caused by a test. Conceding that the privacy intrusion involved in collecting urine could be substantial, the Court nonetheless said that the "operational realities" of the workplace justify job-related intrusions by supervisors that might be unreasonable in other contexts. Certain jobs, moreover, may diminish privacy expectations *vis-a-vis* searches. The Customs workers' diminished expectations and the fact that the testing plan contains safeguards to minimize its intrusion on privacy made the plan reasonable.

The challenge to the plan involved two other claims: it is unjustified because there is no perceived drug problem among Customs workers; and because drug users can avoid detection through abstinence or adulterating samples, it is not sufficiently productive to justify its invasion of privacy. In reply, the Court said that the "extraordinary" safety and national security interests at stake justified attempts to ferret out even casual drug users, and that most employees will test negative did not impugn the plan. Where potential harm is substantial, the need to prevent it may justify reasonable searches designed to advance that goal. To the other argument the Court replied that addicts may be unable to abstain or unaware of the fadeaway effect of some drugs. And because the time it takes for drugs to become undetectable in urine varies with the person, no employee's pattern of elimination for a particular drug can be predicted.

Justices William Brennan and Thurgood Marshall dissented in both *Von Raab* and *Skinner*. They made essentially three points. First, they labeled "unprincipled" the concept that "special needs" justify ignoring the probable cause and warrant language in the Fourth Amendment. The Court should abandon its balancing approach to search cases, they insisted, and apply the amendment as written. Second, they argued that random testing is illegal even under the special-needs or balancing approach, and that individualized suspicion should be a constitutional prerequisite to a test. Finally, they attacked the mechanics and accuracy of current testing methods, especially their inability to measure current impairment as opposed to past drug use.

Justices Antonin Scalia and John Paul Stevens sided with the majority in *Skinner*. While they rejected the claim that the interest in deterring drug use is sufficient to justify the searches involved, they felt that the public interest in assessing the causes of railroad accidents supported the testing rules. The demonstrated frequency of drug use by railroad workers and the link between such use and grave harm, moreover, made random drug testing a reasonable means of protecting society. In *Von Raab*, by contrast, they insisted that neither the frequency of drug use by Customs employees nor a connection with any harm was shown or even likely. To them, the Customs rules were nothing but an "immolation of privacy and human dignity in symbolic opposition to drug use"—a sign, in other words, that the government meant to "get tough" on drug use, and to invade privacy for evidence of it, whether or not there was reason to suspect such use in the industry in question. In a sarcasm-laced dissent joined by Justice Stevens, Justice Scalia asserted that such a program is unacceptable in our society:

I do not believe for a minute that the driving force behind these drug-testing rules was any of the feeble justifications put forward by counsel here and accepted by the Court. The only plausible explanation, in my view, is what the Commissioner himself offered in the concluding sentence of his memorandum to Customs employees announcing the program: "Implementation of the drug screening program would set an important example in our country's struggle with this most serious threat to our national security." ... What better way to show that the Government is serious about its "war on drugs" than to subject its employees on the front line to this invasion of their privacy and affront to their dignity? To be sure, there is only a slight chance that it will prevent some serious public harm resulting from

Service employee drug use, but it will show to the world that the Service is "clean" and—most important—will demonstrate the determination of the Government to eliminate this scourge of our society! I think it obvious that this justification is unacceptable; that the impairment of individual liberties cannot be the means of making a point; that symbolism, even symbolism for so worthy a cause as the abolition of unlawful drugs, cannot validate an otherwise unreasonable search.[16]

What is the current law of drug testing? While it is too early to gauge the full impact of *Skinner* and *Von Raab*, these conclusions seem warranted. (1) Public and some private employment testing involves a "search" within the meaning of the Fourth Amendment. (2) If the Fourth Amendment applies to a drug test, neither a warrant nor probable cause to suspect impairment is needed to conduct it, but it must be "reasonable." This is determined by weighing its intrusion on privacy against its promotion of valid interests, considering its justification, scope and place. (3) If an industry affects the public welfare or has a history of intense state regulation or a drug problem, random testing is legal. The less a job affects the public or is regulated by the state, the more evidence of a drug problem is needed to randomly test; as the job's effect on the public, the amount of state regulation in that area, and the evidence of a drug problem decrease, the basis for suspicionless testing does as well. (4) That tests cannot measure impairment and are not 100 percent accurate is no basis for automatically voiding them, although the more guarantees in a plan, for example, chain-of-custody safeguards, procedures to ensure the confidentiality of results, back-up tests if an initial test is positive, and giving tests under laboratory conditions, the more likely that it will be upheld. (5) Neither advance notice nor employee consent will necessarily validate a test, but they increase the likelihood of its passing muster. The extent to which a plan limits the tester's discretion is also important. (6) The more a plan protects employee privacy, the greater its chances of surviving. The circumstances under which samples are taken will be crucial.

The Fourteenth Amendment

The Fourteenth Amendment requires states to give "due process of law" before denying people life, liberty or property. Procedurally, deprivations must be preceded by notice of the alleged violation and an appropriate hearing; substantive due process bars unreasonable deprivations.[17] Workers fired or disciplined in connection with a urinalysis may have a due process claim if a property or liberty interest is thereby infringed.

Whether an employee has a property interest in her job depends on its nature. "At-will" employees, who serve at their employer's pleasure for an indefinite period, may be dismissed at any time; they have no expectation of continued employment and hence no property interest in their job. But if the law, company policy or a contract, or even verbal assurances create a reasonable expectation of such security, they have a property interest of which they may not be deprived without notice and a hearing. Employee liberty interests are implicated by acts which illegally restrict their freedom or harm their reputation.[18]

The cases say little about the due process implications of urinalysis, but standards can be gleaned from other sources, especially *Cleveland Board of Education v. Loudermill*,[19] which involved the firing of an Ohio civil service employee, with no hearing, for lying on his job application. Noting that Ohio statutes allowed the man to keep his job absent good cause for dismissal, the Court said he had a "property" interest in continued employment, and that absent a need for his immediate removal from the workplace, he was thus entitled to a preremoval hearing. In *Fraternal Order of Police, Lodge No. 5 v. Tucker*,[20] the court applied these standards in finding that the plaintiffs were denied due process because, although they were told they were to be disciplined, they were not given specifics of the charges against them; thus, they had no meaningful chance to rebut the evidence of their drug use.

A urinalysis might also yield a substantive due process claim. A firing based on an unconfirmed positive result could do so, as may the unreliability of testing conditions. In *Von Raab*, for example, the Fifth Circuit rejected a due process attack on the Customs plan, but apparently only because of the storage, handling, and measurement techniques used. The Supreme Court's curt handling of the accuracy-based challenge in *Von Raab*, however, does not bode well for this argument in the future. Based on that case, it seems that there is a chance that a challenge based on the conditions under which a particular test was given might succeed, but next to no chance that an attack based on the inherent reliability of urine tests could do so.

Given the possibility of a due process challenge stemming from a urine test, employers should: (1) Remember that even at-will employees may have a property or liberty interest in their job, and thus be entitled to due process in a disciplinary context, if the law, company policy or their contract, or verbal assurances have created a reasonable expectation of job security; (2) Advise workers of company rules, including policies governing on- or off-the-job substance use; (3) Advise workers that they are subject to testing either periodically or in certain instances, and if the latter, specify them; (4) Give workers notice of the charges against them before firing or disciplining for drug use or for other reasons; (5) Where possible, afford employees an opportunity for a hearing before a dismissal; (6) Ensure that testing plans and mechanisms are as reliable as possible; and (7) Avoid making remarks while administering or implementing the results of a test which may be construed as infringing on an employee's liberty interests.

The Constitutional Right of Privacy

The constitutional right of privacy recognized in 1965[21] has two parts: an interest in autonomy, or freedom from unwanted government intrusions in decisions about one's life, and a right to protect intimate facts. Though they say little about the autonomy implications of urinalysis, cases like *Schmerber v. California* and *Rochin v. California*[22] indicate that minor bodily intrusions will be tolerated and that a balancing approach that considers the nature of and need for a test, its reliability and test conditions, and whether less intrusive options were available will be used to decide privacy claims. Random tests given to detect drug use stand a better chance of violating privacy rights than tests accompanying physical examinations or based on reasonable suspicion.

The right of disclosural privacy is limited, and whether employers who divulge drug test results or insist that employees reveal personal data, for example, medicine taken, violate it depends on whether the interest in disclosure outweighs the intrusion. In *Shoemaker v. Handel*,[23] the court found that the testing plan did not violate disclosural rights because it had been amended to provide that test results would not be disclosed, even to law enforcement authorities. The court stated that although privacy rights in medical information exist, governmental concerns may support the access to such data if it is protected from unauthorized disclosure. Because the racing commission's concern for racing integrity justified its access to data revealed by the tests, the jockeys' privacy concern was limited to preserving the confidentiality of the test results, and the rule did this. If the commission ceased to comply with the rule, said the court, "the jockeys may return to court with a new lawsuit."

URINE TESTING UNDER STATE LAW

Once the courts clarify which public employees may be tested randomly for drug use under the U.S. Constitution, those rules will create a "floor," or a standard below which states may not go. Courts, however, will remain free to decide that state laws and constitutional provisions are more restrictive—that is, afford more protection—than their federal counterparts and may even bar the random testing of employees to whom they apply. Indeed, the last few years have seen several state courts respond to U.S. Supreme Court decisions narrowing individual liberties under the Fourth and Fourteenth amendments to the federal Constitution and the constitutional right of privacy by according greater protection to those liberties under state search-and-seizure, due process, and privacy laws. Cases based entirely on state law are not within the jurisdiction of the Supreme Court to review.

In 1985, for example, a Florida state appeals court found that randomly testing police and firefighters for drugs violated the Florida constitution.[24] In 1986, New York courts ruled that police officers and teachers in that state could not be tested randomly,[25] and in 1987, a New Jersey appellate court said that the city of Newark could not test randomly in a police department narcotics bureau.[26] While *Skinner* and *Von Raab* may prompt some state courts to be more receptive to drug testing plans, it is by no means clear that anti-testing rulings such as those above will no longer be seen. If anything, the opposite may be true: the Supreme Court's refusal to void such plans under the U.S. Constitution may encourage more state courts to invalidate them on state law grounds.

Several states have enacted drug testing statutes. They fall into three categories. The first includes laws such as Rhode Island's, which bans urine testing absent "reasonable grounds to believe, based on specific objective facts, that the employee's use of controlled substances is impairing his ability to perform his job."[27] If the employer has reasonable suspicion, the testing procedures set out in the statute must be followed and employees who test positive must be offered a chance to enroll in a "bona fide rehabilitation program." Employers who violate the law commit a crime and may be sued civilly for damages and attorney's fees. Vermont has a similar statute.[28]

The second group includes laws like Utah's, which allows all employees to be randomly tested for drugs.[29] If tests are given, however, employers and managers must also take them. If a worker tests positive, a more reliable method must be used to validate the initial results. The statute protects employers who follow the prescribed procedure from lawsuits by their employees for invasion of privacy.

Minnesota has a statute which reflects a compromise between these two extreme positions.[30] It permits employers to conduct random or routine tests on employees in "safety-sensitive positions." Other employees may be tested if the employer has a "reasonable suspicion" that the employee is under the influence of drugs or the employee has been in an accident. The statute mandates specific testing procedures and allows workers to sue for damages if the law is violated. Montana has a similar statute.[31]

Union or other contracts also protect many employees against random testing. Generally speaking, arbitrators have found that failing a drug test alone is not "good cause" to dismiss an employee protected by a union contract, because drug tests cannot measure the degree of impairment of the employee. They have also held that employers who wish to begin testing for drugs must first negotiate about this with the union.[32]

PRIVATE SECTOR TESTING CASES

Cases involving private sector testing are on the rise. Typically, they involve claims that testing invades state constitutional, statutory or common law privacy rights. In states that recognize the concepts of "wrongful discharge" or "breach of the covenant of good faith and fair dealing," it is often argued that dismissing an employee for failing or refusing a test is illegal under those theories as well as an invasion of privacy.

In *Luedtke v. Nabors Alaska Drilling, Inc.*,[33] oil rig workers fired for refusing drug tests attacked their dismissal on the grounds noted above. The company responded that the plaintiffs were at-will employees subject to dismissal at any time for any reason, and that even if they could be fired only for "just cause," that existed because the plaintiffs violated company policy in refusing to be tested.

The court traced the evolution of the privacy concept from its inception in 1890 to its incorporation in constitutional, contract and tort law, including "the emerging mixture of theories known as the public policy exception to the at-will" employment doctrine. The court held that a "Right of Privacy" in the Alaska Constitution did not help the plaintiffs, as it applied only to governmental acts. But it also found Alaska to be among the states which recognize an "implied covenant of good faith and fair dealing" in at-will contracts. A public policy violation could breach this covenant, the court said, and protecting employee privacy is such a policy under state law. Finding that the plaintiffs were not hired for a specific term, the court also ruled that they were at-will employees.

The court then held that public policy creates "spheres of employee conduct into which employers may not intrude," and it asked if employer monitoring, via urinalysis, of employee off-duty drug use illegally invades this sphere. Applying the reasoning of Fourth Amendment cases, the Court noted that in *Von Raab*, a Fifth Circuit concurrence had asked how intrusive urinalysis really is, since it involves waste which, if public toilets are used, is yielded under observation, and how different from routine security and background checks a testing plan is if it is based on a "generalized lack of trust and not on a developed suspicion of an individual." This review led the court to conclude that it should assess the legality of urinalysis by focusing on the reason for, not the conduct of, the test.

According to the court, the limits of a privacy sphere are determined by balancing the interests in privacy and in others' safety. The plaintiffs could not claim that whether they use marijuana off duty is private information, because oil rig work is dangerous and marijuana impairs one's faculties; where the public policy favoring privacy in off-duty acts collides with that favoring safety, the court held, the latter prevails. But the court cautioned that because the employer's interest is in monitoring drug use affecting job performance, and not in controlling societal drug use, tests must reasonably coincide with the employee's work time. Notice of the adoption of a testing plan must also be given. Because both conditions were met with regard to the plaintiffs, their employer did not act illegally in imposing the testing rule and in firing them for refusing to abide by it.

In *Jennings v. Minco Technology Labs Inc.*,[34] the company told its employees that they may be required to submit to random drug testing at any time during their employment, for any or no reason. Jennings refused a test and then challenged her subsequent dismissal on privacy grounds. The trial court found that she had suffered no illegal invasion of privacy because she had the choice of consenting to the test or rejecting further employment under the newly-created condition of employment. The state appeals court affirmed. That court also stressed that the plan contained safeguards for accuracy, confidentiality, and modesty, and was administered only on the basis of employee consent.

Not all states recognize the "wrongful discharge" and "implied covenant of good faith" concepts, and their privacy law varies greatly. The analysis and outcome of cases such as *Luedtke* and *Jennings*, therefore, might be quite different elsewhere. These cases, however, offer a useful study of claims often asserted in private sector cases; show how Fourth Amendment analyses may be used to resolve state law issues; reflect the sympathy toward drug testing often found in cases today, while imposing limits on testing to strike a workable balance between worker and employer interests; and stress the utility of obtaining employee consent and of seeking both to ensure testing accuracy and to protect employee privacy. Their approaches will likely be followed in other cases.

In 1972, the California Constitution was amended to include " privacy" among the people's "inalienable rights." The information provided to voters on the ballot said that a vote for the amendment would guarantee protection against private as well as governmental intrusions on privacy. And indeed, courts have since then consistently interpreted this provision in this manner. Two recent rulings illustrate the potential effect of this provision on private employers in California who wish to engage in drug testing.

The first case involved the Matthew Bender Publishing Company in Oakland.[35] It required job applicants to submit to a urinalysis to detect illegal drug use. Several applicants refused to be tested, were not hired as a result, and sued for invasion of privacy. A state appeals court held that the "right of privacy" in the state constitution limits the ability of private employers to invade employee privacy; it then ruled, however, that because the plaintiffs were applicants, not employees, they had no reasonable expectation of privacy that was violated by the company policy. Noting that California law permits private employers to request a medical examination of job candidates and that these examinations often include a urinalysis, the court held that it is reasonable to include a drug test in an examination. The court also felt that the testing process was reasonable and protected adequately the confidentiality of the information to be acquired. The state supreme court refused to review this decision.

The second case involved an employee (not an applicant) who

was fired after refusing a pupillary reaction eye test.[36] This test measures the reaction of eyes to light; the eyes of people impaired by drugs behave differently. The case was on appeal from a summary judgment for the company, and the appeals court remanded for a trial to assess the intrusiveness of this kind of test and to balance that intrusion against the employer's need to ensure the safe and efficient operation of its plant. This balance, the court said, would require detailed fact-finding about the type of test to be used and job to be performed. The court noted that even daily drug testing might be acceptable for employees engaged in very dangerous work, but that any testing might be too invasive where other employees are concerned.

Nine other states have similar privacy provisions in their constitutions.[37] Only time will tell whether courts in these states will follow the approach of the California courts. It must be stressed that in recent years there has been a trend on the part of many state courts toward interpreting civil liberties provisions in state constitutions more broadly than the Supreme Court has lately construed comparable provisions in the federal Constitution. To the extent that state courts so interpret state privacy provisions, employers in that state cannot take advantage of the markedly pro-employer employment screening decisions rendered by the Supreme Court of late. How state courts deal with privacy provisions such as the one in California's constitution will therefore have a major impact on the law of employment screening.

CONCLUSION

In view of the myriad business-related problems caused by employees impaired by drugs, courts are generally sympathetic to employers wanting to conduct workplace drug testing. But courts have not given employers carte blanche to test under whatever conditions they please. In assessing the legality of a plan, courts will consider the extent to which the industry affects the public welfare, has been regulated by the state, and has a history of drug use among workers; how adequately the plan protects privacy and seeks to safeguard both the collection process and the samples obtained; whether employees had advance notice of the tests and validly consented to them; whether there is any reason to suspect impairment among particular employees; and whether efforts have been made to ensure test accuracy. Where employers have made reasonable efforts to address these issues, their testing plans have generally been upheld.

Following is a summary of basic principles relating to drug testing. An employer wishing to develop a drug testing plan or to upgrade his current plan should keep these tenets firmly in mind.

1. Because employers can require job applicants to pass a pre-employment physical examination as a condition of employment, drug testing can be done at that time with the least risk of litigation. In order of increasing risk to the employer, other testing circumstances are: post-accident; "for cause," *e.g.*, based on individualized suspicion of drug impairment; and random. If a job affects the public welfare or has a history of intense state regulation or a drug problem, and if a test is given under a policy tailored to minimize privacy intrusions, random tests will likely be upheld; otherwise, they are legally suspect.

2. Company policies regarding employee drug use and drug testing should be written in detailed but concise form, published, and explained to workers. Courts are more likely to be receptive to testing programs if they provide for rehabilitation of employees with a drug problem. Under the Drug-Free Workplace Act of 1988, government contractors who receive grants or seek government contracts of $25,000 or more must meet these requirements.

3. Drug testing should be done uniformly pursuant to a written policy. Job applicants should be told that a medical examination, including a drug test, is part of the examination procedure, and that if employed they must work unimpaired and may be asked to take a test as a condition of employment. The latter information should be given to current employees as well.

4. Employee consent forms are not dispositive of the legality of a test, but they are helpful. Employees should thus be asked to sign an authorization form consenting to testing for controlled substances.

5. Information acquired in a test should be kept confidential. If another employer asks about a rejected applicant, an employer risks

being sued and held liable for defamation if she reveals that the applicant failed a drug test. Within the company, this information should be revealed only on a need-to-know basis.

6. Urine samples should be taken under conditions that maximize privacy and minimize the chance of sample switching or contamination. The location for collection should provide for controlled access. If collection is done in a restroom, bluing may be added to toilet water to prevent sample dilution; access to sinks may be limited or the water turned off; and after collection, the sample should be examined for unusual color (indicative of dilution or adulteration) or a temperature different from normal body temperature (indicative of urine substitution or dilution).

7. When a sample has been collected, reasonable steps should be taken to ensure that it is not tainted in storage or handling. Testing laboratories will usually assist in this area. Chain-of-custody procedures may include having the employee initial the sample jar and the seal on the jar lid; sealing jars in plastic bags closed with tamper-proof evidence tape; having samples accompanied by a record showing everyone who had custody; and keeping samples under lock and key during shipment, testing and storage.

8. EMIT tests should be used only as an initial screening tool, with positive results confirmed in a GC/MS test. No employee should be disciplined or dismissed based on an unconfirmed test. For a model drug testing policy which has been judicially approved, one should refer to the Customs policy set out earlier in this chapter.

9. The Vocational Rehabilitation Act of 1973, which applies to employers who are government contractors or receive government funds, considers many former and habitual drug users handicapped, and requires that an employer not consider that handicap when hiring, promoting or firing unless the handicap makes the job unreasonably difficult or hazardous to the employee or to fellow workers. People who test positive for drug use may be within the ambit of this act. State or local handicap laws may also afford protection in these cases. In addition, at the time of this writing (early 1990), Congress is considering a new handicap discrimination law that would outlaw discrimination on the basis of handicap by most private employers.

NOTES

1. Drug tests try to find metabolites of drugs to determine if that drug is in the system of the person being tested. Tests for marijuana,

for example, try to find the "THC metabolite." A metabolite is produced by metabolism, "the chemical and physical processes continuously going on in living organisms and cells, comprising those by which assimilated food is built up (annobolism) into protoplasm and those by which protoplasm is used and broken down into simpler substances or waste matter, with the release of energy for all vital processes." WEBSTER'S NEW WORLD DICTIONARY 924 (1968).

2. The *New York Times* recently reported that in 1989, five laboratories that conduct drug tests took in an estimated $173 million from testing, and that it has been estimated that revenues from testing will increase to $340 million, up 48 percent from 1989, in 1990. *Booming Business: Drug Use Tests*, N. Y. Times, Jan. 3, 1990, at D1, col. 3.

3. Other provisions invoked include the Fifth Amendment privilege against forced self-incrimination and the Fourteenth Amendment guarantee of equal protection of the law. Because these claims are so seldom raised and upheld by courts, however, they are not considered here.

4. For more information on how tests operate, *see, e.g., Survey of the Law on Employee Drug Testing*, 42 MIAMI L. REV. 553, 562–67 (1988).

5. 109 S. Ct. 1402 (1989).

6. 109 S. Ct. 1384 (1989).

7. Schmerber v. California, 384 U.S. 757 (1966).

8. 795 F.2d 1136 (3rd Cir. 1986).

9. 850 F.2d 133 (3rd Cir. 1988).

10. 4 IER Cases 1 (3rd Cir. 1988).

11. 844 F.2d 562 (8th Cir. 1988).

12. 809 F.2d 1302 (8th Cir. 1987).

13. 840 F.2d 1139 (3rd Cir. 1988).

14. 846 F.2d 1539 (6th Cir. 1988).

15. 109 S. Ct. 1402, 1404–05

16. 109 S. Ct. at 1399–1401.

17. The notion that the due process clause has a substantive component has been criticized by many commentators, who maintain that the clause, as written, requires only that states follow certain processes before depriving one of his life, liberty or property. *E.g.*, BORK, THE TEMPTING OF AMERICA 31–32 (1990). The Supreme Court, however, has at least tacitly recognized this concept since it decided Dred Scott v. Sandford, 60 U.S. (19 How.) 393 (1857).

18. *E.g.*, Bd. of Regents v. Roth, 408 U.S. 564 (1972).

19. 105 S. Ct. 1487 (1985).

20. 4 IER Cases 168 (3rd Cir. 1989).

21. Griswold v. Connecticut, 381 U.S. 479 (1965). *See supra* chapter 3.

22. 384 U.S. 757 (1966); 342 U.S. 165 (1952).

23. *See supra* note 7 and accompanying text.

24. City of Palm Bay v. Bauman, 475 So.2d 1322 (Fla. App. 1985).

25. Caruso v. Ward, 506 N.Y.S.2d 789 (N.Y. Dist. 1986); Patchogue-Medford v. Bd. of Educ., 505 N.Y.S.2d 888 (N.Y. App. 1986).

26. Fraternal Order of Police v. City of Newark, 524 A.2d 430 (N.J. App. 1987).

27. R. I. 28–6.5–1.

28. Vt. tit. 21, sec. 511–519.

29. Utah Code Ann. §34–38–1 to 15.

30. Minn. Stat. §181.950 to 956.

31. Mont. Code Ann. §39–2-304.

32. *At Work While Under the Influence*, 70 MARQ. L. REV. 88 (1986).

33. 768 P.2d 1123 (Alaska 1989).

34. 765 S.W.2d 497 (Tex. App. – Austin 1989). To the surprise of many, given the importance of the issues raised, the Texas Supreme Court declined to review this decision.

35. Wilkinson v. Times Mirror Corp., 264 Cal. Rptr. 194 (Cal. App. 1989).

36. Semore v. Pool, 266 Cal. Rptr. 280 (Cal. App. 1990).

37. Alaska, Arizona, Florida, Hawaii, Illinois, Louisiana, Montana, South Carolina, and Washington.

9

Honesty Testing

The use of the polygraph as an employment screening tool is a relatively recent aspect of polygraph history. Polygraph testing originated in the 1920's in the field of criminology, as psychologists sought a mechanical, supposedly objective way to assess the guilt or innocence of criminal defendants rather than leave this judgment to jurors, who are fallible to begin with and may be swayed by subjective factors such as race or physical attractiveness. The method developed combines pre- and post-test interviews between examinee and tester with measurements of the examinee's perspiration, heart rate, and blood pressure. By interpreting graphs noting changes in these areas caused when emotional stress is induced in the subject, the examiner presumably is able to gauge the truth of the subject's statements.

Neither commentators nor courts have ever been comfortable with this process. The main difficulty is that deciding if an examinee was honest involves so much judgment on the part of the examiner. If the examiner is unskilled or inexperienced or simply misreads the charts; if he is unduly affected by his subjective perception of the examinee before, during, or after the test; or if he misconstrues the examinee's behavior indications as signs of guilt, erroneous conclusions may follow. Polygraph results are also unlike other kinds of proof, such as fingerprints or blood alcohol analysis, for which there is a proven scientific correlation between the information sought and the physical evidence obtained. A third problem involves the assumptions underlying all truth verification tests: that there is a predictable causal relationship between lying and certain emotional states (the anxiety, tension and stress associated with the fear of detection), and that there is also such a relationship between these states and physiological changes measured by the polygraph (increased blood pressure, sweating and rapid breathing). The responses measured in a polygraph test could stem from other anxieties, such as the fear of being erroneously labeled a liar, surprise at a question or uncertainty about how to answer it, or anger at being tested. Questions may be poorly phrased, and there may be problems with the conditions under which a test is given or with the machine used. Finally, what constitutes an honest answer to a particular question may be hard to determine.

In *Frye v. United States*,[1] the first case involving the use of polygraph results in a criminal prosecution, the court expressed some of these concerns in holding that the test "has not yet gained such standing and scientific recognition among physiological and psychological authorities as would justify the courts in admitting expert testimony deduced from the discovery, developments, and experiments thus far made." Courts today still echo this theme, with the result that most efforts to admit such evidence in criminal proceedings continue to fail.[2] Notwithstanding the many reasons to question the accuracy of polygraphs, however, employers have, in the last two decades, increasingly turned to them for help in assessing employee honesty. The result has been an intense battle pitting those stressing the need for and merits of such testing against those concerned about the reliability of tests and their implications in terms of employee privacy.

Testing proponents claim that the polygraph is a quick, inexpensive way to help employers guard their businesses and property by ferreting out job-related wrongdoing and obtaining needed background data on employees and applicants. Indeed, the polygraph has been used to aid in investigations of employee crimes such as theft; to screen applicants on issues such as drug use or past criminal acts; to inquire about one's work record and attitude toward a job for which he has applied; to learn about mental or physical problems, accident experiences or personal habits; and to deter wrongdoing through periodic screening. In a 1978 survey, a third of the respondents said they tested to verify applications and their employees' "honesty, loyalty, and compliance with company policy."[3]

Invoking many of the arguments against urinalysis, on the other hand, opponents cite the lack of scientific support for the accuracy of polygraphs and claim that tests compromise employee privacy and dignity and pervert the presumption of innocence. They note that testers may conduct fishing expeditions, probing in areas in which they have no valid interest. They also stress the factors, discussed above, which may yield questionable test results. Because of the longstanding doubts about the tests' veracity, courts and legislators have been largely receptive to these claims. The use of polygraphs on the job has been barred in some states, and in others limits of varying degrees of strictness have been imposed. But the most significant action thus far was taken by Congress in 1988, in the form of the Employee Polygraph Protection Act (EPPA).[4]

The EPPA reflects an effort to attain a compromise between the conflicting employer and employee interests noted above. Simply stated, it prevents the use of polygraphs by most private employers without reason to believe that an employee has caused "economic loss," for example, has committed theft or industrial espionage. In that case the law allows the employer to let the worker attempt to prove his innocence through testing. The employee may end the test at any time. Special rules allow wider use of polygraphs by private security firms and employers who distribute or make drugs, but even they cannot use results (or the refusal to be tested) as the sole basis for an adverse employment action, for example, firing or not hiring. Strict rules govern the conduct of tests, and employees may sue employers who violate the law. In view of EPPA, most attorneys are advising employers not to use polygraphs at all: they are not worth the trouble and expense of litigation, and the law has too many technicalities which are too easy to violate.

There are many misconceptions about EPPA. Some, for example, think it covers only polygraphs. In fact, it forbids private employers to "request, suggest, or cause any employee or prospective employee to take or submit to any lie detector test," defining *lie detector* as a "polygraph, deceptograph, voice stress analyzer, psychological stress evaluator, or any similar device (whether mechanical or electrical) that is used, or the results of which are used, for the purpose of rendering a diagnositic opinion regarding the honesty or dishonesty of an individual." Polygraphs—and only polygraphs—may be used in cases involving security personnel, economic loss, or employees engaged in manufacturing or distributing certain drugs.

It is also thought that the law allows all private security firms to test their employees with polygraphs. Actually, such employees may be tested only if their work will involve protecting "facilities, materials, or operations having a significant impact on the health or safety of any State or political subdivision," such as electrical, nuclear, or public water supply facilities; toxic waste materials; public transportation; currency, negotiable securities, or precious commodities; or proprietary data. Even then, results or the refusal to take a test may not afford the sole basis for adverse action against the employee.

Employers who make or dispense certain controlled substances may ask prospective employees to be tested if the job involves direct access to the substances. Current employees, however, may be tested only "in connection with an ongoing investigation of criminal or other misconduct" involving the substances. Again, test results or the refusal to be tested may not be the sole basis for adverse action against an employee.

The EPPA contains several testing prerequisites. There must be a pre-test phase in which the employee receives written notice of the time and place of the test and the fact that he or she may consult with legal counsel before taking it. The employee must sign a notice advising that he or she need not be tested, that statements made during the test may be used against him or her, and that he or she may sue the employer and the examiner based on the test. Before the test, the employee must be allowed to review all questions and told that he or she may end the test at any time. The test must last at least 90 minutes, and degrading questions may not be asked. Questions may not be asked about religion, racial matters, political or union beliefs or activities, or sexual behavior or lifestyle. After the test, the employer must interview the employee on the basis of the results and provide a copy of any opinions or conclusions based on the test. The employee must be given a copy of the questions asked and the chart of the responses. The employer may not disclose data obtained from the test to anyone other than the employee; government agencies, if the results involve an admission of criminal conduct; and others pursuant to a court order.

The EPPA requires examiners to be licensed in the state in which a test is given. State licensing laws typically establish minimum qualifications for licensing, such as education and training requirements; require licensees to pass an examination; provide for license suspension or revocation for acts of misconduct, such as failing to inform the examinee of the voluntary nature of the examination; and authorize the state licensing board to enact other rules. They may prescribe a minimum instrumentation requirement, for example, that a machine be able to measure "permanently, visually, and simultaneously" the subject's cardiovascular, respiratory and galvanic skin response. Finally, they may require certain examination procedures or techniques or forbid some questions, such as those concerning sexual activities or lifestyle, religion, political or labor affiliation, and beliefs concerning racial matters.

The EPPA does not preempt more restrictive state or local polygraph laws. As of early 1990, at least thirteen states[5] and the District of Columbia had such laws, which either prevent most private employers from asking their employees to take a test for any reason or do not allow test results to be used in any way. In these states employers must be careful to ascertain if exemptions in the EPPA also appear in the state law. In New York and the District of Columbia, for example, private employers may not use polygraph test results, regardless of whether the test fits in one of the exceptions in the EPPA. In

Massachusetts, Michigan, Rhode Island and Vermont, employers may not "subject employees to" or "administer" a test. In Alaska, Delaware, Connecticut, Maine, Minnesota, New Jersey, and West Virginia, employers may not "request" that a test be taken. Of the thirteen states and the District of Columbia, only New Jersey, Vermont, and West Virginia make exceptions, and then only for workers engaged in manufacturing and distributing drugs.

The federal government is exempt from the EPPA and any state laws controlling governmental use of lie detection devices. The act also does not apply to state and local government employees. Twenty-one states and the District of Columbia[6] prevent most public employees from having to take a polygraph test, with thirteen of these entities making an exception for police.[7] That a state has no polygraph statute, however, does not mean employers are free to use these devices, for there may be a court case on point. In *Texas State Employees Union v. Texas Dept. of Mental Health and Mental Retardation,*[8] for example, the Texas Supreme Court held that in view of the "right of privacy" in the Texas Constitution, state and local governments in Texas may not require public employees to take a polygraph test. The Court noted that "unique circumstances" may justify an exception for police, but it gave no hint of what such circumstances may be. Other state law causes of action involving the use of polygraphs have included wrongful discharge based on statutory[9] or general[10] public policy factors, negligence in giving a test,[11] and false imprisonment and assault and battery claims.[12]

The polygraph is likely the best known form of honesty testing, but it is not the only one. Other devices include sodium pentathol, or truth serum, and hidden cameras that photograph and measure pupil dilation. Voice stress tests, which purport to measure vocal manifestations of stress, have become popular among employers, as has written honesty testing. With the demise of polygraphs, written testing, already a multi-million dollar industry used by over 5,000 companies,[13] should increase in popularity. More futuristic possibilities include sensing devices implanted in the body and machines capable of mind reading by interpreting cerebral impulses.[14] As discussed above, the EPPA embraces these devices, but individual state laws and court cases will not necessarily do so.

CONCLUSION

Federal and state laws and case law either bar most private employers from requiring their employees and job applicants to submit to a polygraph or other honesty test or severely limit their ability to do so. Even if no judicial or statutory ban on testing exists, however, employers would be well advised to forego it. Test results are problematic for many reasons; the prospects of a judicial challenge, with all of its attendant expense, hassle, and bad publicity, are excellent; and both federal and state courts have proven to be quite receptive to such challenges.

NOTES

1. 293 F. 1013, 1014 (D. C. Cir. 1923).
2. *See generally* 29 AM JUR. 2D, *Evidence* §831.
3. Belt & Holden, *Polygraph Usage Among Major U.S. Corporations*, PERSONNEL J. 81 (Feb. 1978), *cited in* Hurd, *Use of the Polygraph in Screening Job Applicants*, 22 AM. BUS. L. J. 529 (Winter 1985).
4. Pub.L. 100–347, 102 Stat. 646 (1988).
5. Alaska, Connecticut, Delaware, Maine, Massachusetts, Michigan, Minnesota, New Jersey, New York, Oregon, Rhode Island, Vermont, and West Virginia.
6. Alaska, Connecticut, Delaware, Hawaii, Idaho, Iowa, Maine, Maryland, Massachusetts, Michigan, Minnesota, Montana, Nebraska, New Jersey, New York, Oregon, Pennsylvania, Rhode Island, Vermont, Washington, and West Virginia.
7. Alaska, Connecticut, the District of Columbia, Hawaii, Idaho, Iowa, Maine, Maryland, Nebraska, Pennsylvania, Vermont, Washington, and West Virginia.
8. 746 S.W.2d 203 (Tex. 1987).
9. *E.g.*, Perks v. Firestone Tire & Rubber Co., 611 F.2d 1363 (3d Cir. 1979) (applying Pennsylvania law); Heller v. Dover Warehouse Mkt., Inc., 515 A.2d 178 (Del. Super. Ct. 1986) (finding that state laws barring polygraphs in employment created public policy exception to generally prevailing at-will employment doctrine, and that this exception is violated if employee is fired based on polygraph test).

10. *E.g.*, Cordle v. General Hugh Mercer Corp., 325 S.E.2d 111 (W. Va. 1984), holding that although state constitution and statutes did not prohibit the discharge of employees for refusing to take a lie detector test, state public policy was violated when a worker was fired for that reason.

11. *E.g.*, Ivey v. Sayre Corp., *reported in* 23 A.T.L.A. L. Rep. 415 (Nov. 1980).

12. *E.g.*, Walden v. General Mills Restaurant Group, Inc., 508 N.E. 2d 168 (Ohio App. 1986).

13. Sackett and Harris, *Honesty Testing for Personnel Selection: A Review and Critique*, 37 PERSONNEL PSYCHOLOGY 221 (1984).

14. *E.g.*, Craver, *The Inquisitorial Process in Private Employment*, 63 CORNELL L. REV. 1 (1977).

10

AIDS Testing

A decade ago, AIDS was nearly unknown in the medical community. Now, approximately two million people have been identified as seropositive for AIDS, and the disease is referred to as the public health crisis of our time.[1] Since most victims are between the ages of 20 and 50, and since the disease is incurable, AIDS is having a major impact in the workplace. While the possibility that the disease may be acquired through the kind of contact experienced by co-workers is almost nil, many employees insist on not working with people infected with the virus. Infected workers may also periodically need time off to recuperate from AIDS-related health problems, which may be costly to employers and disrupt normal business operations. Employers are thus facing the dilemma of whether to test for AIDS and what to do if a test is positive.

Employers' responses to AIDS implicate several societal concerns, some of which are legally protected. Those coping with the presence or potential presence of AIDS in their businesses, therefore, must be aware of the implications of their acts and of the laws governing acceptable responses.

CAUSES OF AIDS

AIDS is caused by the Human Immunodeficiency Virus (HIV), which selectively attacks lymphocytes, the body's white blood cells that initiate the production of antibodies. When those lymphocytes, called T-4 helper cells, are destroyed, infection can occur, since the body's ability to fend off disease is compromised. The condition known as "full-blown" AIDS is characterized by malignancies that attack the acquired deficiencies in the body's immune system. These malignancies, which otherwise are found only rarely in the population, are called opportunistic diseases because they take advantage of the body's inability to combat them.

People with AIDS can remain in apparent good health and fit for work for years from the time of diagnosis. At times, however, they may suffer from the debilitating effects of opportunistic infections. At these times—and it may be many times for one person—a recuperative period may be needed. The treatment for the malignancies can be nearly as devastating physically as the malignancies themselves. And the grim reality is that most persons diagnosed as having AIDS die within two years.

Full-blown AIDS is only one way in which the human immunodeficiency virus is manifested. Indeed, it has been estimated that only 2 to 3 percent of all people exposed to the virus ever experience full-blown AIDS. People may be infected with the virus without showing any symptoms; they are identified through a blood test to detect the presence of antibodies to the virus. If the test is positive, the person is said to be seropositive. These people are considered infectious, or able to transmit the virus. Researchers' estimates of the number of these people who will develop AIDS range from 25 to 35 percent in five to ten years, to 100 percent with no time limit.[2]

People may also have the virus but exhibit a less devastating syndrome called AIDS-related complex (ARC). This condition is characterized by fever, lethargy, weight loss, sweating, coughing, diarrhea, and generalized swelling of the lymph nodes. Although these people experience the clinical symptoms of AIDS, they do not develop the opportunistic infections associated with full-blown AIDS. It is not known how many people have ARC, as ARC is not currently a reportable condition.

There is no evidence that the AIDS virus can be transmitted through the kind of casual contact that occurs at the workplace. It cannot move from one person to another, for example, through mere touching, sneezing, hugging, or shaking hands. People cannot catch AIDS by sharing an office, desk, water fountain, bathroom, or cafeteria with an infected person. On the contrary, it can be acquired only through either sexual contact where semen or blood is exchanged or the purposeful or inadvertent exchange of blood or blood products, such as when a contaminated needle is used for intravenous injection, when one receives a blood transfusion with contaminated blood, or when a hemopheliac is given blood products to aid in clotting which are later found to have been made with contaminated blood. The virus has also been transferred perinatally from a pregnant woman to her fetus. Although the virus has been isolated in many bodily fluids, including blood, semen, breast milk, saliva, tears, urine, and cervical secretions, only the first three have been implicated in its transmission.[3]

AIDS TESTS

The most common way to detect the presence of antibodies to HIV is through an enzyme-linked immunoabsorbent assay (ELISA) test. This test, which is highly sensitive and fairly inexpensive, uses a blood sample drawn from the subject which is mixed with a deactivated virus. First one, then another, antibody is added to test for binding reactions that can be measured by a light meter. The test does not reveal whether the AIDS virus is present in the subject's blood; rather, it detects antibodies to HIV. It can produce results in a few hours.

The suggested protocol is to repeat ELISA tests on blood samples which produce positive results. If a repeat positive occurs, a confirmatory test is recommended. The most common such test is the Western Blot technique, which also detects the presence of antibodies rather than the AIDS virus itself. The Western Blot is more selective than the ELISA, making its rate of false positives lower than ELISA's. It is also more expensive and more difficult to perform, making it less suitable for a first screening test.

The main problem with ELISA involves its penchant for yielding false positives—positive results when the blood tested lacks antibodies to HIV—which makes its exclusive use as a job screening device dangerous. If a confirmatory test is not performed, the subject could be denied employment and also suffer extreme emotional distress based on false data. On the other hand, the Western Blot yields a high rate of false negatives—negative results when the blood is contaminated with antibodies—which also makes its exclusive use problematic. Used in connection with the ELISA, however, the Western Blot is considered very accurate. One study reported that the results obtained with two ELISAs followed by a Western Blot are over 99 percent accurate.[4] Other problems with these tests involve their use out of sequence, which can produce erroneous results; misinterpretation of results; the fact that it takes time for one's body to produce antibodies to a virus after being exposed to it, so that testing during the lag time may yield inaccurate results; and the inability of a test to determine if an infected person will develop AIDS or ARC or remain an asymptomatic carrier of the virus, and if the former, when symptoms might appear. A case of AIDS diagnosed today, for example, may be the result of HIV exposure from up to seven years before.[5]

AIDS AND THE WORKPLACE

Employers have a number of concerns regarding AIDS. One is whether an infected employee can work, and if so, for how long. An employer's business may be incapable of functioning smoothly when even one person is absent repeatedly due to sickness and hospitalization, or a job may demand such extensive training that hiring someone with a limited life expectancy may be unduly burdensome. This problem is compounded by the inability of current technology to ascertain if or when an infected person will develop AIDS or HIV. Courts have not favored the practice of firing or refusing to hire someone because an illness may render him unable to perform the job in the future.

In addition, under the common law of master-servant relationships and under federal law, employers have a duty to maintain a safe workplace. An employer may be concerned that retaining an employee with AIDS would violate that duty. While the courts seem inclined to hold otherwise, some employers and co-workers fear that AIDS is too new and that too much is unknown about it to rely on medical advice. That authorities maintain that AIDS cannot be transmitted through casual workplace contact may not allay their fears, which puts pressure on employers to fire or take restrictive action concerning HIV-infected employees.

What does an employer do if he has an employee with AIDS and others refuse to work with that person? Fair employment and work safety laws will likely support a decision to discipline recalcitrant employees, but the employer still faces a disruption of work. Of more concern is the possibility that clients or customers will react adversely. The employer has some legal and economic leverage to exert on unwilling co-workers, but he can do little about nervous customers.

Employees with AIDS or who test HIV-positive also have valid concerns. Aside from the obvious health threat they face, they may legitimately fear overreaction by co-workers and employers. Such overreaction may also prompt employers to engage in a crude form of AIDS screening by excluding from their workforces anyone who "looks like" they may have the disease, such as gay males or any male thought to be gay. People subjected to AIDS screening also have valid fears about accuracy and privacy. While testing under optimal conditions is highly accurate, tests are not always performed flawlessly, and confirmatory tests are not always given. One may thus lose a job or a chance for one when another test might have shown that an initial positive result was incorrect. One may also be improperly labeled an AIDS-carrier based on an inaccurate test, which can have disastrous consequences for that person's personal life. And even if a test is accurate, that one has AIDS does not always warrant the conclusions to which people tend to jump: that the individual is gay or has engaged in homosexual sex.

At least four states—California, Florida, Maine and Wisconsin—have enacted laws which prohibit or seriously curtail the use of serological tests to detect the presence of antibodies to the AIDS virus as a condition of hire or of continued employment. These laws also generally make it unlawful to disclose test results to anyone other than the subject without that person's consent. Several cities have ordinances to the same effect.

Some states afford less protection. Hawaii, for example, bans testing for antibodies to HIV without the subject's consent.[6] Maryland prohibits employers from asking applicants about physical disabilities or treatments unrelated to the applicant's ability to perform the job.[7] Because laws such as these are new, they have not yet received much judicial attention, so their parameters and possible effect remain unclear. Cases have arisen involving employees discharged for refusing to submit to blood tests, but so far they have been in jurisdictions without laws banning antibody testing by employers. Cases dealing with job screening through HIV tests have also been filed with state and city civil rights agencies.[8]

Most AIDS-related employment court cases seek relief under federal or state handicap laws. In 1987, the U. S. Supreme Court decided *School Board of Nassau County, Florida v. Arline*,[9] which held that a person with a communicable disease may be handicapped under the 1973 Vocational Rehabilitation Act. Although this decision did not squarely resolve the status of AIDS victims under the act, it has been read to mean that such victims are protected. Even before *Arline*, most state agencies charged with implementing state anti-discrimination laws had announced that they would consider AIDS a handicap under state law.[10] The most common definition of "handicapped person" in these laws is the same as or similar to the one in the federal act. It prohibits job discrimination against anyone who has a physical or mental impairment which substantially limits one or more major life activities; has a record of such impairment; or is regarded as having such impairment, whether or not the perception is true. Even people who test seropositive for HIV infection but are asymptomatic seem to fall within this definition, either because of physical impairment—infection with a communicable virus—or because of perceived impairment due to the myths and fears that people have about AIDS.

If a person is handicapped, the next inquiry under most laws is whether she is "otherwise qualified" for the job at issue. This decision is made on an individual basis. In the context of a contagious disease, the Supreme Court has said that the inquiry should include "[fact findings] based on reasonable medical judgments given the state of medical knowledge, about (a) the nature of the risk (how the disease is transmitted), (b) the duration of the risk (how long is the carrier infectious), (c) the severity of the risk (what is the potential harm to third parties) and (d) the probabilities the disease will be transmitted and will cause varying degrees of harm."[11] The federal law and many state laws also require employers to decide if the handicapped person would be otherwise qualified if offered "reasonable accommodation." Reasonableness is judged in the light of the size of the employer's operation, the cost of the accommodation, and the hardship which might result to the employer if accommodation is offered. It is unclear what accommodations might be needed for an employee with AIDS, but they might include flexible job scheduling, at-home work, reassignment of duties, and the like.

State fair employment laws typically ban discrimination based on race, color, sex, national origin, religion, age, and often handicap—thus mirroring the combined coverage of Title VII and the federal Age Discrimination in Employment and Rehabilitation Acts—and people with AIDS or HIV would appear to be within their ambit. Some states also protect such categories as marital status, ancestry, juvenile criminal record or sexual orientation, and these laws may apply in situations involving AIDS. In one employment benefits discrimination case, a litigant claimed that the employer's exclusion of AIDS-related benefits from an employee benefits package was unlawful discrimination under the Oregon Civil Rights Law. The hearing officer agreed, finding that over 90 percent of people with AIDS, nationally and in Oregon, were men, and that the policy, which was gender-neutral on its face, thus had a disparate impact on men.[12] The employer unsuccessfully argued that the employee was actually raising a sexual orientation discrimination case.

The constitutional provisions that bear most directly on AIDS in the workplace are the guarantees of due process, equal protection and privacy. The validity of an employer's testing program may also be challenged on the basis of the Fourth Amendment's protection against unreasonable searches, or its state counterpart, as it is undisputed that the taking of blood to be tested for HIV antibodies involves a "search."[13] For a testing plan to pass muster, an employer would have to show that the interests to be served by testing outweigh privacy expectations. Two court cases on this issue have come out differently, one finding that the government's interests in testing were paramount,[14] and the other holding that those interests were not served by the tests at issue.[15]

Privacy issues may also surface in other than the testing context. Once an employer learns about an employee's or applicant's HIV status—whether through employment-based antibody tests, self-disclosure or other methods—constitutional, statutory or common law principles may dictate what may be done with that data. Laws controlling the confidentiality of medical and personnel records, and specifically HIV antibody test results, may also come into play. If an employer decides to keep this information on file, she must safeguard access to it. In *Cronin v. New England Telephone Co.*,[16] the plaintiff was asked to tell his employer why he sought time off for doctor's visits. After receiving assurances of confidentiality, he told his supervisor that he was being treated for symptoms of ARC. Despite these assurances, the supervisor told his superiors of the plaintiff's condition. They organized group meetings with all employees who had ever worked with the plaintiff, to tell them he had AIDS. Cronin sued under the Massachusetts privacy law, and his claim survived a motion to dismiss before finally being settled.

Federal and state laws regulating workplace safety and the common law will also play a role in the formulation of AIDS employment policies. They require employers either to provide working conditions reasonably safe for workers or to warn them of unsafe conditions not discoverable through the exercise of reasonable care. The Federal Occupational Safety and Health Act mandates that each employer "furnish to each of his employees employment and a place of employment which are free from recognized hazards that are causing or are likely to cause death or serious physical harm to his employees."[17] These laws prohibit an employer from taking adverse action against employees who protest working in areas or situations which they reasonably believe pose a danger of serious bodily harm or death. This right, however, usually carries certain duties. An employee must ask the employer to correct the allegedly hazardous situation through normal channels, if there is time to do so, and the protest must be made in good faith, based on a "reasonable" belief.

Does an employer have a duty to warn employees if a co-worker or customer has AIDS or HIV infection? Does he or she violate legal duties to keep a safe workplace by retaining an HIV-infected employee? Is a co-worker's refusal to work with an employee with AIDS a protected health and safety protest? The present consensus among health and labor experts is that if the workplace is not one in which there is a risk of an exchange of bodily fluids, the answers to the above questions are "No."

CONCLUSION

AIDS is a major national health concern. In the workplace, it causes innumerable fears among employers and co-workers, who often seek to be separated from those infected with the virus—and those who look like they may be infected—even if they display no symptoms. Various federal and state laws, however, prohibit or severely limit such action, at least in areas involving no exchange of bodily fluids. Often these laws also require employers to reasonably accommodate workers with AIDS. These laws rest on the premise that people should be allowed to work as long as they can, not be treated adversely because of a debilitating condition, and not be the victims of unwarranted stereotypes, prejudices and myths.

NOTES

1. The data on AIDS in this section was taken from reports of the Centers for Disease Control. One states that men comprise 93 percent of adults with AIDS and that 90 percent of those men are between the ages of 20 and 49. *Update: Acquired Immunodeficiency Syndrome—United States.* 35 MORBIDITY & MORTALITY WEEKLY REP. 757–66 (1986).

2. 25 to 35 percent within ten years: Sevak & Wormser, *How Common is HTLV-III Infection in the United States?* 313 NEW ENG. J. MED. 1352 (1985). 50 percent within 15 years: Results of study by Dr. M. Rees, *reported in* 2 AIDS POLICY & LAW (BNA), No. 6, at 10 (April 8, 1987). 100 percent with no stated time limit: Remarks of Dr. M. R. Schwarz, chair of the AIDS Task Force of the American Medical Ass'n., at AMA Meeting, Chicago, Ill., April 21–22, 1987.

3. Centers for Disease Control, *Human T-Lymphotropic Virus Type III/Lymphadenopathy-Associated Virus: Agent Summary Statement,* 35 MORBIDITY & MORTALITY WEEKLY REP. 540–42, 547–49 (1986).

4. Centers for Disease Control, *Recommendation for Prevention of HIV Transmission in Health-Care Settings,* 36 MORBIDITY & MORTALITY WEEKLY REP. 13S-14S, Table 2 (1987).

5. Centers for Disease Control, *Trends in Human Immunodeficiency Virus Infection Among Civilian Applicants for Military Service—United States, October 1985 – December 1986,* 36 MORBIDITY & MORTALITY WEEKLY REP. 273–76 (1987).

6. S. B. 1007, *reported in* 2 AIDS POLICY & LAW (BNA), No. 19, at 8.

7. Md. Ann. Code art. 100, §95A(a) (1985).

8. *See, e.g.,* discussion of nine cases involving employment-based testing in Eisnaugle, *New York State Div. of Human Rights—AIDS Based Discrimination: A Summary of Reported Instances Sept. 1983–Oct. 1985.* (Nov. 8, 1985).

9. 107 S. Ct. 1123 (1987).

10. Ritter and Turner, *AIDS, Employer Concerns and Options,* 38 LAB. L. J., No. 2 at 73 (1987).

11. 107 S. Ct. at 1131, *quoting* Brief of American Medical Association as *Amicus Curiae* 19.

12. Oregon Civil Rights Div., Bureau of Labor, Case Em-HP-870108-1353 (Jan. 8, 1988).

13. Schmerber v. California, 384 U.S. 757 (1966).

14. Local 1812, Am. Fed'n of Gov't Employees v. U. S. Dept. of State, 662 F. Supp. 50 (D. D. C. 1987).

15. Glover v. Eastern Neb. Community Office of Retardation, 686 F. Supp. 243 (D. Neb. 1988).
16. 1 IER Cases 651 (Mass. 1986).
17. 29 U.S.C. §254 (1982).

11

Genetic Testing

Although there have been many astounding scientific break-
throughs in recent years, we are not yet able—thankfully, most
would say—to produce employees physiologically or psychologically tailored for certain jobs. But we can screen workers and
applicants to minimize the risk that those with or predisposed
to physical, mental or emotional illnesses may be exposed on
the job to factors that might make the problems manifest or
exacerbate their severity. Current knowledge about medical
testing can also lessen the risk of susceptible employees being
exposed to substances that might cause health problems in
their children.

As is true of testing for employee honesty and drug use,
that employers are capable of engaging in genetic screening
does not necessarily mean that they should do so. They must
weigh the perceived benefits of testing against the full range
of costs involved, which embrace not only the expense of a
test but also the risk of litigation and of the bad will it might
engender among employees. These benefits and costs are explored below.

PREMISES OF GENETIC TESTING

One's genetic makeup is determined at conception, but it does not always remain static. Genes can be mutated, or fundamentally altered, because mistakes occur naturally when cells reproduce or because exposure to environmental factors causes these mistakes. Substances in the environment capable of inducing genetic mutations are called *mutagenic*. Certain types of radiation are mutagenic, for example, meaning that exposure to a sufficiently high dose of them may cause genetic mutations. Scientists think mutagens are linked with cancer, although the nature of this linkage is the subject of much debate.

Some mutations are confined to people exposed to the mutagen, while others may be passed on to their children. Substances may be *teratogenic*, meaning that although they may or may not cause mutations in workers exposed to them, they can cause developmental abnormalities in embryos of pregnant workers thus exposed. Many substances in the workplace may be mutagenic, and proper screening should theoretically enable employers to limit worker exposure to these substances to a level that would not cause permanent damage. A drawback of this theory, however, is that screening can only test the past effects of exposure to a substance; thus, future harm to other workers may be prevented, but those monitored effectively serve as human guinea pigs. Another is that while screening can detect cellular abnormalities in people exposed to a substance, it cannot predict whether systemic damage will occur. It also cannot determine if the abnormalities were caused by the exposure or by other environmental factors to which the person may have been exposed, either on the job or elsewhere.

Scientists have identified hundreds of diseases which are genetically-based and may be affected by substances at the job site.[1] Among them are blood diseases, including various kinds of anemia; lung diseases such as cancer and emphysema; and other maladies such as bladder cancers, cystic fibrosis, and a rare form of optic atrophy. Links between genetic makeup and both mental illness and personality also seem to exist. It has been suggested that diabetes and drug and alcohol dependency may be influenced by hereditary traits. Finally, a predisposition to certain diseases may be linked to racial or ethnic background. Blacks, for example, are more susceptible to sickle-cell anemia than other races; for that matter, no racial or ethnic group is without its own predisposition to disease.

GENETIC TESTING AND THE WORKPLACE

Why might employers be concerned about the genetic makeup of their workforce? For one thing, most don't want to see their employees become incapacitated through exposure to harmful substances. But there are also economic incentives for genetic tests: an employee with a disease traceable to his job, for example, can usually collect workers' compensation. Although the employer will likely have insurance to cover any liability in this regard, her premiums will increase, maybe prohibitively, if too many workers are disabled by occupationally caused diseases. Premiums for health and disability insurance may be similarly affected, even if a link between the job and the disease cannot be shown. Finally, great cost may be involved in training replacements for employees unable to work after contracting a genetically linked disease.

But there are downsides to testing. First, an employer could be sued for negligent or deliberate acts associated with it. Such cases are unlikely, because workers' compensation statutes usually contain "exclusive remedy" provisions barring employees from suing employers for a work-related physical injury, at least one caused by negligence. But recent cases suggest some risk of liability in this area. Employees with work-related asbestosis, for example, have alleged that their employers knew of the dangers of asbestos exposure but deliberately concealed them and failed to warn workers whose physical examinations showed that their respiratory systems had already been damaged by exposure. Some courts have held that, if proven, these claims would establish a cause of action for deliberate injury, which is not barred by exclusive remedy provisions. An employer performing genetic screening may thus have a duty to warn employees whose tests indicate that they may contract a genetically linked disease. And this may create a Catch-22: if the employee is not warned of the danger and given a chance to escape the hazardous environment, the employer may be liable in tort; if, however, the employee is transferred to a less dangerous but lower-paying job, he may qualify for partial disability benefits on the ground that he has already sustained a work-related injury.

Another possible basis for employer liability involves pre-employment testing. Normally, if an injury is sustained during a pre-employment physical exam, the employer is liable for workers' compensation benefits and thus is protected by the exclusive remedy provisions of the relevant statute. But she may not be protected from liability if an injury is incurred because of the exam. Assume, for example, that screening reveals—or would have revealed, had it been properly done—that an applicant has a genetic defect that would make it dangerous for him to be exposed to a substance. If the applicant is not warned of or is mistakenly told he does not have the defect, and if he then goes to work for someone else in a job where he is exposed to the substance, the workers' compensation exclusivity bar may not shield the first employer from liability for its failure to warn or for its misdiagnosis.[2]

Another problem with genetic tests involves federal and state handicap laws. An applicant or employee with a genetic deficiency but no signs of it could be determined to be handicapped if a genetic test were positive. The applicant would thus be entitled to the full range of protection given by these laws, including the right not to be subjected to an adverse employment action based on the risk of future injury or incapacitation and the right to be allowed to show that, with reasonable accommodation, she can do the job.

There are two types of genetic tests. Cytogenetic monitoring involves testing employees to see if their chromosomes have been affected by exposure to radiation or toxic chemicals on the job. This is similar to other physical exams to which workers are routinely subjected and are an attempt to discover physical harm as quickly as possible. There are few legal problems with this test. The second, and most troubling, kind of test tries to predict susceptibility to injury by examining the genes and even the DNA profile of prospective employees. There are at least two problems with these tests. First, many genetic traits are related to race or sex, which raises the specter of bias claims if employees or applicants are treated adversely based on such testing. Second, as has been noted, discrimination against one with a genetic deficiency may be handicapped discrimination.

If genetic traits are linked with an increased risk of injury in some jobs, is exclusion from the workforce allowed? The leading case on this question is *E. E. Black Ltd. v. Marshall.*[3] Crosby, a 31 year old carpenter, sought work at a construction company. He had previously suffered two back injuries, and a physical examination taken in connection with his application disclosed a congenital back defect. Fearing that Crosby might suffer further harm, the company rejected him, although doctors disagreed over the extent of the risk of future injury. Crosby challenged this rejection, but the court held that this risk may justify the rejection of a qualified handicapped individual based on "the likelihood of injury, the seriousness of the possible injury or the imminence of the injury." The court said that, "[i]f, for example, it was determined that if a particular person were given a particular job, he would have a 90 percent chance of suffering a heart attack within one month, that clearly would be a valid reason for denying that individual the job, notwithstanding his status as a qualified handicapped individual. A job requirement that screened out such an individual would be consistent both with business necessity and the safe performance of the job."[4] The court remanded the case to the Labor Department for a determination of the likelihood of future injury to Crosby if he took the job.

In 1986 a court allowed New York City to reject a police candidate who had suffered four shoulder dislocations and had had corrective surgery. The odds of his sustaining another, potentially disabling dislocation during the course of his work were deemed high. The court held that because "there is a chance of a new dislocation, and its consequences could be unacceptably costly, the regulation is reasonable in including the apparently few who statistically have this risk from such employment."[5]

The Ninth Circuit Court of Appeals has held that a job requirement may screen out qualified handicapped individuals on the basis of possible future injury, but only if there is a "reasonable probability" of "substantial harm."[6] In one case, the city of Los Angeles wanted to reject a diabetic who sought work as "building repairer." The court found insufficient evidence that the job would significantly increase the risk of substantial harm to the applicant. In the other, the U.S. Post Office refused to hire an epileptic as a letter sorter machine operator. The Ninth Circuit remanded the case to the trial court to decide if the epilepsy posed "a reasonable probability of substantial harm" that could not be minimized by reasonable efforts at accommodation.

The West Virginia Supreme Court allowed a coal mine to reject a female applicant with psoriasis.[7] A doctor who gave a pre-employment physical exam had concluded that working in the mine would "inevitably aggravate" the psoriasis and "had a high likelihood of leading to secondary infection that would require extensive treatment." The court held that "the fact that an applicant's handicap creates a reasonable probability of a materially enhanced risk of substantial harm to the handicapped person or others is a legitimate, nondiscriminatory reason for an employer to reject the applicant." But it cautioned that in making this decision, employers may not rely on "general assumptions or stereotypes" but must consider the actual condition of the person and threat posed by the work. The employer must also be able to demonstrate that no "reasonable accommodation" would ameliorate the risk of injury.

POTENTIAL PREGNANCY AS A HANDICAP

In 1989, the Seventh Circuit Court of Appeals issued a decision which, if it survives on appeal, will rank among the most pivotal court rulings on Title VII. While most commentators regard *Int'l. Union of United Auto Workers v. Johnson Controls, Inc.*[8] as a sex discrimination case, one might also argue that it is a genetic-handicap case. The Supreme Court has agreed to review the decision, so its status will be in doubt until late 1990 or early 1991.

The case involves the battery making division of Johnson Controls. For years company doctors had monitored the level of lead in the blood of plant workers, and they decided that the average level was potentially harmful to fetuses. Accordingly, the company decreed that women capable of becoming pregnant could not work on the battery assembly line or in jobs which might result in a promotion to that line. In a court challenge to this policy alleging gender discrimination in violation of Title VII, the Seventh Circuit judges voted seven-to-four that no violation had occurred because protecting potential damage to future generations is a "business necessity" that justifies the discrimination. It will be recalled that otherwise illegal discrimination is justifiable under Title VII if the employer can prove a valid need for it.[9]

A dissenting opinion by Judge Easterbrook received quite a bit of media attention, in part because he is a conservative judge appointed by President Reagan. Easterbrook made several points that the Supreme Court will be hard-pressed to ignore. First, he noted that Congress amended Title VII in 1978 to deal specifically with discrimination based on "pregnancy, childbirth, or related medical condition." This amendment, often called the Pregnancy Discrimination Act, forbids such discrimination unless the women involved are unable to do the work at issue, and in *Johnson Controls* it is undisputed that the women can make batteries. Judge Easterbrook argued that it is the role of Congress, not the courts, to create any "fetal protection" exception to this rule thought desirable and to establish the relevant medical standards.

Easterbrook also suggested that the proper analysis in this sort of case is similar to that used to decide whether preventing harm to handicapped people justifies discriminating against them. He would have remanded the case for trial—it was decided on summary judgment—to assess the probability and amount of any harm. Observing that potentially pregnant women are much less susceptible to lead poisoning if they use respirators while working, the judge found the presumption that such women would not use this protective device just another "stereotypical belief" that federal law supposedly outlaws in the workplace.

If this decision stands, other companies will have a green light to enact similar prohibitions without worrying about violating Title VII. As many as 20 million jobs could thus be foreclosed for potentially pregnant women—clearly a disastrous result in an economy in which jobs are already sparse. Of course, there always exists the chance that such prohibitions could violate the laws of individual states.

CONCLUSION

Just as more employers are engaging in drug, honesty and AIDS testing, more want to learn about the likelihood that an employee or applicant will become ill through exposure to harmful substances at the workplace. Their concern is attributable to the heightened risk of litigation in this area, the dramatic increase in the costs of employee benefits and health insurance, the desire (and the need) to make the job site safer, and care for their workers. Court cases thus far indicate that if people with certain genetic traits have a significantly higher probability of substantial injury if they work at a certain job, and if that probability cannot be reduced by reasonable efforts at accommodation, an employer might be able to exclude them from the workforce. Hard-and-fast rules are not yet possible, however—each case has to be judged on its own merits. But one thing is clear: employers who impose genetic standards should be ready to defend them in court, as judicial attacks are highly likely in this area.

NOTES

1. *Screening and Counseling for Genetic Conditions: The Ethical, Social and Legal Implications of Genetic Screening, Counseling and Education Programs*, President's Commission for the Study of Ethical Problems in Medicine and Biomedical Behaviorial Research (Feb. 1983).

2. *E.g.*, Esters v. Gen. Motors, 246 Cal. Rptr. 566 (Cal. App. 1988) (holding that an employee can sue an employer for medical malpractice because doctor failed to diagnose cancer during pre-employment physical. Since employee was not employed at time of physical, exclusive remedy did not preempt suit). *See also*, *e.g*, Bryand v. Fox, 515 N.E.2d 775 (Ill. App. 1987); Davis v. Stover, 366 S.E.2d 670 (Ga. 1988) (employee allowed to sue company doctor for malpractice).

3. 497 F. Supp. 1088 (D. Hawaii 1980).
4. *Id.* at 1104.
5. Mahoney v. Ortiz, 645 F. Supp. 22 (S.D.N.Y. 1986).
6. Mentolete v. Bolger, 767 F.2d 1416 (9th Cir. 1985); Bentivegna v. United States Dept. of Labor, 694 F.2d 619 (9th Cir. 1982).
7. Ranger Fuel Corp. v. W. Va. Human Rights Comm., 376 S.E.2d 154, 160 (W. Va. 1988).
8. 886 F.2d 871 (7th Cir. 1989).
9. *See* chapters 2 and 5.

12

Ability Testing

In 1941, when World War II began, our government faced an enormous task: deciding quickly for which jobs millions of people were best suited. Many individuals had been out of work for years due to the Depression, and there were neither reliable references nor past experience to use in making hiring decisions about them. Many had to be trained rapidly for technical work. A large number were women who had never worked in a factory.

Industrial psychologists came to the rescue with a battery of tests. They measured basic intelligence and physical agility so that fighter planes would be entrusted to pilots best able to shoot down enemy aircraft. They tested aptitude so that those selected for specialized training could make the most of their new skills. They gauged achievement so that those needing no special training could be put right to work. And they assessed personality traits so that men with leadership ability could be sent to officers' candidate school. In 1945, this testing strategy was declared a great success: we won the war, didn't we?

Having observed first-hand how useful aptitude testing could be, many of those who became employers and supervisors after the war began using it in the workplace. Over the next two decades, management did less testing on its own, as schools assumed this task; indeed, these years saw ever larger numbers of job applicants arrive at employers' doorsteps armed with high school and college transcripts containing a battery of test scores. In 1964, however, Title VII of the federal civil rights act became law, and court cases interpreting it soon applied brakes to aptitude testing. The extent to which aptitude and psychological testing in the workplace is now permissible is the subject of this chapter.

INTELLIGENCE TESTNG

As chapters two and five discussed, Title VII of the 1964 Civil Rights Act bars covered employers from discriminating based on race, color, sex, religion or national origin in recruiting, hiring, classifying, promoting, compensating or discharging employees, and in establishing other conditions of their employment. It prohibits "disparate treatment" of racial minorities and allows treatment based on sex, national origin or religion only if such a classification is a "bona fide occupational qualification" (BFOQ).[1] The BFOQ standard has been strictly construed. One court, for example, defined it as requiring that an employer who did not want to hire a woman for a job prove a factual basis for believing that "all or substantially all women" could not have performed the job.[2] Others have restricted the classification to cases in which secondary sex characteristics, as opposed to characteristics which correlate with a particular sex, were essential to job performance.[3] In 1977, the U.S. Supreme Court resolved this issue in favor of the former standard, while at the same time emphasizing that the standard would apply only in rare instances.[4]

The act also bans the use of neutral rules whose effect is to discriminate against a protected group. Court rulings in these "disparate impact" cases have permitted facially neutral but factually discriminatory rules only if they are, within the meaning of section 703(h) of the act, part of a "bona fide" seniority or merit system, or if they are justified by "business necessity." The business necessity defense is a court-created defense to a *prima facie* case of disparate impact; to be defensible on this basis, a policy must be job-related.[5] As with the BFOQ, this concept has been interpreted restrictively. One court, for example, said the test is "not whether there exists a business purpose for the challenged practice, but rather whether there exists an overriding legitimate business purpose such that the practice is necessary to the safe and efficient operation of the business."[6] As has been noted, however, some commentators believe that the recent Supreme Court decision in *Wards Cove Packing Co. v. Antonio* may have effectively sounded the death knell for disparate impact litigation, by requiring plaintiffs to perform the nearly impossible task of identifying the specific employment policy or practice that allegedly caused any disparate impact that can be shown to exist in the particular employment setting.[7]

To grasp how Title VII affects ability testing, one must understand three basic concepts: test reliability, test validity and job validity. A test is reliable if it can be given to the same subject at different times with the same results. A test is valid if it actually measures what it claims to be able to measure. Tests cannot be valid if they are unreliable. Assume, for example, a machine designed to measure one's Q factor. A woman puts her hand in the machine and waits 60 seconds. A number between 0 and 100—the Q factor—appears on the digital readout. The woman then puts her hand in the machine three more times, and scores of 3, 48 and 87 result. This machine is not reliable, because the same subject with a Q factor which should remain constant had vastly different scores. In this circumstance, it is unnecessary to ask what the machine is measuring, because the answer obviously is nothing. If a measuring device is unreliable, it is not valid, and if it measures nothing, what it should measure becomes irrelevant.

Now assume scores of 47, 49 and 51. This test would be reliable, with a reliability factor of $+/-2$. It clearly measures something, but with a hit-or-miss factor of 2—someone who scored 49, in other words, might score between 47 and 51 at another time. In this case, the validity question may be asked: what is the test measuring? This is hard to answer. Intelligence tests purport to measure intelligence, but what is intelligence? Is it one trait, or are there different kinds?

In the employment world, "true" validity matters little if a test has "job validity." Simply put, whether a test has job validity depends on whether it can predict who will most likely do well at a job years after the test is given. The army, for example, once tested to choose people for vital but repetitive tasks. They selected their most intelligent recruits, but within two years most quit because of boredom. Their extensive and costly training was wasted. Ultimately, the testers realized that people of average intelligence were the most likely both to stay on the job and to do a good job. In this scenario, the intelligence test had job validity, but only when people in the average range were given the job in question.

Griggs v. Duke Power Co.[8] was the first major ruling on the meaning of Title VII in the aptitude test context. This case involved the Duke Power Company, which required a passing score on the Wonderlic Intelligence Test and the Bennett Mechanical Comprehension Test before it would consider a job candidate. While the policy appeared evenhanded, in that all candidates had to take the same tests and make the same base score, statistics showed that the tests excluded more blacks than whites from consideration for jobs. The Court found this to be illegal discrimination. An employer may use tests having an adverse impact on protected groups, the Court said, but only if the test has job validity or is "job-related." Tests, in other words, must assess an applicant's suitability for the job sought, or, as the Court put it, must "measure the person for the job, not the person in the abstract."[9]

There are two ways for a test to have job validity. First, it can measure an applicant for a skill plainly related to the job sought. A typing test, for example, would be in order for a person seeking employment as a secretary, as would a swimming test for one wanting to be a lifeguard. The other way is to predict job performance. In this instance, there must be a significant correlation between a high score on the test and good job performance. The only way to see if this correlation really exists, however, is to test a group of applicants, hire all of them, and then evaluate them two years later to see if those who scored highly are the best performers on the job. Since few employers have the resources to conduct this kind of job validation study, this route is not feasible.

Courts have allowed employers to use tests without scientific validation if they measure something obviously required for job performance. But the courts do not always agree on what is "obviously required." The California Supreme Court, for example, ruled that the ability to pass an agility test was obviously related to being a good police officer.[10] But in a case with similar facts, the Ninth Circuit Court of Appeals required proof that agility correlated with job performance.[11]

Griggs and its progeny made aptitude testing so onerous for employers that most simply quit doing it. By the 1980's, many employers had begun using subjective measures, such as interviews by supervisors, to make hiring and promotion decisions. Two Supreme Court cases handed down at the end of the decade, however, raised doubts about the viability of these methods. The first was *Johnson v. Santa Clara County, California*,[12] which involved an opening for a road dispatcher job. A panel of evaluators had interviewed candidates and given each a score. Although Paul Johnson, a white male, scored 75, the county gave the job to Diane Joyce, who scored 73. Johnson sued, claiming sex discrimination. The Court ruled in the county's favor, finding that Joyce's promotion was the result of a valid affirmative action plan. But the Court ducked this question: What was the reliability factor of this subjective measurement device? If it was +/−1—a very reliable test—then the scores of 75 and 73 were, scientifically speaking, identical. More employers are now realizing that they cannot use just any test to make this kind of fine distinction between job candidates. While a test can tell if someone is not qualified for a job, it usually cannot tell who is best qualified.

Watson v. Ft. Worth Bank & Trust Co.[13] involved a black woman repeatedly denied a promotion by a bank. When she finally sued, she did so on behalf of all blacks who had ever applied for a job or promotion with that bank. The bank used subjective job interviews, not objective tests, to make personnel decisions, but statistics showed that although 16.7 percent of the white applicants got the job or promotion sought, only 4.2

percent of black applicants did. At trial, a statistician testified that the odds of this happening by chance were 10,000 to 1. Based on this, the Court found illegal discrimination. While it did not rule out the use of subjective tests, even if they discriminate against a minority group, the Court put the burden on employers to show that they validly predict job performance. Given the nature of subjective tests, this is almost impossible to prove.[14]

Employers must also be cognizant of the degree to which a test invades an employee's privacy. Generally, courts will allow such an invasion only if the employer can prove a valid connection between the information acquired and the dictates of the job. In the 1970's, for example, the New York Transit Authority asked if applicants for bus driver positions were on methadone maintenance and rejected those who were. Not only did this practice invade privacy, but it kept a higher percentage of minority applicants from being hired. The U.S. Supreme Court upheld the practice, however, accepting the Authority's claim that the public would stop riding buses if they knew that former drug addicts were driving them.[15] Another possible danger is that test results may get into the wrong hands and cause a suit for "publication of private facts" or "false light" privacy, or for defamation.

In view of these potential problems, employers may well ask: if every test and even job interviews may lead to a suit for discrimination, invasion of privacy or defamation, how should they select and promote employees? The answer is that there is no good substitute for giving those who meet minimum qualifications a chance to do the work and then watching to see if they perform effectively. Observing and supervising employees may be costly, burdensome and less effective than some kinds of testing are thought to be, but with the increasing chances and costs of litigation in this area, it is the only truly feasible option.

PSYCHOLOGICAL TESTING

Psychological testing, especially that purporting to assess personality traits, is a large Pandora's box waiting to be opened.

This form of testing can be done in two ways: through paper and pencil tests that require the employee to answer a series of multiple choice or true/false questions, or through interviews with psychologists during which the professional forms an opinion of the examinee's suitability for a job. Many states require a psychological evaluation before one can assume certain public positions, such as police officer. Private companies often use paper and pencil tests to decide if an employee or applicant has management potential or is fit for certain jobs, such as security guard or salesman. But these tests pose large problems in terms of reliability and validity. For example, while it may be conceded that having only mentally stable police officers is desirable, why should it be assumed that the psychologist who conducts a test is really equipped to make that determination? In addition, a candidate for police officer could circumvent the testing process simply by shopping around until she finds a psychologist who deems her fit for service. Informal surveys suggest that it is not excessively difficult to do this.

One of the most widely used paper and pencil tests is the Minnesota Multi-Phasic Personality Inventory Test (MMPI). Its use, however, raises many potential problems. In 1979, for example, a Mr. Horowitz was denied a job as a probation officer with the city of New York because his MMPI test showed he was "possibly prone to worry" and that he might be "passive and dependent." He filed a discrimination complaint, and the city's Division of Human Rights found the test improper and awarded damages.[16] Recently, suit was filed in California against Target Stores on behalf of all people denied employment because they failed the MMPI test given to applicants for certain jobs, such as security guard.[17] The lead plaintiff was so offended by the questions on his test that he sneaked over to a copy machine and duplicated all 704 of them. Included were such true/false statements as, "I have been in trouble one or more times because of my sex behavior," "I have strong political opinions," "I have no difficulty starting or holding my urine," "I have never indulged in any unusual sex practices," "I believe in the second coming of Christ," "Women should not be allowed to drink in cocktail bars," and "I am strongly attracted to members of my own sex."

This lawsuit charges an invasion of the right to privacy recognized by the California Constitution, a right which California courts have held applies to both private and public employers. But "invasion of privacy" is not the only basis for attacking the MMPI. The federal handicap discrimination act and many state laws define handicap to include anyone "regarded as having" an impairment. Certainly employers who refuse to hire people as a result of this and similar tests do so because they regard the person as less than fully healthy. If the courts find that those who fail the MMPI are handicapped or that even requiring applicants to take a test invades privacy, employers may have to prove the test is "job valid" and that these people with "personality handicaps" cannot be "reasonably accommodated" in the workplace. Having to defend the job validity of the sorts of questions included in the Target test is something few lawyers would welcome. As Neil Martin, with the Houston law firm of Fulbright & Jaworski, said recently, "This area of employee and applicant testing is subject to the most imprecise and subjective scoring, and the least objective defense."[18]

Although it will take months for the Target suit to be resolved, one can anticipate the trial testimony by considering what books on psychological testing have to say about the MMPI test. In the sixth edition of her text, for example, Anne Anastasi reports that some sections of the test have a very low reliability rate, with some people scoring 50 and 90 on a 100 point scale at different times.[19] Kaplan and Saccuzzo say that age, race, residence, intelligence, education and socioeconomic status can affect test results and that "two exact MMPI profile patterns can have quite different meanings depending on the demographic chracteristics of each subject."[20] Murphy and Devidshofer summarized their discussion of the MMPI as follows: "Given the widespread use of the MMPI and the veritable mountain of data which is available regarding this test, the test itself is a bit disappointing." They noted that "the clinical scales are based on an outmoded set of diagnostic categories," that norms "are widely viewed as unrepresentative [and that] evaluations of the measurement properties of the test are not altogether encouraging," and that "the reliability of scores on individual clinical scales is disappointingly low."[21] The introduction of comments such as these at trial would hardly make the prospects of winning a suit look good.

CONCLUSION

Faced with the specter of litigation and the spiraling cost of insurance and employee benefits packages, employers understandably want to learn as much as possible about their employees' and applicants' aptitude, chances of doing well at a job, and prospects of contributing to a harmonious work setting. However, just as there are serious questions about the implications of drug, honesty, AIDS and genetic testing in terms of accuracy, privacy, and discrimination and handicap laws, aptitude and psychological testing raises doubts on these counts. Growing concern about lawsuits and "costs of doing business" have caused some courts to side with employers facing challenges to these tests; that employers win some battles, however, does not warrant the inference that victory in the war is at hand. And even if the right to use aptitude and psychological tests in making personnel decisions is upheld on occasion, the cost of its vindication in terms of litigation expenses, time for depositions and courtroom appearances, and decreased employee morale will likely make the triumph hollow at best.

NOTES

1. Section 703(4), as codified at 42 U. S. C. §2000e(2)(e).

2. *E.g.*, Weeks v. Southern Bell Tel. & Tel. Co., 408 F.2d 228 (5th Cir. 1969).

3. *E.g.*, Rosenfeld v. Southern Pac. Co., 444 F.2d 1219 (9th Cir. 1971).

4. Dothard v. Rawlinson, 433 U.S. 321 (1977).

5. Griggs v. Duke Power Co., 401 U.S. 424 (1971).

6. Robinson v. Lorillard Corp., 444 F.2d 791 (4th Cir. 1971), *cert. denied*, 440 U.S. 1006 (1971).

7. *See supra*, chapter 2, n. 7 and accompanying text.

8. 401 U.S. 424 (1971). *See supra* chapter 2, n. 6 and accompanying text.

9. 401 U.S. at 436.

10. Hardy v. Stumpf, 145 Cal. Rptr. 176 (Cal. 1978).

11. Blake v. City of Los Angeles, 595 F.2d 1367 (9th Cir. 1979).

12. 107 S. Ct. 1442 (1987).

13. 108 S. Ct. 2777 (1988).

14. Again, however, statements in *Wards Cove* cast doubt on the view that employers bear the burden of proof regarding "job performance." There, the Court said: "In this phase, the employer carries the burden of producing evidence of a business justification for his employment practice. The burden of persuasion, however, remains with the disparate-impact plaintiff. . . . '[T]he ultimate burden of proving that discrimination against a protected group has been caused by a specific employment practice remains with the plaintiff *at all times*.' Watson, *supra*. . . ." 109 S. Ct. at 2126 (emphasis in original). *See also supra*, chapter 2, n. 7 and accompanying text.

15. New York Transit Authority v. Beazer, 440 U. S. 568 (1979).

16. Martin, "Employee Selection and Testing," paper delivered at Employment Law Institute, South Texas College of Law (1989).

17. San Jose Mercury News, Sept. 8, 1989 at 13D, 14D.

18. Martin, *supra* note 17.

19. ANASTASI, PSYCHOLOGICAL TESTING, at 2 (1988).

20. KAPLAN AND SACCUZZO, PSYCHOLOGICAL TESTING, at 377 (1989).

21. MURPHY AND DEVIDSHOFER, PSYCHOLOGICAL TESTING, at 357–58 (1988).

PART IV

EMPLOYER SCREENING PRACTICES: ON-THE-JOB SURVEILLANCE

The need for workplace surveillance, employers maintain, does not stop with the hiring of employees. On the contrary, they assert, the kinds of problems discussed previously, including the possibilities of employee theft and industrial espionage, direct and vicarious employer liability for accidents and shoddy products attributable to workers ill-equipped to perform their tasks, and even simple goofing-off by employees, necessitates, if anything, heightened scrutiny of on-the-job activities. Surveillance tools now include searches of employees' vehicles, desks, lockers, and even persons, and close monitoring of workers through computer, telephone, and video technology.

Many employees, however, are equally firm in opposing the use of these techniques. Invoking the arguments used to fight drug and other forms of invasive testing, workers insist that most forms of job-related surveillance are demeaning, unnecessary and even counterproductive, and involve illegal searches and invasions of their privacy. Some who accept the legitimacy of employee surveillance in principle object to the types of monitoring used in particular instances. This portion of the book will examine the competing claims in this area and the legality of the most commonly used workplace surveillance methods.

13

Searches

This chapter discusses the legality of employer searches of employees' offices, desks, lockers and persons. Throughout the discussion, readers must bear in mind that courts which have considered the legal implications of workplace searches have drawn two important distinctions. First, because monitoring people is thought to be far more intrusive than examining places, courts treat the two contexts differently, affording greater protection in the former case. Second, courts consider whether public or private employment is involved, as the constraints of the Bill of Rights in the U.S. Constitution apply only to employers engaged in "state action."[1] These distinctions account for the separate treatment in this chapter of different types of searches, and they cannot be overlooked by employers and supervisors interested in developing legally acceptable search policies.

In many respects, the principles explored in the discussion of the legality of drug testing in chapter eight apply to the workplace searches considered here. Public employees, for example, often invoke the Fourth Amendment and the "right of constitutional privacy" in challenges to employer inspections of their offices, lockers, desks and vehicles, just as they do when the permissibility of being forced to undergo a urine test is at issue. Private employees subjected to searches of these areas in the workplace also tend to join their drug-tested counterparts in basing their attacks on the tort theories of wrongful discharge, invasion of privacy, and intentional infliction of emotional distress, as well as on the "implied covenant of good faith and fair dealing" found in the contract law of some states. Because, however, the courts are inclined to regard urinalysis as a unique form of search, given the involvement of an excretory function and the overall invasiveness of the process, the rules governing its legality are unique. In a nutshell, those rules are stricter than those applicable to other kinds of searches, with the result that one cannot simply assume that the principles reviewed in chapter eight apply *in toto* to the searches dealt with in this chapter, even those involving an employee's person.

SEARCHES OF PLACES: OFFICES, DESKS AND LOCKERS

Employers have many reasons for wanting to search the lockers, desks, and offices of their employees. They may be concerned with office security, suspected drug or alcohol use by the employee, theft, or industrial espionage. Questions of national security or possible terrorist activity are not beyond the pale. Employees, however, often argue that while the privacy interest in these areas may not be as great as it is when personal searches are involved, there nonetheless exists some interest deserving of some protection.

Public Employment

In *O'Connor v. Ortega*,[2] the U.S. Supreme Court ruled for the first time on the legality of searches in public employment. The case involved a psychiatrist in charge of a residency program. When hospital officials became concerned with charges that residents may have been coerced into contributing to the purchase of a computer to be used in the program and that the psychiatrist had harassed female employees and improperly disciplined a resident, they placed the psychiatrist on paid leave and launched an investigation. Among other things, the hospital administrator who conducted the inquiry decided to search the psychiatrist's office. He entered the office several times and seized various items from the desk and files. These items were used in a state administrative proceeding that resulted in the psychiatrist's discharge.

The psychiatrist sued in federal district court, which granted summary judgment for the hospital on the basis that a need to secure state property existed which justified the searches of the plaintiff's office. The Ninth Circuit Court of Appeals reversed, concluding that the search violated the Fourth Amendment, that the plaintiff was entitled to summary judgment on the issue of liability, and that the case should be remanded to the lower court for a determination of damages.

The U.S. Supreme Court, however, reversed the Ninth Circuit. In her plurality opinion,[3] Justice Sandra Day O'Connor said that the case raised two questions: (1) Did the psychiatrist, as a public employee, have a reasonable expectation of privacy in his office, desk, and file cabinets? (2) What is the proper standard under the Fourth Amendment for an employer's search of areas in which an employee has a reasonable expectation of privacy? In answer to the first question, the plurality found that "the operational realities of the workplace ... may make some employees' expectations of privacy unreasonable" when intrusion is by a supervisor rather than a law-enforcement officer, and that such expectations also may be reduced "by virtue of actual office practices and procedures, or by legitimate regulation." But it rejected a claim that public employees never have a reasonable expectation of privacy in their place of work. The plurality concluded that the psychiatrist had such an expectation extending at least to his desk and file cabinets.

The plurality then turned to the issue of reasonableness. Finding "surprisingly little case law" on the standards of reasonableness for a public employer's work-related search of employees' offices, desks, or file cabinets, O'Connor said that the proper resolution of this issue required a balancing of the "employees' legitimate expectations of privacy" against the government's "need for supervision, control and the efficient operation of the workplace." No search warrant is needed in this context, because imposing "unwieldly" warrant procedures on supervisors would be "unduly burdensome" for employers and would "seriously disrupt the routine conduct of business." "Probable cause" to conduct the search is also unnecessary. This requirement would impose "intolerable burdens" since the work of agencies providing "myriad services" to the public would suffer if probable cause were required for entry of an employee's desk to find a file or piece of office correspondence. The plurality concluded:

> [P]ublic employer intrusions on the constitutionally protected privacy interests of government employees for noninvestigatory, work-related purposes, as well as for investigations of work-related misconduct, should be judged by the standard of reasonableness under all the circumstances . . . both the inception and the scope of the intrusion must be reasonable . . . Ordinarily, a search of an . . . office by a supervisor will be "justified at its inception" when there are reasonable grounds for suspecting that the search will turn up evidence . . . of work-related misconduct, or that the search is necessary for a noninvestigatory work-related purpose such as to retrieve a needed file.

The plurality held that there was a factual dispute about the character of the search and that, because the district court had erroneously assumed that the search was conducted pursuant to hospital policy, no finding on the scope of the search had been made. The Court thus remanded the case to the trial court to evaluate the justification and scope of the search.

Concurring in the judgment, Justice Scalia said that the plurality had applied a legal standard "so devoid of content that it produces rather than eliminates uncertainty in this field." Offices of government employees, and a fortiori drawers and files within those offices, are protected by the Fourth Amendment; thus, the question was whether the search was reasonable. Searches to retrieve work-related materials or to investigate violations of workplace rules do not violate the Fourth Amendment, Scalia argued, saying that these kinds of searches are "regarded as reasonable and normal in the private-employer context." Because the evidence here could not conceivably support a summary judgment that the search lacked a validating purpose, Scalia concluded, the plurality was correct in reversing the Ninth Circuit.

Four justices dissented, arguing that the psychiatrist had an expectation of privacy in his office, desk, and file cabinets and that the investigatory search conducted by the hospital was not characterized by a "special need" sufficient to dispense with the warrant and probable-cause requirements of the Fourth Amendment. They further maintained that the standard applied by the plurality "makes reasonable almost any workplace search by a public employer."

The full import of *Ortega* cannot yet be appreciated, as lower courts are just now sifting through the various opinions in the case and applying their reasoning in specific contexts. But the case does settle some questions. Previously, for example, courts had split over whether public employees have a privacy expectation sufficient to trigger the Fourth Amendment in employer-furnished desks, lockers, and offices. Some had found no expectation in a government-provided locker[4] or desk,[5] while others held that a reasonable expectation does exist in a police officer's locker[6] and a school guidance counselor's desk.[7] *Ortega* makes it clear that such an expectation may exist, although agency policy may negate this expectation by informing employees that their desks and similar areas in the workplace are subject to random searches. It should be stressed that public employers who want to search these areas should notify employees of this before they are hired, or at least before the day of any search. If they fail to do so, and employees thus have a reasonable expectation of privacy in these areas, *Ortega* establishes that the places may be searched only on the basis of a "reasonable suspicion" that they contain items forbidden by law or agency policy. Finally, the case indicates that advance consent by employees will not be sufficient to validate a search. This is because public employees cannot be made to consent to the loss of their constitutional rights.[8]

Private Employment

Private employers have more leeway regarding searches. They may, for example, condition employment on an employee's consent to a search, and even a search conducted without consent will likely be upheld, at least if at-will employees are involved. At-will employees, for that matter, may generally be fired if they refuse to consent to a search. But to be on the safe side, searches should be conducted pursuant to valid, uncoerced consent. To eliminate any doubt about whether consent was obtained and its scope, the employer should have the employee sign a consent form before starting work. They should also see that search policies are communicated to and understood by employees. Finally, the employer should not say or do anything that might reasonably lead employees to think that they were no longer subject to a search or had a reasonable expectation of privacy in the area in question.

In *K-Mart Corp. Store No. 7441 v. Trotti*,[9] for example, a store manager testified that all of his new employees were told that their lockers could be searched randomly. Other company executives, however, said they were unaware of this policy, as did Ms. Trotti, an employee. Some workers were given company locks to use on their lockers, but Ms. Trotti was allowed to bring her own lock from home. When she found her locker open one day and her purse ransacked, she learned that company security personnel had searched her locker without her consent, despite their having had no reason to believe she had stolen anything. A jury awarded her $108,000 in damages for invasion of privacy. The Court of Appeals affirmed, ruling that when the company allowed her to bring her own lock to secure her belongings, they gave her an expectation of privacy in her locker.

Cases such as *Ortega* and *K-Mart* suggest that the real issue in litigation involving both public and private sector employer searches of lockers, desks and offices is not whether consent to the searches was obtained, but rather is whether actions or policies of the employer have created a "reasonable expectation of privacy" in the affected area. In *K-Mart*, the act of allowing the plaintiff to bring her own lock created an expectation of privacy in the contents of her locker. In *Ortega*, the lack of notice or a policy stating otherwise gave the employee a reasonable expectation of privacy in his desk. The message is clear: if employers want to search, they should give advance notice of that fact. This lessens, if not eliminates, any basis for claiming a privacy expectation. Rules, regulations, signs and consent forms all help to establish that the employees involved were put on notice that given areas are subject to search. While a search absent such notice may be validated on other grounds, that may require a trip to court, which is costly and time consuming. $108,000 will pay for a lot of signs and policy manuals.

BODY SEARCHES

Body searches, including pat-downs and strip searches, are rare in the employment context, but the need to conduct them is at times thought to exist. Because they involve an examination of people rather than places or inanimate objects, body inspections are deemed the most intrusive form of search and must be counterbalanced by a strong need. After a threshold inquiry into the justification for this search, courts will consider the methods by which it was conducted and whether other, less intrusive means were available and would have accomplished the same result.

In one case,[10] a strip search in an employment context resulted in a tort suit by a part-time retail store checker who was ordered to disrobe after a customer accused her of taking $20 the customer had left on the counter. A female assistant manager and the customer watched while the checker stripped to her underwear in the women's public restroom. The checker subsequently filed a tort action for outrageous conduct against the store and the customer. The Oregon Court of Appeals ordered the case tried by a jury, concluding that the employer had a special relationship with the employee under which recovery for emotional distress might be justified. A jury could find, the court said, that the store manager put the clerk through a degrading and humiliating experience to satisfy a customer and that this conduct exceeded the bounds of social toleration.

In *McDonell v. Hunter*,[11] a federal appeals court upheld strip searches of officers at correctional institutions if based on reasonable suspicion—not just on mere suspicion—in light of the legitimate governmental interest in maintaining security. But the same court concluded that asking employees to strip before giving a urine specimen was unjustified, since less intrusive measures could be taken to insure the validity of the specimen. And another federal appeals court invalidated a New York Department of Corrections random-search policy for strip and body cavity searches, holding that a reasonable suspicion directed to a specific person is required.[12] Both cases, it should be stressed, predated the recent *Skinner* and *Von Raab* decisions by the U.S. Supreme Court;[13] thus there is some doubt about the validity of their holdings on the reasonableness of the policies involved, especially the need for individualized suspicion in those contexts.

In light of their highly intrusive nature, the strong possibility that the employee will litigate the matter, and the uncertainty over what legal standards apply to such searches, the best advice to employers is to avoid body searches of employees unless, for some reason, no viable alternative is thought to exist. In that event, the employer may consider contacting the local police for their assistance.

VEHICLE SEARCHES

Vehicle searches are far more common in the employment setting than body searches, and employees usually are not able to state a cause of action for searches of their vehicles while parked on the employer's property. For one thing, such searches involve places, which do not attract the intense level of judicial scrutiny accorded to inspections of people. That the vehicle is on company property furnishes another basis for allowing an examination of it, in the form of a kind of "implied consent" to the search resulting from the employee's having voluntarily chosen that spot for parking.

In *Gretencord v. Ford Motor Co.*,[14] the court rejected a challenge to an employer's policy of randomly searching employee vehicles prior to their exit from his property. The plaintiff alleged that this practice involved an invasion of privacy, false arrest and imprisonment, outrageous conduct, and reckless and wanton disregard by the employer of the employee's right to be let alone. Because the employee had refused to allow the employer's agents to search his vehicle, the court found that no intrusion had occurred and, accordingly, that there were no grounds for a lawsuit.

In *McDonell v. Hunter*,[15] the court upheld a correctional institution's policy of searching without cause vehicles parked within its confines and accessible to prison inmates, although it stated that the searches must be done uniformly or by systematic random selection. The court also ruled that the institution could search on a random basis employees' vehicles parked outside institutional confines if inmates had unsupervised access to those vehicles, or on the basis of a reasonable suspicion that the vehicle to be searched contained contraband.

That the plaintiff was covered by a collectively bargained agreement furnished the grounds for dismissal of the suit in *Penrith v. Lockheed Corp.*[16] The employer's security guards had searched the employee and his camper truck, located on company premises, after which the employee was arrested, suspended, and then fired. The suit alleged false arrest and imprisonment, assault and battery, invasion of privacy, breach of fiduciary duty, negligence, negligent hiring, and wrongful discharge.

CONCLUSION

Searches of employees or their possessions are regarded by employers as a necessary evil to prevent theft and to control their operations, and by many of the affected employees as an invasion of privacy. The legality of a search hinges essentially on the manner, scope, justification and location of it. Searches of people attract greater judicial scrutiny than inspections of places, given the higher level of intrusiveness involved. Public employers have somewhat less latitude in conducting searches than private employers, as the former are subject to the commands of the U.S. Constitution. In both contexts, the central issue usually boils down to whether the employee had a reasonable expectation of privacy in the area in question. Advance notice that searches may be conducted and obtaining employee consent to searches are two ways to lessen and perhaps negate any such expectation, thus making it more likely that the legality of the search will be upheld.

NOTES

1. *See supra* chapter 1 for a discussion of the "state action" doctrine and the issue of which employers are subject to federal constitutional constraints.

2. 107 S. Ct. 1492 (1987).

3. Principles announced in Supreme Court cases are binding on other courts only if at least five of the nine justices endorse them. In some cases, although a majority of the Court will agree with a certain outcome, they will do so for different reasons; if no justice can get a majority to subscribe to his views, a plurality opinion and various concurrences and dissents will likely be issued. Griswold v. Connecticut, 381 U.S. 479 (1965), the landmark case which first recognized a right of constitutional privacy, *see supra* chapter 3, is another major case in which no majority opinion was issued.

4. United States v. Donato, 269 F. Supp. 921 (E.D. Pa. 1967), *aff'd per curiam* 379 F.2d 288 (3rd Cir. 1967); United States v. Bunkers, 521 F.2d 1217 (9th Cir. 1975).

5. Williams v. Collins, 728 F.2d 721 (5th Cir. 1984).

6. United States v. Speights, 557 F.2d 362 (3rd Cir. 1977).

7. Gillard v. Schmidt, 579 F.2d 825 (3rd Cir. 1978).

8. *See also, e.g.*, McDonell v. Hunter, 612 F. Supp. 1122 (S.D. Iowa 1985), *aff'd as modified* 809 F.2d 1302 (8th Cir. 1987): "The consent form [authorizing random drug testing], which it appears plaintiff McDonell and others signed as a condition of employment... cannot be construed to be a valid consent to any search... [im]permissible under the Fourth Amendment. Public employees cannot be bound by unreasonable conditions of employment.... Advance consent to future unreasonable searches is not a reasonable condition of employment." 612 F. Supp. at 1131.

9. 677 S.W.2d 632 (Tex. App. - Houston [1st Dist.] 1984), *writ ref'd n.r.e.* 686 S.W.2d 593 (Tex. 1985).

10. Bodewig v. K-Mart, Inc., 635 P.2d 657 (Or. App. 1981).

11. *See supra* note 8.

12. Sec. & Law Enforcement Emp., Dist. C. 82 v. Carey, 737 F.2d 187 (2nd Cir. 1984).

13. *See supra* chapter 8.

14. 538 F. Supp. 331 (D.C. Kan. 1982).

15. *See supra* note 8.

16. 1 IER Cases 760 (D.C. Cal. 1986).

14

Non-Electronic and Electronic Surveillance

NON-ELECTRONIC SURVEILLANCE

In general, employers cannot be successfully sued for invading privacy rights because they or their agents simply follow an employee around either at work or in public places. Observing employees at work is among the legitimate functions of an employer. Watching people in public places does not constitute an illegal invasion of privacy, because when someone chooses to go out into the world he voluntarily allows himself to be seen by anyone, including his employer.

One case in this area involved an employer whose employee was hurt on the job.[1] After the employee was treated, medical experts decided he could do light work, but the employee said that even this was too painful and continued to file for workers' compensation payments. The employer hired a private investigator who followed the employee around after work and took movies of his "public activities." These included using a heavy rototiller in his garden at home and mowing the yard. The investigators did not question any of the employee's neighbors or friends and did not observe him anywhere that could be deemed private. The employee sued for invasion of privacy, but the Oregon Supreme Court rejected this contention since the employee had in effect "opened the door" to others' viewing of him.

In another case,[2] investigators hired by an employer observed an employee having an extramarital affair and reported this to the employee's union and to his wife. The investigators had generally done nothing more than watch the employee in public places and listen to what had occurred, although there was some evidence that they had also put a listening device on a motel door. The Maryland Appeals Court ruled that the public surveillance did not involve an invasion of privacy, but it remanded the case to the trial court to rule on the propriety of the listening device.

These and similar cases stand for the proposition that employers, like anyone else, have the right to walk in public and observe employees who are there. They can also hire private investigators to do their watching for them. If they do not intrude on the employee's private space or use electronic surveillance, they stand little chance of running afoul of privacy laws.

Employers can generally observe their own employees at the job site free of invasion of privacy concerns, although California does have a special law governing the use of "spotters."[3] This is an outside investigator brought in to spy on employees. If a spotter is used to spy on a public utility employee and that results in the employee being discharged, the employee must be given an opportunity to defend himself at a hearing. He must also be told of the accusations against him and allowed to present testimony in his defense. Nevada law requires employees accused of dishonesty or rules violations by spotters or detectives to be given a hearing and allowed to confront the person who made the report.[4]

In commercial, retail and service establishments in California a different rule applies. If a worker is about to be interviewed, disciplined or dismissed because of information contained in a "shopper's" report, she must be given a copy of the report before the interview is over and before the discipline or discharge occurs. California law defines a "shopper" as one who comes in from the outside and is not a full-time employee of the employer.[5]

Union Activity

If an employer or his agents want to observe a union meeting, the same rules do not apply. Federal labor law permits unions to exclude employers from union meetings.[6] An employer who attends a union meeting but leaves when asked to do so does not violate federal law.[7] A court reached the same conclusion where union officials asked if any of the members objected to the presence of management at a meeting, and when no one did a company supervisor was allowed to stay.[8] On the other hand, when an employer was found just sitting in a parked car outside a union hall entrance during a meeting, the National Labor Relations Board held that federal labor law had been violated.[9]

These cases involved union meetings held away from work. Typically, an employer may lawfully observe union activity that occurs on the job. For example, moving a supervisor's desk so that he could keep an eye on union members and see that they were working instead of spending time on union activity has been found legal.[10] Observing union activity that takes place in public is lawful. The same is true of watching union representatives pass out literature or solicit members on public streets or in parking lots.[11]

In both union and non-union contexts, the same general rule applies. An employer has the right to watch what occurs at work or in public places. Trying to observe union meetings or activities taking place in private, on the other hand, will usually be illegal.

Mail

It is a federal crime to open other people's mail.[12] In the employment context, mail sent to a place of business may generally be opened by anyone having reason to believe that the contents are relevant to their business activity. The problem arises when clearly personal mail arrives. Opening this mail does not usually result in a criminal prosecution, but it may lead to a lawsuit. In one case, for example, a court allowed an employee to recover damages from another employee for invasion of privacy.[13] The court ruled that the fellow employee was simply snooping around and had no legitimate business reason to open the plaintiff's mail.

ELECTRONIC SURVEILLANCE

The monitoring of employees through a variety of technological means is increasing, but there is widespread disagreement over its scope and effectiveness.[14] Computer, telephone, and video technology are the most common types of electronic surveillance in the workplace, but they are not the only ones. Biometric identification, such as hand geometry and retinal patterns, is being used to secure rooms and sensitive equipment and information. Hand geometry is the bone structure and webbing between the fingers that is thought to be unique in each individual, while retinal patterns are the configuration of blood vessels in the retina.

One reason why it is difficult to determine how much of this sort of monitoring occurs is that people may not be aware of it. Anytime computers or telephones are used on the job there is the potential for surveillance. If an employer engages in computer monitoring for performance evaluation or time-motion studies, he may not sense that it qualifies as monitoring, but his employees will see it as such. As the available technology becomes more sophisticated and less expensive, its use will almost assuredly increase. One recent report cited a survey by a professor who examined data and word processing and customer-service operations in 110 worksites and found that 98 percent already use computers to track the movements of workers.[15] It also noted an estimate by the National Institute of Occupational Safety and Health that two-thirds of the users of visual display terminals are monitored.

Computer and telephone monitoring in the service industries are the types of surveillance noted most often, with the insurance and newspaper industries cited as places where it is occurring. Airline reservation clerks and telephone-directory-assistance operators are also mentioned, as is video monitoring on assembly lines as an anti-theft precaution. Jobs that involve word processing lend themselves well to monitoring. Computer monitoring counts the number of keystrokes per hour or day and indicates how often an employee does certain activities or uses a terminal. Some monitoring may be done as an afterthought, when vendors selling computer equipment to organizations show them the add-on monitoring capability. In other instances, buyers obtain software with an eye toward monitoring, to protect the organization against lawsuits and to ensure the quality of service. The purchasers know exactly what they are getting.

Keeping tabs on the quality of service, enhancing productivity, and detecting dishonesty are the most common reasons for employer monitoring. But monitoring may in fact be counterproductive, given the animosity and stress that it prompts in employees. Judging by complaints from employees and unions, the general feeling among workers is that monitoring threatens their privacy, intrudes on their personal affairs or work in progress, and will lead to their being evaluated on criteria which they don't understand. Some employees avoid new computer applications because of the threat of this kind of surveillance. And some companies have put monitoring in place and then stopped because they discovered how counterproductive it could be.

Employees are finding ways to counter attempts at monitoring. When keystrokes are monitored, for example, a key can be held down continuously to make the count go up—although a particular software program can detect this deception. Telephone operators who are monitored can often tell if a call is going to be difficult; they may disconnect the call or give bad information so they can terminate the call in the time necessary to meet statistical norms. Where video monitoring is done, employees have spray-painted the camera lenses.

Some employees, offended by what they perceive as a sudden lack of trust, reduce their work efforts to the bare minimum needed to get by. Middle managers avoid monitoring by filling in their electronic schedules with meetings, since employers tend to think managers are productive if they are in meetings. Other employees, however, are pleased that their work is being observed, because they want to be rewarded for their efforts. Monitoring is most successful if a bonus is given for working above a certain level. And when monitoring is used to evaluate work, it is possible for a machine to be fairer than a person, since machines, for example, are color-blind and do not recognize gender. Of course, employers generally wish to learn from evaluations and to be able to interpret and explain if necessary, and that cannot be done with machines.

Wiretapping and Bugging

Because electronic surveillance is relatively new, court cases concerning them are only now appearing. Most have involved the monitoring of employees' telephone calls and conversations and have alleged a violation of Title III of the Omnibus Crime Control and Safe Streets Act of 1968, which, among other things, makes it a crime to "intentionally intercept . . . any wire, oral or electronic communication."[16] This means that as a rule *wiretapping*—using an electronic device to intercept wire communications—and *bugging*—using such a device to intercept an oral communication—are federal crimes. In addition to criminal penalties, civil penalties—actual and punitive damages and attorney's fees and court costs—are provided. Employers can avoid these penalties if their activity is within either of two narrow exceptions: (1) the use of a telephone extension by an employer during the "ordinary course of business" is permissible, and (2) companies that provide a communication service may monitor it to check for quality of transmission.

Employers who monitor their employees' telephone conversations come within the "ordinary course of business" exception if they listen at their place of business and reasonably believe that the communication is business related. In one case, a woman brought a civil action alleging a violation of the act arising out of her ex-employer's monitoring of a personal call to her.[17] The employer claimed that the employee's acceptance of employment with knowledge that the employer monitored calls as part of its regular training program constituted consent to the interception of her call. The court, however, said that the employee had consented to a policy of monitoring sales, not personal calls, and that this consent included inadvertent interception of a personal call, but only for as long as needed to determine its nature. The court found that the interception in this case went beyond the point necessary to determine the nature of the call and thus exceeded the scope of the employee's consent. To be shielded from liability, the court ruled, the employer must rely on the business-extension exemption and must show that the interception of the call beyond the initial period was in the ordinary course of business.

In another case, an employer had a policy of listening in on employee phone calls to help employees improve their relations with customers.[18] Employees knew that this was occurring. The court found that this satisfied the "ordinary course of business" requirement. And where an employer secretly listened in on an employee's phone conversations at work because he believed that the employee was giving trade secrets to a competitor, the court found a justifiable business reason for the privacy invasion.[19] In view of the special nature of the situation, the court allowed the monitoring to take place without prior notice to the employee.

A chief of police and a lieutenant were found to have violated the act by placing a microphone and transmitter in a briefcase in the office of the assistant chief, who was suspected of leaking damaging information.[20] The court found that the assistant chief had a reasonable expectation of privacy that normal conversations in his office could not be overheard. In another case, a regional chief of security for a department store chain was prosecuted under the act for monitoring and recording conversations occurring on the chain's privately operated communication system.[21] He was found not guilty. The court said that random monitoring of private telephone installations is not forbidden, that employees misusing a private phone system do not have a reasonable expectation that the communication will not be intercepted, and that the security chief was operating in the normal course of his employment in seeking to "protect the system, the rendition of service, and the rights and property of his employer."

The federal law does not require that the customer on the other end of the line be informed that the conversation is being monitored. Legislation has been proposed in several states and in Congress to require the use of an "audible beep" when phone conversations are being monitored. This would inform both the employee and the customer of the interception. So far, none of these proposals has become law, despite strong lobbying efforts by the Communications Workers of America and the American Civil Liberties Union.

At least thirty-seven states have laws controlling wiretapping, but in general they are consistent with the federal law. Statutes in California, Delaware, Illinois, Michigan, Oregon, Pennsylvania and Washington require the consent of both parties before a phone conversation can be listened to or recorded.

Bugging differs from wiretapping in that there is no "ordinary course of business" exemption. Without the consent of at least one party to the conversation, listening in on or recording an oral conversation anywhere, even at work, by electronic means would probably be a crime and be subject to a civil lawsuit under the federal law.[22] The law is violated if the conversation involves people who think it is not being overheard, in circumstances that would reasonably justify this belief.

State laws differ widely on the subject of bugging. The states listed above that require the consent of both parties before a phone may be tapped also do so before an oral conversation may be monitored or recorded. Connecticut has a law prohibiting the use of electronic devices, including bugs and video cameras, in areas designed for the health and comfort of employees or the safeguarding of their possessions.[23] Many states make it a crime even to possess bugging equipment. An employer wishing to bug her employees, even with their consent, should consult with a lawyer regarding the laws in effect in that state, and managers and supervisors should do so before secretly recording a conversation with an employee. In one case, a supervisor taped an exit interview with an employee and found himself and his company being sued under the Illinois Eavesdropping Act.[24] The judge decided that the company could not be held liable because its higher executives had neither known nor approved of the supervisor's act. But that did not shield the supervisor from personal liability.

Video Cameras

At least three states—Connecticut, Delaware, and Michigan—ban the use of hidden cameras in areas of the workplace in which people reasonably expect privacy.[25] In addition, the use of cameras in restrooms and locker areas, where a reasonable expectation of privacy certainly exists, might be deemed a common law invasion of privacy. Most of the laws regarding the interception of oral and electronic communications, however, do not address the issue of hidden cameras. But if a camera is also recording sound, the eavesdropping laws would apply. For example, a group of congressional investigators found themselves sued by an insurance salesman whom they secretly videotaped during his sales presentation.[26] The court found that the sound recording made by the taping machine violated Maryland's Electronic Surveillance Act.

The debate over whether state laws against intercepting and recording "communications" apply to video-tape recordings became more interesting in late 1989 with a California Appeals Court ruling that the state Supreme Court declined to review. *People v. Gibbons*[27] involved a California man who had a habit of picking up young women in bars and bringing them to his residence for sexual intercourse. He used a hidden camera to record these encounters. When one woman learned what had occurred, she filed criminal charges. The California Penal Code makes it illegal to intentionally "eavesdrop upon or record" a "confidential communication" without the "consent of all parties" involved. The case thus raised two questions: does the phrase "eavesdrop upon or record" include a video-taping that records no sound, and does sexual intercourse involve a "confidential communication?" The court answered both questions in the affirmative. In view of this, employers in California and elsewhere who think they may use video cameras to monitor the actions of their employees—or their customers, for that matter—without fear of violating state laws against eavesdropping might wish to take a fresh look at the matter.

Video Display Terminal Monitoring

As noted previously, the use of video display terminals is becoming a part of the work routine of millions of workers. More employers are also finding it helpful to monitor what their employees do with their computers. In 1986, a court held that the Omnibus Crime Control Act does not apply to the interception of electronic data transmitted over telephone lines or by radio wave.[28] As a result of this decision, Congress amended the act to include electronic communications, broadly defined as embracing electronic mail, digitalized transmissions, and video teleconferences. Congress also included private communications systems and intra-company networks in the act. The "ordinary course of business" exception, however, still applies. To date, there has been no reported litigation challenging the monitoring of video display terminals by employers. Presumably, monitoring that serves a legitimate business purpose will be permitted.

SURVEILLANCE AS A MANAGEMENT TOOL

To get the most benefit from the use of electronic surveillance as a managerial tool requires minimizing its adverse effects in terms of employee morale and stress. Following are some recommendations in this area:

1. Explain to employees how, why, and when their work may be monitored. When installing computer systems, involve employees at the planning stage to allay their fears at the outset.
2. When using monitoring for employee evaluation, give employees access to their records, regular feedback, and the right of rebuttal before the evaluation goes on the record.
3. Measure only items essential to meeting organizational goals, and be certain that those goals are carefully and clearly defined.
4. Use statistics to spot problems early and take action on them.

5. Anticipate and allow for individual differences, and let people regulate their work environment as much as possible.
6. Reward individuals appropriately.
7. Do not continually drive up production standards.
8. Be sensitive—don't monitor restrooms or employee lounges.

CONCLUSION

Employers who simply observe their employees at work or in public run little risk of committing a legal wrong. Watching employees on the job is a legitimate employer function, and watching them in public can essentially be deemed to have been invited by the employee. One exception to this rule exists in states with special laws in this area, such as California's "spotters" law; another applies to union meetings occurring away from the workplace. An employer who opens employee mail that appears clearly relevant to business activities should also not be vulnerable to suit.

Monitoring employees electronically can be a useful management tool, but it can also backfire by increasing employee stress and resentment and thus lowering morale and productivity. Legally, such surveillance might run afoul of state common law and statutory privacy laws as well as the federal Omnibus Crime Control and Safe Streets Act of 1968. This is, therefore, an area in which employers must tread especially lightly. The bottom-line question is this: Given the nature of work involved, will the benefits of monitoring employees through computer, telephone, or video technology likely outweigh the risks of litigation and of decreased employee morale and output resulting from the surveillance?

NOTES

1. McLain v. Boise Cascade Corp., 533 P.2d 343 (Or. 1975).
2. Pemberton v. Bethlehem Steel Corp., 502 A.2d 1101 (Md. App. 1986), *cert denied* 508 A.2d 488 (Md. 1986), 107 S. Ct. 571 (1986).
3. Cal. Pub. Utilities Code §§8251 and 8252.
4. Nev. Rev. Stat. §613.160.

5. Cal. Labor Code §2930; Cal. Bus. and Prof. Code §§7521, 7522, 7523.

6. 29 U.S.C. §§151–169.

7. Litton Educational Publishing, 214 N.L.R.B. 413 (1974).

8. NLRB v. Computed Time Corp., 587 F.2d 790 (5th Cir. 1979).

9. Custom Coating & Laminating Corp., 249 N.L.R.B. 765 (1980).

10. East Side Shopper, Inc., 204 N.L.R.B. 841 (1973).

11. J. H. Block & Co., 247 N.L.R.B. 262 (1980); Phillips Indus. Components, 216 N.L.R.B. 885 (1975).

12. 18 U.S.C. §1702.

13. Vernars v. Young, 539 F.2d 966 (3rd Cir. 1976).

14. The information in this chapter was obtained largely from surveys and interviews cited in the "Surveillance" section of the INDIVIDUAL EMPLOYMENT RIGHTS MANUAL, A PUBLICATION OF THE BUREAU OF NATIONAL AFFAIRS, INC.

15. *Computer Monitoring and Other Dirty Tricks*, 9-to-5, National Association of Working Women (1988).

16. 18 U.S.C. §2511 (1)(a).

17. Watkins v. L. M. Berry & Co., 704 F.2d 577 (11th Cir. 1983).

18. James v. Newspaper Agency Corp., 591 F.2d 579 (10th Cir. 1979).

19. Briggs v. American Filter Co., 630 F.2d 414 (5th Cir. 1980).

20. United States v. McIntyre, 582 F.2d 1221 (9th Cir. 1978).

21. United States v. Christman, 375 F. Supp. 1354 (N.D. Cal. 1974).

22. 18 U.S.C. §2511(1)(d).

23. Conn. Gen. Stat. 31–48b(b).

24. Cebula v. Gen. Elec. Co., 614 F. Supp. 260 (D.C. Ill. 1985).

25. Conn. Gen. Stat. 31–48b(b); Del. Code. Ann. Tit. 11, §1335 to 1336 Ann. 11–1335 to 1336; Mich. Stat. §750.539d.

26. Benford v. Amer. Broadcasting Co. Inc., 554 F. Supp. 145 (D. Md. 1982).

27. 263 Cal. Rptr. 905 (Cal. App. 1989).

28. United States v. Gregg, 629 F. Supp. 958 (W.D. Mo. 1986).

15

Employee Records

EMPLOYEES' ACCESS

Although a federal Privacy Protection Study Commission formed in 1977 considered the need for such a law, no federal statute now requires the average employer to provide employees with access to their personnel files. Over a dozen states, however, have such laws.[1] Illinois had an employee-access statute, but the state Supreme Court invalidated it.[2] The law allowed employees to have access to their files but not to "management planning" documents, and the Court found that term too vague to be enforceable.

One of the major issues in this area has been the extent to which college professors considered for tenure or promotion should be allowed to examine information about them. Over the loud protests of university officials across the country, the U.S. Supreme Court recently resolved a longstanding conflict over this issue among the federal circuit courts of appeal by holding that the Equal Employment Opportunity Commission may obtain files on professors to see if a tenure or promotion decision involved gender or race discrimination. The case, however, does not stand for the proposition that the professor may inspect the files.[3] A Pennsylvania court, on the other hand, has ruled that professors may obtain information written about them by their colleagues.[4] The state law allows "letters of reference" to be withheld from employees, but the court held that reports of colleagues are "performance evaluations" rather than letters of reference, and thus are subject to required disclosure.

In states without a statute controlling employee access to their records, the common law prevails. The New Jersey Supreme Court, for example, held that wrongful discharge occurred when a female employee was fired after asking to see her personnel file, ostensibly to investigate possible sexual discrimination.[5] The court found that public policy in New Jersey supports the right of employees to examine their own files to investigate suspected violations of the law. Because any employee who wants to see his file can claim this as a motive, this decision is an open invitation to the inspection of their files by employees in that state. And the same logic might apply in federal court. The Tenth Circuit Court of Appeals, for example, has ruled that an employer violated federal law in dismissing a female employee for asking how much male employees at her company earned.[6] Like her counterpart in New Jersey, the employee asserted that she was simply checking on whether the company engaged in sex discrimination.

Public employers are subject to state Open Records Acts as well as to any privacy statutes that might exist in that state. Many of these "sunshine" acts afford governmental employees a right of access to their personnel files. Some not only allow access, but also permit employees to correct or explain information in their file which they believe is erroneous or misleading. On the other hand, some state laws specifically place personnel files off limits to employees. As construed by the state Attorney General, for example, the Texas Open Records Act affords governmental employees in that state no "special right of access" to their files, and it allows governmental bodies to withhold, even from the subject of the file, personnel file data within one of the act's exceptions to the mandatory public disclosure of information.[7]

DISCLOSURE OF INFORMATION ABOUT EMPLOYEES

Federal Laws

In 1974, Congress passed the Privacy Act, which restricts the records maintained on individuals by federal agencies.[8] Other federal statutes also protect employee privacy rights. The Federal Fair Credit Reporting Act,[9] for example, regulates the use of credit reports to investigate employees. If an employer receives a credit report on an applicant and does not extend a job offer because of its contents, the applicant must be informed of the name of the credit agency. She may also contest the accuracy of the data and require a reinvestigation. The Occupational Safety and Health Act[10] and the Vocational Rehabilitation Act[11] also have provisions governing individual medical records.

Invasion of Privacy

Employers risk being sued for invasion of privacy if, without the employee's consent, they reveal information in a personnel file to people not legally entitled to it. As chapter 3 observed, privacy rights may be violated if the material disclosed puts the employee in a false light or is intimate, even if it is true. One case in this area involved a United Airlines flight attendant who sought a waiver of the weight limit imposed by the airline. Her personal physician gave her medical records to the airline's doctor who was dealing with her gynecological problems and contraceptive methods. That doctor discussed the information in the records with the woman's male supervisor and commented about it in the presence of other supervisors. A jury found this to be an invasion of privacy and awarded $14,000 in damages.[12] In another case, IBM allowed employees with psychological problems to obtain counseling through a company program. A doctor who examined an employee told his supervisor that the employee was paranoid and needed psychiatric treatment. This and other statements about the employee were disclosed to his supervisor and to other executives in the company. A federal circuit court of appeals found that the disclosures could constitute an invasion of privacy and remanded the case to the trial court for a jury decision on the issue.[13]

Supervisors who need to know what is in personnel files will usually be allowed to examine them. The Oklahoma Supreme Court, for instance, found no privacy invasion where some other workers and managers in a company examined an employee's file and found information about the employee's psychiatric treatment. The Court decided that the limited number of co-workers who had seen the information and thus knew of the condition kept this from being a case of unreasonable publicity.[14] Another case dealt with a chemical plant employee who used a counseling service provided by his employer.[15] A counselor informed the employee's supervisor that the employee was suicidal and a possible threat to his and others' safety. The court ruled that these people had good reason to discuss this problem, that there was no real publication of private facts, and that the supervisor had a privilege to protect the safety of the plant and its employees.

Defamation

Employers are facing a dramatic upsurge in the number of claims filed by present or former employees for defamation and related torts. The risk of liability attaches whenever any statement is made by an employer to an employee—when, for example, the employer tells the employee the reason for his discharge, communicates that reason to co-workers, or supplies it to a prospective employer in a job reference. Under the theory of "compelled self disclosure" some states permit a defamation action for false statements made only to the employee upon his discharge, on the theory that in seeking another job the employee will be compelled to state the reason for the discharge given by the previous employer.

Defamation occurs when a communication by X harms Y by lowering Y's reputation in the community or by discouraging others from associating with him. The statement must be communicated to a third person. Except under the compelled self disclosure theory, traditional defamation principles hold that derogatory words expressed only to the plaintiff, and not communicated to another person, provide no basis for a defamation claim. Two types of defamation exist: libel, which is defamation by writing, and slander, which involves speaking. In employment terminations, statements indicating that employees cannot perform their duties or lack integrity may be considered defamatory. The same is true for any statement implying that an employee has a communicable disease, such as AIDS.

Truth is an absolute defense to a defamation action. In one recent case, a physician sued a hospital for defamation based on statements that he had assaulted another physician and had been placed on probation.[16] The court held that the statements could not be defamatory because they were true. Defamation also requires that a statement be "published." Unlike "publicity" in a privacy claim, "publication" requires communication to only one other person. Some courts have held that the placement of statements regarding employees in their personnel files does not constitute defamation if the statements are not given to a third party.[17] If, however, a statement is communicated to other employees, even within the company, the element of publication can be established.

In most defamation and "false light" cases, employers will be allowed to assert a qualified business privilege. This privilege exists when a statement is made in good faith, concerns a subject in which the person making it has a legitimate interest, and is made to a person with a corresponding interest. Communications in the workplace about an employee are usually privileged if they are between the employee's supervisor and managers, who have a duty to the company. For example, a plant supervisor's accusation that an employee committed vandalism made in the presence of a manager[18] and a supervisor's communication of poor evaluations to his superior[19] have been held to be conditionally privileged because they served the employer's legitimate interests.

The qualified privilege can be lost through excessive publication to co-workers or other employees with no interest in the matter. Yet in several cases when an employer has communicated to a large group of employees the reasons for an employee's dismissal, courts have found the speeches privileged. *Gonzalez v. Avon Products, Inc.*,[20] for example, involved eight employees fired after an investigation into theft from the company. A few days later the plant manager gave a speech to all 900 employees at the plant to explain his decision to fire the employees and to reassert the company's policy of terminating only for cause. In a defamation action, the court held that the employees' termination was a matter of common interest for both the employer and those who heard the speech, and that the speech was not motivated by spite or ill will. This defense is not accepted in all states.

Most states also recognize a qualified privilege to allow an employer to communicate his opinion of a former employee's conduct or performance in a reference given to a present or prospective employer. The rationale is that the prospective employer has an interest in obtaining information about the employee, and the former employer has an interest in the former employee's work.[21] As a practical matter, however, one should carefully analyze the truth of statements, and the employer's ability to prove their truth, before embarking on litigation over the privilege. Most states hold that the conditional privilege is abused and thus lost when a statement is made with malice, spite, or ill will toward a former employee.[22] Juries, moreover, tend to infer malice when an employer cannot prove that a statement is true.

Guidelines for Employment References

Because employers understand how they can be held liable for releasing information in employee personnel files and other information pertaining to employees, many now refuse to provide references at all, except to furnish employees' names, positions, and years of employment. Indeed, one survey found that prospective employers do not check references of nearly 75 percent of their job candidates because they feel that former employers will not cooperate for fear of potential litigation.[23] In the long run, however, refusals to provide references hurt both employees seeking new jobs and employers who need to obtain information about potential employees to make accurate hiring decisions. As chapter four observed, employers who fail adequately to inquire into employees' and applicants' backgrounds risk being held liable for negligent hiring or retention if the person is later responsible for a work-related accident or for making goods or providing services in a shoddy way. While the possibility of a legal challenge based on disclosure of information about employees cannot be eliminated, these actions can lessen that risk:

1. When employees are terminated, make certain that they know the reason for the termination and explain the company policy on providing references.

2. Obtain a written, signed consent from the employee that authorizes the company to disclose relevant information to prospective employers.

3. When giving references, be truthful and provide whatever explanation is necessary about the discharge so that the reasons cannot be misunderstood. Be sure to distinguish opinions from facts.

4. Most importantly, be fair and impartial and, when possible, note the good qualities of the employee.

If employers give references in good faith, and if their employment records can substantiate the statements they make, little risk of liability exists under any theory.

OBTAINING INFORMATION ABOUT EMPLOYEES

Most states have laws dictating who has a right of access to medical and other kinds of information about employees. Many allow employers to ask employees for permission to inspect their medical files. The California Confidentiality Act,[24] for example, requires employers to create procedures guaranteeing that medical information about employees is protected from unauthorized use. The act also bars the disclosure of medical data kept by employers without the written permission of the employee and limits the kind of data that an employer can receive from an employee's physician without the employee's permission.

The issues of obtaining and revealing information about workers often arises in the drug testing context. In *Shoemaker v. Handel*,[25] for example, the court considered a plan to randomly test horse racing jockeys in New Jersey. Two of the jockeys' concerns about the plan were whether test results would be revealed and the requirement that jockeys fill out a form indicating medicines being taken and similar personal information. The court, however, dismissed a challenge to these features of the plan alleging a violation of constitutional privacy rights, on the ground that the New Jersey Racing Commission had amended the plan so that it adequately took care of privacy concerns. The court said that although privacy rights exist in medical information, governmental concerns may support the access to such data if it is protected from unauthorized disclosure. Because the commission's concern for racing integrity justified its access to facts revealed by the tests, the jockeys' privacy interest was limited to preserving the confidentiality of the test results, and the rule did this. If the commission ceased to comply with the rule, said the court, "the jockeys may return to court with a new lawsuit."

In *Capua v. City of Plainfield*,[26] the court struck down a testing plan for city police and firemen. Among other things, the court was troubled by the fact that the policy forced employees to "divulge private, personal medical information unrelated to the government's professed interest in discovering illegal drug abuse." The court noted that "[a]dvances in medical technology make it possible to uncover disorders, including epilepsy and diabetes by analyzing chemical compounds," and said that employees "have a significant interest in safeguarding the confidenitality of such information whereas the government has no countervailing legitimate need for access to this personal medical data." Comparing the plan to the one involved in *Shoemaker*, the court stressed that there the court had

> based its ruling on the fact that such confidentiality concerns had been carefully addressed in statutory regulations strictly limiting the use and publication of test results so as to guarantee the jockeys utmost confidentiality.... The court's decision...is

thus readily distinguishable from the case at hand. Plainfield had not established any procedural guidelines to govern the urine testing, and in particular had not taken any precautions to vouchsafe confidentiality. Quite to the contrary, following the suspension of those fire fighters who had tested positive for drugs, the City of Plainfield publicized its actions to the media. While no individuals were identified by name, the exposure has subjected all Plainfield fire fighters to public suspicion and degradation.[27]

These cases underscore the importance of requiring employees to divulge highly personal information and of disclosing such information about employees only if a demonstrable need exists and the resulting privacy intrusion is minimized as much as possible. The New Jersey Supreme Court, for example, has said that the state could require job applicants to sign a form authorizing the release of records held by "courts, banks, employers, government agencies and educational institutions" only if it instituted procedures to ensure that the records obtained would be kept private and that the employee would be notified of any release of that information.[28] This is good advice for all employers.

AVOIDING LEGAL PROBLEMS

In 1977, the Privacy Protection Study Commission issued guidelines for access to employee information.[29] These guidelines recognized the need to keep references and test scores confidential; recommended that employers grant employees access to performance evaluations, security investigations placed in their personnel files, and credit, medical, and insurance records; encouraged employers to let employees request the correction of inaccurate information and place a notice of dispute in the record if their idea of what was accurate did not conform with the employer's; and suggested that payroll, security, medical, and insurance records be kept separate from personnel files and made available to others within the company only on a need-to-know basis. Some of these recommendations have become law in some states, although laws vary greatly and employers must thus consult an expert in their area to learn the parameters within which they may operate. From a managerial standpoint, the recommendations remain sound ones to follow.

NOTES

1. California, Connecticut, Maine, Massachusetts, Michigan, Nevada, New Hampshire, Oregon, Pennsylvania, Rhode Island, South Dakota, Washington, and Wisconsin.
2. Spinelli v. Immanuel Luth. Evan. Cong., 515 N.E.2d 1222 (Ill. 1987).
3. Univ. of Pennsylvania v. E.E.O.C., 110 S. Ct. 577 (1990).
4. LaFayette College v. Dept. of Labor, 546 A.2d 126 (Pa. Cmwlth. 1988).
5. Velantzas v. Colgate-Palmolive, 536 A.2d 237 (N.J. 1988).
6. EEOC v. Gen. Lines, 865 F.2d 1555 (10th Cir. 1989).
7. Tex. Rev. Civ. Stat. Ann. art. 6252-17a (Vernon 1989).
8. 5 U.S.C. 552a.
9. 15 U.S.C. 1681.
10. 29 U.S.C. 651 *et. seq.*
11. 29 U.S.C. 701 *et. seq.*
12. Levias v. United Airlines, 500 N.E.2d 370 (Ohio App. 1985).
13. Bratt v. Int'l. Bus. Machines, 785 F.2d 352 (1st Cir. 1986).
14. Eddy v. Brown, 715 P.2d 74 (Okla. 1986).
15. Davis v. Monsanto Co., 627 F. Supp. 418 (S.D.W.Va. 1986).
16. Wright v. Southern Mono Hospital District, 631 F. Supp. 1294 (E.D. Cal. 1986).
17. Wyant v. SCM Corp., 692 S.W.2d 814 (Ky. App. 1985).
18. Lawson v. Howmet Aluminum Corp., 449 N.E.2d 1172 (Ind. App. 1983).
19. Lewis v. Equitable Life Assur. Soc., 389 N.W.2d 876 (Minn. 1986).
20. 648 F. Supp. 1404 (D. Del. 1986).
21. Walsh v. Consolidated Freightways, Inc., 563 P.2d 1205 (Or. 1977).
22. Smith v. Greyhound Lines, Inc., 614 F. Supp. 558 (W.D. Pa. 1984), *aff'd* 800 F.2d 1139 (3rd Cir. 1986).
23. National Law Journal (May 4, 1987), at 30.
24. Cal. Civ. Code § 56.21.
25. 619 F. Supp. 1089 (D.N.J. 1985), *aff'd* 795 F.2d 1136 (3rd Cir. 1986), *cert denied* 107 S. Ct. 577 (1986). *See supra* chapter 8.
26. 643 F. Supp. 1507 (D.N.J. 1986).

27. *Id.* at 1515.
28. In re Martin, 447 A.2d 1290 (N.J. 1982).
29. REPORT OF THE PRIVACY PROTECTION STUDY COMMISSION, July 1977, U.S. Government Printing Office.

PART V

INTERFERENCE WITH LIFESTYLE AND NON-WORK RELATED ACTIVITIES

16

Theories of Liability

Thus far this book has been concerned almost exclusively with the right of privacy in the context of employee and applicant testing and surveillance. It has been seen that employers who screen or search in the wrong way or for the wrong reason may find themselves in court charged with violating privacy rights. In this part of the book, the focus shifts to another, equally controversial aspect of employee privacy: lifestyle choices and non-work related conduct. The potential for employers being held liable for dismissing or disciplining employees or not hiring applicants based on disapproval of their appearance, living habits, or off-the-job activities is great and growing. Before examining specific problems, it is necessary to consider in general terms the kinds of legal issues that might arise in this area.

CONTRACTS, HANDBOOKS AND CIVIL SERVICE LAWS

Whether an employee is working under a contract or at-will was often irrelevant in the preceding chapters. This issue now becomes highly relevant. As chapter 2 observed, at-will employees can be fired for any or no reason. Half of the American workforce is in this category. The other half work under a contract, handbook or federal or state civil service law that limits their employer's right to fire. In most instances these workers can be fired only for "good cause," with that term usually defined as involving adverse behavior having a direct bearing on job performance. While significant misconduct at work will usually qualify, there are differences of opinion about what constitutes good cause.

A recent case from Boston illustrates this point.[1] The case involved a policeman fired by the Police Commissioner, reinstated by the Civil Service Commission, and fired again by the Massachusetts Court of Appeals. The disagreement was over whether the officer's conduct was sufficiently bad to afford good cause for dismissal, or if some punishment short of dismissal was appropriate. On the night in question, the officer and his partner were called to pick up a woman of "questionable sobriety." They took her to her place of employment, but she refused to get out of the car. At that point one of the officers decided to take his meal break and took the woman with him to a private club. There the policeman had a beer (he was still on duty, so this violated work rules), later shed his clothes in a back room in the club (being out of uniform violated work rules), and then had sex with the woman, at her suggestion. After the woman returned home, regained her sobriety, and fully comprehended what had happened, she called the police department to report a "voluntary rape." In upholding the commissioner's finding that this constituted good cause for dismissal, the court observed that the civil service law is designed to protect efficient public employees from partisan politics, not to prevent the removal of incompetent or unworthy employees.

Among other things, this case shows that whether an employee's behavior constitutes good cause for dismissal may eventually be decided, not by the employer, but by a commission, arbitrator, or judge, and will hinge on the specific facts of the case viewed objectively from the standpoint of the supposedly disinterested, neutral third party. There is a great deal of room for interpretation and disagreement in this area—what one judge or arbitrator considers good cause may not be so regarded by another. Of course, the obvious difficulty with this is that even the best-intentioned and diligent employer will be hard-pressed to know the bounds within which he must operate in making employment decisions which he thinks are in the best interests of his business.

Most union employees now work under a written contract that requires good cause for dismissal. Most public workers are covered by some kind of civil service law that affords this protection. More private sector employees, particularly executives and professionals, have employment contracts requiring good cause before the employee can be dismissed during the term of the contract, although when that term expires the employee can be let go just like other at-will employees. Finally, millions of employees are covered by employee handbooks which state that their employment will be terminated only for good cause and provide a discipline procedure for the employer to follow. At the end of 1989, thirty-three state supreme courts had ruled that these promises in handbooks must be treated as if they were contracts and enforced. Only the supreme courts of Delaware, Massachusetts, Missouri and New York had ruled otherwise.[2]

STATE "PUBLIC POLICY" AND WRONGFUL DISCHARGE

Since the late 1950's, and especially in the 1980's, state courts have been increasingly willing to let employees sue their employers for common law wrongful discharge. The first case in this area illustrates the point.[3] Mr. Petermann was an official of the California Teamsters Union. Ordered to lie to a committee of the California legislature, Petermann instead told the truth and was fired. In a subsequent suit, a California appeals court ordered the union to pay damages to Petermann for having "wrongfully discharged" him for refusing to commit perjury. Since then many other state courts have adopted and broadened this concept, so that now a variety of statutory and common law wrongful discharge theories exist.

Courts allow these suits only if the employee did something deemed by the court to be supported by state *public policy*, an extremely nebulous and elastic term capable of as many definitions as there are judges. Many wrongful discharge cases, for example, have involved a refusal to obey an order that is or is reasonably thought by the employee to be illegal. Courts feel that employees should be encouraged to obey the law, that permitting them to sue if they are dismissed for refusing to disobey the law will achieve that goal, and that the overall public policy interests of society are not served when employers are allowed to discharge employees on this basis. Many wrongful discharge cases involve employees fired for activities away from the workplace. In 1975, for example, the Supreme Court of Oregon ruled that it was wrongful for an employer to fire an employee who had to serve on a jury.[4] Fifteen years later employees in almost all states are protected by statute or court decision from being discharged based on jury service.

These decisions stand for the proposition that some behavior by citizens must be tolerated and legally protected even if it provokes the displeasure of their employers. Courts often guard this behavior because they feel that the political and legal systems must have citizens free to perform certain roles, such as candidate, jury member, witness, voter, or outspoken citizen. Louisiana, for example, has a statute that protects the right of employees to run for public office.[5] When a Mr. Davis decided to run for the city council against a candidate supported by his employer, he soon found himself in the unemployment line. The employer, however, found himself in court, where he was ordered to pay $24,000 in damages.[6]

CONSTITUTIONS AND STATUTES

Employees also enjoy federal and state constitutional and statutory protection against arbitrary dismissal in many instances. In 1968, for example, the U.S. Supreme Court held that a government employer may not fire an employee simply because the latter said something that the employer did not like.[7] The case involved a teacher dismissed for criticizing the school board in a letter to the local newspaper. Noting that the "right of free speech" in the First Amendment of the U.S. Constitution protects speech involving issues of public concern, the

Court said that "teachers are, as a class, the members of a community most likely to have informed and definite opinions as to how funds allotted to the operation of the school should be spent. Accordingly, it is essential that they be able to speak out freely on such questions without fear of retaliatory dismissal." Since then, other cases have clarified the kinds of speech, including symbolic expression, that cannot legally support the dismissal of an employee, and also identified other constitutional provisions that may come into play when employees are dismissed for engaging in certain activities. In *Briggs v. Northern Muskegon Police Dept.*,[8] for example, the Sixth Circuit Court of Appeals upheld a ruling by a federal trial court that the dismissal of a married, part-time officer for cohabiting with a woman who was not his wife violated the officer's right of constitutional privacy.

Most state constitutions also protect the right of free speech. Some go further in doing so than the federal Constitution—at least, as the latter has recently been applied by the U.S. Supreme Court. Many also protect other constitutional rights, even, in some cases, as against private individuals. Not only may these provisions be used directly to protect employees, but they may also form the basis for a judicial decision concerning what behavior is supported by state "public policy" and thus worthy of protecting through the common law wrongful discharge concept. In 1983, for example, a court accepted the claim that because the Pennsylvania Constitution protects free speech, the dismissal of a private employee for speech—actually, in that case, nonspeech—reasons violates state public policy and thus involves a wrongful discharge.[9] The Nationwide Insurance Company had sent its employees a memorandum asking them to lobby the legislature for the creation of a no-fault insurance system. A Mr. Novosel argued that he was fired because he refused to support this effort. The court agreed and ruled that this kind of interference with a private employee's right to speak or not speak on political issues was illegal and that the employee could sue for wrongful discharge.

Many state statutes protect employees in different ways, either directly or indirectly by expressing a public policy that judges are increasingly willing to enforce through wrongful discharge lawsuits. Several states have statutes protecting such things as the right of employees to leave work to vote or to report illegal activities of the employer to the proper authorities ("Whistleblower" statutes).[10] Some states and even some large cities protect various aspects of an employee's private life from being used by employers as a justification for discharge. State and local civil rights laws, for example, often protect against discrimination based on marital status, parenthood, political affiliation, arrest records, dishonorable military discharge, sexual orientation, and whether or not the person has been on welfare. Some deal with the right of citizens to belong to the National Guard and to attend guard activities without suffering penalties at work.

Two cases illustrate how even very general civil rights statutes can be used to protect activities outside of work. In one, a white female employee was fired because she had a social relationship with a black man. The court found this to be a form of racial discrimination in violation of Title VII of the Civil Rights Act of 1964.[11] In the other case, the court found that a white employee was the victim of discrimination when he was fired for selling his house to a black.[12] Again, this was deemed to constitute race discrimination in violation of Title VII.

UNEMPLOYMENT COMPENSATION

In some instances there is no question of invasion of privacy, breach of contract, or wrongful discharge. The employee was working at-will and the employer who fired her had every right to do so. Then the issue becomes whether the former employee is entitled to unemployment compensation while looking for another job. Employers usually try to prevent former employees from collecting this compensation because their insurance rates rise with each claim for benefits. In most states, however, a discharged employee is entitled to collect unless he was guilty of work-related misconduct. Whether behavior was misconduct and was work-related are ultimately for an agency hearing officer or judge to decide. If there is a trend in recent years, it is to allow employees to collect unemployment compensation unless their conduct had a tangible negative impact on the work environment.

Claim of Apodaca[13] illustrates this point. A young lady with purple hair who worked at a fast-food restaurant was ordered by her employer to re-dye her hair. When a week went without her getting a new color, she was fired. The New Mexico Supreme Court allowed her to receive unemployment compensation, finding no evidence of customer complaints or other negative impact on the business resulting from her purple hair. The employee's life style included purple hair, and the employer simply did not like it. While refusing to dye her hair was technically insubordination, the court felt that the woman's hair color was not any of the employer's business as long as it did not affect his business in any tangible way.

OTHER CLAIMS

Defamation is another basis for litigation in this area. An employer may be sued, not for firing an employee for non-work related activities, but for making statements about those activities which harm the employee's good name or reputation. This legal theory was explored in the preceding chapter. Commenting about an employee's behavior may also place the employee in a false light in the public eye and create a cause of action under this branch of privacy law. Finally, during the last two decades the tort of "intentional infliction of emotional distress" has come into its own. It allows employees to sue employers if they engage in outrageous behavior that a reasonable person should have known may cause extreme emotional distress. Recently employers have been sued on this basis when, for example, they fired an employee for having a romantic relationship with a competitor's employee,[14] required an employee to submit to a polygraph examination,[15] and forced an employee to undergo a strip search in front of a customer.[16]

In most cases the behavior of the employer or supervisor has not risen to the level of *outrageous*, but it must be stressed that the definition of this term seems to be changing as more judges and juries decide that employers should be held to a higher standard when dealing with their employees. In one case, for example, a department store employee found herself subjected to a threatening and intense interrogation in an attempt to get her to confess to theft. The court ruled that a jury should be allowed to decide if this "deliberate and systematic tactic" of interrogating employees based on little real evidence that they were involved in theft was outrageous behavior.[17]

CONCLUSION

Federal and state courts and legislative bodies are narrowing the right of employers to discipline or fire workers for behavior and lifestyle choices as well as activities occurring outside the workplace. Even at-will employees may have, by virtue of contract or employee handbook provisions, the right not to be treated adversely unless "good cause" exists, and courts are increasingly finding that the failure to conform one's lifestyle to some standard set by the employer does not provide such cause. The theory of "wrongful discharge" may also afford protection for non-work related acts. Federal and state constitutions and statutes may be invoked. Other causes of action that employees may assert include defamation, invasion of privacy, and intentional infliction of emotional distress. Finally, an employee who is discharged for activities outside the workplace may be entitled to receive unemployment compensation.

NOTES

1. Police Comm'r. of Boston v. Civ. Service Comm'n., 494 N.E.2d 27 (Mass. App. 1986).
2. Alabama: Hoffmann-La Roche, Inc., 512 So.2d 725 (1987); Arizona: Leikvold v. Valley View Comm. Hosp. 688 P.2d 170 (1984); Arkansas: Gladden v. Children's Hosp., 728 S.W.2d 501 (1987); California: Hepp v. Lockheed-California Co., 150 Cal.Rptr. 408 (1978); Colorado: Continental Airlines v. Keenan, 731 P.2d 708 (1987); Connecticut: Finley v. Aetna Life and Cas. Co., 520 A.2d 208 (1987); Delaware: Heideck v. Kent Gen. Hosp., 446 A.2d 1095 (1982); Hawaii: Kinoshita v. Canadian Pac. Airlines, 724 P.2d 110 (1986); Idaho: Watson v. Idaho Falls Consol. Hospitals, 720 P.2d 632 (1986); Illinois: Duldulao v. St. Mary of Nazareth Hosp., 505 N.E.2d 314 (1987); Iowa:

Cannon v. Nat'l. By-Products, Inc., 422 N.W.2d 638 (1986); Kansas: Morris v. Coleman Co., Inc., 738 P.2d 841 (1987); Kentucky: Shah v. Amer. Synthetic Rubber Corp., 655 S.W.2d 489 (1983); Maine: Libby v. Calais Reg. Hosp. 554 A.2d 1181 (1989); Maryland: Staggs v. Blue Cross of Maryland, 486 A.2d 798 (1985); Massachusetts: Jackson v. Action for Boston Comm. Develop., Inc., 525 N.E.2d 411 (1988); Michigan: Toussant v. Blue Cross & Blue Shield of Mich., 292 N.W.2d 880 (1980); Minnesota: Pine River St. Bank v. Metille, 333 N.W.2d 622 (1983); Missouri: Johnson v. McDonnell Douglas Corp., 745 S.W.2d 661 (1980); Montana: Gates v. Life of Montana Ins. Co., 668 P.2d 213 (1983); Nebraska: Morris v. Lutheran Med. Center, 340 N.W.2d 388 (1983); Nevada: Southwest Gas Corp. v. Ahmad, 668 P.2d 261 (1983): New Hampshire: Panto v. Moore Bus. Forms, Inc., 547 A.2d 260 (1988); New Jersey: Wooley v. Hoffman-La Roche, Inc., 491 A.2d 1257 (1985); New Mexico: Vigil v. Arzola, 687 P.2d 1038 (1984); New York: Sabetay v. Sterling Drug Co., 506 N.E.2d 919 (1987); North Dakota: Aasmundstad v. Dickinson St. College, 337 N.W. 2d 792 (1983); Ohio: Mers v. Dispatch Printing Co., 483 N.E.2d 150 (1985); Oregon: Simpson v. Western Graphics Corp., 643 P.2d 1276 (1982); South Carolina: Small v. Spring Ind., Inc., 357 S.E.2d 452 (1987); South Dakota: Osterkamp v. Alkota Mfg., Inc., 332 N.W.2d 275 (1983); Vermont: Metalcraft, Inc. v. Pratt, 500 A.2d 330 (1985); Virginia: Blake v. Hercules, Inc., 356 S.E.2d 453 (1987); Washington: Thompson v. St. Regis Paper Co., 685 P.2d 1081 (1984); West Virginia: Cook v. Heck's, Inc., 342 S.E.2d 453 (1986); Wisconsin: Ferraro v. Koelsch, 368 N.W.2d 666 (1985); Wyoming: Mobil Coal Producing, Inc., v. Parks, 704 P.2d 702 (1985). *See generally* PERRITT, EMPLOYEE DISMISSAL LAW AND PRACTICE (2d ed. 1989).

3. Petermann v. Int. Brotherhood of Teamsters, 344 P.2d 25 (Cal. App. 1958). For additional information regarding the theory of wrongful discharge, *see e.g.*, McWHIRTER, YOUR RIGHTS AT WORK Ch. 6 (1989); *supra* chapter 2.

4. Nees v. Hocks, 536 P.2d 512 (Ore. 1975).

5. La. Rev. Stat. Ann. §23:961.

6. Davis v. Louisiana Computing Corp., 394 So.2d 678 (La. App. 1981), *cert denied* 400 So.2d 668 (La. 1981).

7. Pickering v. Bd. of Education, 391 U.S. 563 (1968).

8. 563 F. Supp. 585 (W.D. Mich. 1983), *aff'd* 746 F.2d 1475 (6th Cir. 1984), *cert. denied* 473 U.S. 909 (1985).

9. Novosel v. Nationwide Ins. Co., 721 F.2d 894 (3d Cir. 1983).

10. *See generally* McWHIRTER, YOUR RIGHTS AT WORK, ch. 6, 10 (1989).

11. Whitney v. Greater N. Y. Corp. of Seventh-Day Adventists, 401 F. Supp. 1363 (S.D.N.Y. 1975). For a discussion of Title VII, *see supra* Chapters 2 and 5.

12. DeMatteis v. Eastman Kodak Co., 511 F.2d 306 (2d Cir. 1975), *on reh.* 520 F.2d 409 (2d Cir. 1975).

13. 769 P.2d 88 (N.M. 1989).

14. Rulon-Miller v. Int'l. Bus. Mach. Corp., 208 Cal. Rptr. 524 (Cal. App. 1984).

15. M.B.M. Co., Inc. v. Counce, 596 S.W.2d 681 (Ark. 1980).

16. Bodewig v. K-Mart, Inc., 635 P.2d 657 (Or. App. 1981), *reh. denied* 644 P.2d 1128 (Or. 1982).

17. Hall v. May Dept. Stores, 637 P.2d 126 (Or. 1981).

No-Spouse Rules

The term *nepotism* denotes favoritism, undeserved rewards, or unfair discrimination in granting employment or other advantages to relatives.[1] Few people would disagree with anti-nepotism rules that companies adopt to prevent such favoritism and the employment of clearly unqualified people. Companies favoring anti-nepotism rules also argue that relatives, especially spouses, may compromise the business by talking about business matters outside the workplace. Anti-nepotism and no-spouse rules, however, may breed practical and legal issues. In practice, the exclusion of talented and creative individuals who happen to be married or related to employees or managers shrinks the pool of available skilled labor. Where the excluded worker is the spouse of an employee, the employer may lose the services of two qualified employees if the couple find work with another employer, possibly a competitor, who does not impose spousal restrictions.

Anti-nepotism policies range from broadly sweeping rules that bar the employment of any employee's relatives to more liberal ones that prohibit one relative from supervising another. In between are rules barring the employment of relatives at the same facility or allowing relatives at the same site but not in the same department. The tentative manner in which many employers approach this subject was mirrored by Congress when it authorized the president to "prescribe rules which shall prohibit, as nearly as conditions of good administration warrant, discrimination because of marital status" in federal employment.[2]

CONSTITUTIONAL CHALLENGES

Married couples affected by anti-nepotism policies imposed by public employers have challenged them on constitutional grounds. Because the Fourteenth Amendment to the U.S. Constitution prevents states from denying citizens "equal protection" under the law, states must treat similarly situated persons in a similar manner. To establish a violation of the equal protection clause, plaintiffs must prove that a public employer purposefully discriminated against them. Thus, for example, a no-spouse rule that applies to women but not men would be invalid.

Governmental no-spouse rules also may not abridge the fundamental interests protected by the Fourteenth Amendment due process clause, which prohibits states from depriving citizens of life, liberty, or property without due process of law. Constitutional challenges arise when anti-nepotism rules threaten to deprive couples of their jobs when they contemplate marriage. In numerous cases, the U.S. Supreme Court has stressed the fundamental nature of the "right to marry." *Zablocki v. Redhail*,[3] for example, involved a Wisconsin law requiring non-custodial parents under child support orders to seek court permission before marrying. The Court held that the law violated the fundamental, constitutionally protected right to marry. Rules that "directly and substantially" interfere with the right to marry are subject to strict scrutiny, the Court stated, while those that do not should be judged under a rational basis standard.

The federal courts have considered whether no-spouse rules infringe on the right to marry in two cases. In *Keckeisen v. Indep. School Dist. 612*,[4] the court held that a school rule prohibiting the employment of spouses in an administrator-teacher context did not substantially infringe on a principal's constitutional rights or impair his freedom to marry a teacher at that school. The court observed that the rule did not deny employees the right to marry, but only barred the employment of married couples in a particular superior-subordinate relationship. This indirect interference was justified because the rule furthered the school district's legitimate interest in providing good education, preventing potential favoritism, and maintaining the morale of other teachers. *Southwestern Community Action Council, Inc. v. Community Services Admin.*[5] reached the same conclusion. There, the court considered a rule prohibiting federal agencies from employing any person if an immediate relative would be in a position to supervise her. In upholding the regulation, the court stressed that the rule interfered only indirectly with the right to marry and did not significantly interfere with any fundamental right. Both cases indicate that limited no-spouse rules adopted by public employers involving a superior-subordinate relationship do not illegally infringe on the right to marry. Existing judicial decisions do not indicate whether sweeping rules prohibiting spouses from working in the same agency would be found unconstitutional.

TITLE VII CHALLENGES

Title VII of the Civil Rights Act of 1964, discussed in chapters 2 and 5, prohibits discrimination by covered employers based on sex. Most anti-nepotism rules are neutral, barring the hiring of a spouse of any employee, male or female. Many no-spouse rules allow spouses who marry after they start work at the firm to choose which one will resign. Although Title VII objections have been raised, the courts have hesitated to conclude that no-spouse rules discriminate against people based on sex.

Plaintiffs can attack no-spouse rules under both disparate treatment and disparate impact theories. Under the former, the plaintiff must show that the employer has intentionally treated some applicants less favorably than others because of their sex.[6] While neutral rules cannot easily be challenged on this basis, a no-spouse rule that discriminates against one sex (such as refusing employment only to the wives of male workers) normally will be struck down under Title VII.[7]

In a disparate impact case, the main concern is the effect of the employer's policies rather than the underlying motivation for them. A prima facie case of unlawful discrimination may be established by showing that a policy has a substantially adverse impact on a protected group, even if its terms are neutral. An employer may rebut the alleged adverse impact by showing that a non-discriminatory "business necessity" justified the policy.

This theory was used to defend a no-spouse rule in *Yuhas v. Libby-Owens-Ford Co.*[8] The plaintiff claimed unintentional discrimination because seventy-three female applicants and only three males were denied employment under the rule. The trial court felt that the statistical imbalance was evidence of a *prima facie* violation of Title VII. To establish business need, the defendant stated that spouses who work together are often tardy or absent, that it is difficult to schedule vacations when spouses are jointly employed, and that the presence of spouses undermined employee efficiency and morale at the company. The trial court was not persuaded by this justification and voided the rule. The Seventh Circuit Court of Appeals reversed, however, finding that these were legitimate job-related reasons for a no-spouse rule.

A different problem arises in challenges to rules that ban the continued employment of spouses who marry after they are employed by the same company. The number of employees affected by such rules may often be too small to enable a plaintiff to show statistical significance. The plaintiff in *Harper v. Trans World Airlines, Inc.*[9] faced this problem when the airline terminated her employment after she married an employee in the same department. The airline's anti-nepotism policy barred spouses from working in the same department but allowed them to decide who would resign. Since neither Harper nor her husband was willing to resign, the company fired her. Although in four of five previous situations the wife had voluntarily left the airline, the court held this evidence was insufficient to prove a violation of Title VII. Finding no statistical or other persuasive evidence that the policy was discriminatory, the appeals court did not address the trial court's finding that the airline had implemented its policy to prevent conflicts of interest.

STATE LAWS

No-spouse rules of public and private employers may violate state laws barring discrimination in employment based on marital status. Over twenty states and the District of Columbia have enacted such laws.[10] The Oregon law, for example, prohibits firing or hiring anyone because a member of their family works for the employer, although it does permit employers to refuse to hire anyone who would exercise "supervisory, appointment, or grievance adjustment authority" over a relative.[11] Washington and California restrict no-spouse rules to situations involving compelling business interests or supervisory relationships.[12]

Challenges to no-spouse rules under state law have achieved mixed results due to the varied definitions of and judicial interpretations given to the term "marital status." A no-spouse rule is more likely to be invalidated under a law prohibiting discrimination based on the identity or situation of a spouse than under one barring employers from considering marital status (married, single, divorced or separated) in making employment decisions. In *Kraft, Inc. v. State*,[13] four part-time employees were denied full-time jobs because Kraft prohibited the full-time employment of more than one family member at any company office. The plaintiffs sued, claiming that the policy constituted a discriminatory practice based on marital status within the meaning of the Minnesota Human Rights Act. The Minnesota Supreme Court ruled that discrimination based on "marital status" encompasses discrimination based not only on one's status as married, single or divorced, but also on the "identity or situation of one's spouse." The court rejected a narrower reading of the law which would have allowed the company to continue hiring all married individuals except those married to full-time Kraft employees.

The New York Court of Appeals took the opposite view in *Manhattan Pizza Hut, Inc. v. New York State Human Rights*

Appeals Bd.[14] The plaintiff was discharged under a rule forbidding an employee from working under a relative's supervision. The court held that the protection afforded by the New York Human Rights Law is limited to discrimination based on "marital status" and does not extend to employment restrictions affecting relatives, including the spouse, of an employee.

CONCLUSION

Courts have been disinclined to invalidate employer no-spouse rules on the federal grounds of sex discrimination or impermissible interference with the right to marry. This is especially so where the rule bars only marriages that would result in one spouse having supervisory authority over the other. No-spouse rules may violate state law, with these laws varying dramatically in terms of what constitutes protected "marital status."

NOTES

1. Wexler, *Husbands and Wives: The Uneasy Case for Antinepotism Rules*, 62 B.U.L. REV. 75 (1982).
2. 5 U.S.C. §7202(a).
3. 434 U.S. 374 (1978).
4. 509 F.2d 1062 (8th Cir.), *cert. denied* 423 U.S. 833 (1975).
5. 462 F. Supp. 289 (S.D.W.Va. 1978).
6. Int'l. Brotherhood of Teamsters v. United States, 431 U.S. 324 (1977).
7. *See* McArthur v. Southern Airways, Inc., 404 F. Supp. 508 (N.D. Ga. 1975), *vacated on other grounds*, 556 F.2d 298 (5th Cir. 1977), *dismissed*, 569 F.2d 276 (5th Cir. 1978).
8. 411 F. Supp. 77 (N.D. Ill. 1976), *rev'd* 562 F.2d 496 (7th Cir. 1977), *cert. denied* 435 U.S. 934 (1978).
9. 525 F.2d 409 (8th Cir. 1975).
10. Alaska, California, Connecticut, Delaware, District of Columbia, Florida, Hawaii, Illinois, Maryland, Michigan, Minnesota, Montana, Nebraska, New Hampshire, New Jersey, New York, North Dakota, Oregon, Washington, and Wisconsin.
11. Or. Rev. Stat. §659–340.

12. Wash. Admin. Code §162–16–150; Cal. Admin. Code Tit. 2, R. 80 §7292.

13. 284 N.W.2d 386 (Minn. 1979)

14. 415 N.E.2d 950 (N.Y. 1980).

18

Off-Duty Relationships and Lifestyle Issues

Most employees believe that no area is more private and less relevant to the employment relationship than their off-duty, personal relationships. Legal challenges to employer policies or actions affecting these relationships focus, in dramatic ways, on the issue of what employers can or should do about workplace policies and whether they should apply those policies to situations occurring outside the workplace. Employers have legitimate interests in maintaining a reputable and credible work environment that is capable of meeting the organization's goals of productivity and efficiency. At the same time, society recognizes and encourages the right of employees to associate freely and pursue personal relationships that do not adversely affect their job performance. Many employees cannot accept an employer's interference with their off-duty relations or sexual preferences. Regardless of the law, their reaction often is: "That's none of your business!"

The courts, caught in the middle of this tension, have tended to favor the employees' right to pursue personal relationships without interference unless they conflict seriously with job performance. As the employment-at-will doctrine continues to erode, employers can expect further challenges to their power to fire workers whose relationships are viewed as a threat to the company or offend the sensibilities of company officials and customers.

DATING CO-WORKERS AND COMPETITORS' EMPLOYEES

Like no-spouse rules, policies forbidding employees from dating co-workers or competitors' employees are designed to avoid conflicts of interest that may arise when people involved in close relationships work together or in competition with each other. This concern has motivated many employers to impose significant restraints on intra- and inter-office dating. Whether the employer is a public or private entity, it may be engaging in a tortious invasion of employees' privacy rights when it interferes with their personal relationships.

The leading case in the private sector is *Rulon-Miller v. Int'l. Business Machines Corp.*[1] Rulon-Miller began dating a co-worker named Blum while both worked for IBM. The next year Blum left IBM to join a competitor, and several years later IBM told Rulon-Miller that because of a perceived conflict of interest she must stop dating Blum. She refused and was fired. In a suit alleging wrongful discharge and intentional infliction of emotional distress, the plaintiff received $100,000 in compensatory and $200,000 in punitive damages.

In analyzing the wrongful discharge claim, the court noted that IBM's written personnel policies prohibited its employees from becoming involved in conflicts of interest, but not from socializing or entering into relationships with competitors' employees. In addition, IBM had a stated policy of not interfering in an employee's private life unless it "reduced his ability to perform regular job assignments, interfered with the job performance of other employees, or ... affected the reputation of the company in a major way." IBM argued that it had the right to inquire into managers' personal relationships even if no evidence existed that those relationships interfered with job performance, because the morale of the managers' subordinates might be affected. The court, however, found no evidence to support this argument. It also pointed to a memo written by a former company chairman and distributed to all employees which stated that IBM's "first basic belief is respect for the individual, and the essence of this belief is a strict regard for his right to personal privacy. This idea should never be compromised easily or quickly."

The court based its decision on a contractual privacy right granted by IBM's personnel policies, finding that those policies gave IBM employees a legitimate expectation of privacy in personal relationships. The court also found sufficient evidence that IBM's conduct caused Rulon-Miller emotional distress and was so extreme and outrageous that it went beyond all possible bounds of decency. Finally, the court relied on management's flagrant disregard of IBM policies and its statements implying that Rulon-Miller could not act for herself and that IBM therefore would decide for her that her relationship should be terminated.

Some employees have challenged rules prohibiting co-employee dating under state laws barring discrimination based on marital status. One federal court, analyzing such a claim under Michigan law, ruled that no state had extended statutory protection to employee relationships. The court refused to extend the scope of the law, noting that the strong policies protecting the marital relationship do not apply to a mere dating situation.[2]

An employer's interference with the personal relations of its employees will continue to raise privacy challenges. If, as in *Rulon-Miller*, established company policies have created an expectation that employees' privacy will not be impaired, a challenge could succeed under a contract theory, at least in states which recognize the "wrongful discharge" or "implied covenant of good faith and fair dealing" concepts. Conversely, explicit written policies prohibiting certain relationships and setting out the consequences may provide employers with some legal protection. The most defensible policies are those governing superior-subordinate relationships or other obvious conflicts of interest.

OFF-DUTY SEXUAL BEHAVIOR

Employers often adopt, and courts usually uphold, no-spouse and inter-office dating prohibitions because of employer concerns about conflicts of interest. This rationale, however, does not apply to many cases where an employee is fired for off-duty sexual behavior that an employer views as inappropriate or immoral, including cohabitation, adultery, or homosexuality. In these cases, a claim that the discharge violates constitutional or common law privacy protections is quite certain; the outcome, unfortunately, is not.

Constitutional Rights of Public Employees

Although issues concerning the regulation of the private conduct of public employees have arisen quite often, courts have divided sharply both in their results and analytical approaches. Several have declared that the U.S. Constitution does not contain a fundamental privacy right for two people, one of whom is married, to live together. One of these cases, *Hollenbaugh v. Carnegie Free Library*,[3] involved two library employees living together in "open adultery," where a child was born out of wedlock. The court, citing the employer's concern that it not give tacit approval to the relationship, found no constitutional violation. Similarly, in *Suddarth v. Slane*,[4] a state trooper was fired for adultery under a department rule barring "criminal, infamous, dishonest, immoral, or other conduct prejudicial to the Department." In rejecting the trooper's claim that his First Amendment right to freedom of association and his right of privacy had been violated, the court held that by engaging in adultery the trooper had pursued an activity unprotected by the First Amendment and had violated state law and department regulations.

Other courts have taken the opposite position. In *Briggs v. Northern Muskegon Police Dept.*,[5] for example, a federal appeals court upheld a lower court ruling that dismissal of a married, part-time officer for living with a woman not his wife violated the officer's right to privacy. The trial court rejected the claim that regulation of a public employee's conduct could be justified by general community disapproval and held that while the police department has a valid interest in regulating the personal sexual activities and living arrangements of its employees when they affect job performance, this case involved no such adverse impact. The court also rejected the argument that the officer's conduct violated a criminal law making unlawful the cohabitation of unmarried persons in a "lewd and lascivious" manner.

In *Thorne v. City of El Segundo*,[6] the court also found an invasion of privacy where a female applicant for a police department was asked, during a polygraph examination, numerous questions about her sexual activities, including an affair with a married officer. The court found that the interest in the privacy of her sexual activities was within the zone protected by the Constitution, and that absent any showing that off-duty activities protected by the constitutional guarantees of privacy and association adversely affect an applicant's on-the-job performance, and absent specific, narrowly-drawn policies in this area, the police department could not rely on those activities to deny employment.

School districts have also had to deal with the off-duty sexual conduct of their employees. Again, the question involves the impact of the conduct on job performance. In one case involving a teacher fired because of alleged immoral conduct committed in his home with the two school-aged daughters of the woman with whom he lived, a court decided that the right of privacy was outweighed by the potential negative impact on job performance and upheld the discharge.[7] Another court, however, ruled that a teacher's right to be pregnant and bear children out of wedlock was greater than the school district's need to protect school children from the sight of an unmarried and pregnant school teacher.[8] A federal appeals court would not permit a school district to fire a teacher simply because she allowed a man to stay at her apartment overnight.[9]

Court cases are also inconsistent regarding employment decisions that involve public employees who engage in homosexual conduct. Several courts ruled in the early 1970's that employees cannot be dismissed from public employment because they are homosexual, unless that adversely affects job performance.[10] In 1986, however, the U.S. Supreme Court, in *Bowers v. Hardwick*,[11] rejected a constitutional challenge to a Georgia law criminalizing sodomy. The law was attacked by an adult homosexual prosecuted for engaging in consensual sodomy in his home with another adult homosexual. In finding that homosexual sodomy is not entitled to constitutional protection, the Court stressed that numerous state laws outlawing sodomy reflect general societal disapproval of such conduct. The Court concluded that the constitutional right of privacy does not extend to sodomy when committed behind closed doors, because sodomy is analogous to other crimes, such as illegal drug use, that do not escape the law merely because they are committed at home. Four justices dissented, arguing that this was primarily a case about personal autonomy, not homosexuality, and that the constitutional right of privacy does embrace intimate personal relationships and private, consensual sexual activity.

Relying on *Bowers*, a federal appeals court held in *Padula v. Webster*[12] that the Federal Bureau of Investigation did not violate the constitutional rights of an openly homosexual job applicant by refusing to hire her as an agent. The court stressed that agents who engage in conduct deemed criminal in half of the states would undermine law enforcement credibility. It would not, therefore, be irrational for the bureau to conclude that the criminalization of homosexual conduct coupled with general public opinion toward homosexuality exposes many homosexuals to possible blackmail.

The question of whether any form of sexual conduct outside the marital relationship is entitled to constitutional protection is a highly divisive one. The opinions of the majority and the dissenters in *Bowers* illustrate the fundamentally different approaches to this issue. Some courts have tried to take an intermediate approach, finding that private sexual conduct, while not entitled to the same protection as political expression, is entitled to some protection, and that the reasons given for infringing on the right in discharge cases must be more than minimally justified.[13] Which of these approaches ultimately prevails may depend largely on the composition of the Supreme Court when one of the public employee cases is reviewed.

Private Sector Employees

In the private sector, the effect of common law privacy protections in cases involving employees fired for off-duty sexual activity is no clearer. One court rejected an employee's claim that his discharge violated public policy after he attended a business convention with a woman other than his wife—but whom he introduced as his wife—finding this to be no threat to "some recognized facet of public policy."[14] Other privacy claims, focusing on the way in which employers have learned of off-duty sexual behavior, have been more successful. *Conway, Inc. v. Ross*,[15] for example, dealt with a woman hired to be a topless stripper with a nine week contract and then fired after three weeks for being a prostitute on her own time. The court said that this activity occurring away from the workplace did not violate any express terms of her employment contract and did not have any negative impact on the employer's business; thus, it did not rise to the level of "good cause" justifying discharge.

The tort of intrusion is designed to prevent any surveillance or invasion of a person's home, regardless of who may be inside. The public disclosure of an employee's sexual activities would also be actionable. The likelihood of extensive legislation in this area, however, is not great. A few jurisdictions, notably Wisconsin and the District of Columbia, include sexual orientation among the protected classifications of anti-discrimination laws.[16] But many states still have criminal prohibitions against fornication, adultery, sodomy, and other private, consensual conduct. As long as those laws are on the books and the Supreme Court has not clearly extended the constitutional right to privacy to private consensual conduct, courts in most states are not likely to find a clear, protectable privacy interest in such acts. It should be noted, however, that legal philosophy and arbitration decisions support the idea that the "right to be let alone" is fundamental, and that any off-duty behavior or activities that do not affect an employee's performance or injure the employer should not be the basis for discipline. Eventual judicial recognition of this fact as a matter of public policy is not inconceivable.

RELIGION

Title VII of the Civil Rights Act of 1964 and the civil rights laws in forty states[17] outlaw discrimination based on religion in public and private sector employment. There is, however, some confusion about what constitutes a religion. The U.S. Supreme Court has said that a religion does not have to be an established denomination or organized sect—it is enough that the individual has a "sincere and meaningful" religious belief.[18] But this raises the thorny problem of how to define "sincere and meaningful." What must one do to demonstrate that he holds a belief sincerely or meaningfully? Can beliefs held by one person qualify, or must others hold them as well? Beliefs that are "patently devoid of religious sincerity" are not protected, courts have held; atheism, on the other hand, is protected.[19] Within these extremes it is often difficult to determine what is safeguarded.

Title VII and most state laws allow religious discrimination if the employer cannot "reasonably accommodate" the employee's religious observance without "undue hardship" to his business. Courts have held, for example, that employers need not force employees with seniority to work so that the religious employee can have his Sabbath day off.[20] On the other hand, if other employees are willing to work so that a religious employee can have his Sabbath off, the employer must allow this.[21]

Courts differ over what constitutes "reasonable accommodation." In 1986, the U.S. Supreme Court allowed a school district to deny a teacher six days off for religious observance.[22] District rules allowed teachers to take up to three days off for religious observance, and although teachers also had sick and personal business leave days, the district did not allow them to be used for religious observance. The Supreme Court upheld the rules. The Massachusetts Supreme Court, on the other hand, has held that not allowing an employee a week off for a religious observance constitutes discrimination under the state civil rights law.[23] The court observed that the employer could have shifted other employees around to accommodate the needs of the religious employee. This case can be viewed as another of several instances in recent years in which state courts, apparently feeling that the U.S. Supreme Court has interpreted the U.S. Constitution and federal civil rights statutes too narrowly of late, have read corresponding state constitutional and statutory provisions more broadly to afford more protection to civil liberties. Decisions by state courts based on state law are not subject to review by the U.S. Supreme Court.

One point on which courts agree is that employers cannot treat different religions differently. Where, for example, an employer let one worker have Saturday off to observe his Sabbath but did not allow another to have Sunday off to observe hers, the court said that impermissible discrimination had occurred.[24] In another case, the court allowed an employer to continue to hold religious services at work, but ordered him to excuse employees who did not wish to attend and not to retaliate against them for making this decision.[25]

The federal and most state constitutions require governments not to interfere with people's religions, including discriminating against public employees on this basis. At the same time, they require the government not to encourage one religion over another. These requirements often conflict.[26] When, for example, Janet Cooper, a public school teacher in Oregon, became an adherent of the Sikh religion, she began wearing white clothes and a turban to school. Pursuant to an Oregon law barring teachers from wearing religious dress at school, the state revoked her certificate. The Oregon Supreme Court recognized Cooper's right to freely exercise her religion, but also observed that as a teacher Cooper was an authority figure representing the government. Concluding that the government must be neutral in religious matters and that Cooper's wearing of religious dress compromised that neutrality, the court upheld the revocation decision.[27] In another case, the court upheld a teacher's dismissal because she talked of devils, demons and God much of the time.[28] And in 1985 the U.S. Supreme Court invalidated a Connecticut law because it encouraged the "establishment of religion." The law gave all employees an absolute right to take their Sabbath day off from work and required private employers to honor that right.[29]

Title VII allows religious organizations to discriminate on religious grounds. This exception extends to employees hired to work for a church or a church school, and the U.S. Supreme Court has also said that it applies to other nonprofit activities carried out by a church.[30] The Mormon Church in Salt Lake City ran a gymnasium that was open to the public but hired only Mormons to work there. The Court said that this was permissible under Title VII, but left open the question of whether a church engaging in for-profit activity may discriminate on the basis of religion.

In recent years the most interesting court cases have involved religion and unemployment compensation. The Indiana Supreme Court, for example, ruled that a man who quit work for religious reasons when he learned that the parts he was making would be used in military equipment deserved compensation.[31] The Oregon Supreme Court held that an employee fired for using peyote as part of a religious ceremony must be compensated.[32] And in 1988, the Fourth Circuit Court of Appeals handed down a ruling with far-reaching implications. Generally courts have held that spouses forced to quit work to move with their transferred spouse did not have good cause to leave and thus could not collect unemployment compensation. In this case, the wife argued that her religion required her to live with her husband and, therefore, to quit her job to move when her husband was transferred. She asserted that denying her unemployment benefits would interfere illegally with her religious practices and beliefs. The federal court agreed.[33]

If there is any trend in this area, it is toward requiring employers to make a greater effort to accommodate the religious beliefs and practices of employees. Increasingly, employers risk facing discrimination charges and a bill for unemployment compensation if they do not do so.

RESIDENCY REQUIREMENTS

Some employers find it desirable to impose residency requirements on employees. For private employers this is strictly a matter of contract: if an employee accepts a job knowing that he must live in a certain place, no legal issue is raised. In general, it is noted, private employers do not seem to care where their employees live as long as they get to work on time and in condition to work; local governments, however—particularly cities and school districts—do care. They often argue that their employees must live in the city or district to understand its problems and to be available in case of an emergency. This burdens employees, who may wish to live in a nearby district or city.

Under the equal protection clause of the Fourteenth Amendment to the U.S. Constitution, state and local governments may not require people to be residents of the state or district to apply for a government job.[34] Unless a statute or local ordinance limits this power, however, it is permissible to require employees to become residents of the area within a reasonable time after they accept employment. One court upheld a 90-day move-in period,[35] while another found 120 days to be reasonable.[36] Some states have statutes controlling the ability of cities and school districts to impose residency rules. Pennsylvania law, for example, prevents some districts from requiring their employees to live in the district.[37] If an employer institutes a residency requirement, it must give its current employees sufficient time to move into the area. In one case, a county college gave current employees four years to move into the county, and a court decided that this was adequate time.[38]

Residency rules encounter two problems, one financial, the other familial. Some government entities are discovering that people cannot afford to move into the area on the salaries paid by the entity. In 1987, for example, Westchester County, New York abandoned its residency rule because county employees could no longer afford to live in the county. In some cases, husbands work for one city while the wife works for another. Most cities give one of these employees an exemption from the residency requirement. It remains unclear whether the constitutional right of privacy would require a city to do so in this case.

Cities and school districts with union contracts present another problem. If the contract is silent on this issue and the city has an ordinance dealing with residency, can the ordinance be enforced? In one case, the city signed a collective bargaining agreement that did not mention residency. The city, however, had a pre-existing ordinance that required city employees to live in the city. When a union member employed by the city moved elsewhere, he was fired. An arbitrator ruled that the ordinance was a work rule that was not reasonably related to job performance and ordered the city to reinstate the employee.

The Wisconsin Supreme Court disagreed, ruling that the ordinance was still in force and did not conflict with the union contract. The court upheld the dismissal of the employee.[39]

OUTSIDE EMPLOYMENT

The extent to which employers can control their employees' outside employment is a question of contract law in both the private and public sectors. As long as employees are told of restrictions on outside employment when they are hired, there should be no problem. Outside employment can affect an employee's ability to perform work for the employer by consuming energy that would otherwise be used to further the employer's interests. In 1988, for example, the California Supreme Court ruled that a statute limiting the off-duty employment of police was not designed to strip cities of legislative authority in this area. California cities thus remain free to impose tighter restrictions than those in the statute.[40]

CONFLICT OF INTEREST

Most public and private employers have conflict of interest rules. Cases in this area typically involve either government employees or workers under a union contract. The rules vary greatly. The Pennsylvania Ethics Act, for example, requires civil servants to file a financial interest statement. A Pennsylvania court ruled that failing to report some rental properties was good cause for dismissal regardless of whether this posed a direct conflict of interest.[41]

In many cases courts have upheld the dismissal of civil servants found guilty of direct conflicts of interest even without the violation of a specific law. Where, for example, a civil servant accepted $600 worth of free work from a contractor, the court said that good cause for his dismissal existed.[42] In another case, a town's planning and zoning contractor failed to disclose his financial interests in a real estate development, and the court agreed that this was good cause for dismissal.[43]

Obvious conflicts of interest have been found to afford sufficient cause for dismissal in the context of private employers and union contracts. The *New York Post*, for example, was allowed to discharge a sports writer who became part-owner of a race horse. Although he did not pick favorites when his horse was racing, that other horses owned by his partners would be racing created a clear conflict of interest.[44] Because private employees not covered by a contract usually work at-will and can be fired for any reason, they clearly can be dismissed for conflicts of interest. Employers must be careful, however, not to say anything in their handbooks, company policies, or otherwise that would eliminate this right to discharge for this reason. As *Rulon-Miller*[45] illustrates, at-will employees who are told that they will be fired only for a direct conflict of interest have a right in most states to rely on that promise.

DUTY OF LOYALTY

Related to the conflict of interest question is the fact that in most states courts have held that employees have a duty of loyalty to their employer. If they violate this duty, they can be discharged even if they are covered by a contract. Many cases involve employees who prepare to compete with their employer while still employed by him. This causes a dilemma. On the one hand, our economic system depends on free competition, and often the only people capable of competing in a particular area are those experienced in that area. On the other hand, employees owe their employer a duty of loyalty while working for him. The question is whether an employee's acts went beyond "preparation to compete" and involved actual competition. In one case, an employee's wife incorporated competing company *B* while her husband, still employed by company *A*, tried to convince customers of *A* to switch to *B*. The court not only held that the employer was justified in firing the employee, but also issued an injunction barring the employee from selling to *A*'s customers.[46]

Preparations to compete must take place on the employee's own time. If they occur during working hours, not only may dismissal of the employee be warranted, but the employer may be able to refuse to pay the employee for the work done.[47]

OFF-DUTY MISCONDUCT

When employees engage in off-duty misconduct, a number of issues are raised. If the employee is protected by a civil service law or a contract, the question is whether his or her off-duty behavior constitutes good cause for dismissal; in the public sector, a discharge may implicate the constitutional right of privacy. Employees unprotected by contracts or civil service laws can usually be fired for any reason, but not for an illegal reason. In this instance, the issue would be whether the employee's behavior is such that it would violate a recognized public policy to permit dismissal for that reason. Finally, the question of whether the employee is entitled to unemployment compensation is also raised where an employee is discharged for off-duty misconduct.

Where public employees are involved, the issue is to what extent their employer may expect them to be role models away from work. In one case, a male teacher invited two female students to a party where everyone drank and smoked marijuana. A Michigan court found that this afforded good cause for the teacher's dismissal.[48] A Pennsylvania court, however, ruled that a policeman's threat to kill the city's mayor did not constitute cause for the officer's discharge.[49] The policeman was found to be insane at the time and the court allowed him to use what amounted to an insanity defense.

For private sector employees under contracts, the issue is not whether the employee is a role model, but whether the off-duty conduct might negatively affect the workplace. An arbitrator, for example, allowed a union worker to be discharged when it was found that he was the acting grand dragon of the Ku Klux Klan.[50] Several cases have involved employees discharged for "streaking" or "mooning" while off duty, and this has usually been found not to be good cause for dismissal.[51] Off-duty conduct that threatened the ability of supervisors to maintain discipline at work, however, has been deemed to afford good cause. In one case, an employee assaulted his supervisor while both were at a restaurant; in another, the employees kept others from aiding their foreman while he was being assaulted at a party.[52]

Off-duty criminal conduct usually justifies dismissal. Many civil service laws allow employees to be fired if they are found guilty of "crimes of moral turpitude." In the private sector, the issue often turns on the extent to which the employee works with the public and is associated in the public mind with the employer. In one case, a peace officer admitted smoking marijuana while off-duty. This was enough to justify dismissal.[53] Where an off-duty milkman was arrested in a raid on a night club and charged with pandering and conducting obscene exhibitions, an arbitrator allowed his suspension pending the outcome of the trial because the milkman contacted customers on a daily basis and was identified in the public's mind with his employer.[54]

Many civil service laws require employees to be warned before dismissal if the misconduct is "remedial." The purpose of this requirement is to protect employees from the realities of bureaucratic life. Most government agencies have so many rules that employees break at least one every day, and statutes requiring warnings give employees another chance to avoid dismissal based on hypertechnical violations. Supervisors, however, do not have to warn if the behavior is criminal or immoral. For example, a nurse discharged for giving shots to students without parental consent was ordered reinstated by an Illinois court.[55] This is the kind of rule violation that would justify a warning. But criminal or immoral conduct is not deemed remedial. Illinois and Minnesota courts have upheld the discharge without prior warning of teachers convicted of stealing from students and swindling co-workers.[56]

Whether the off-duty misconduct justifies withholding unemployment compensation depends on its impact on the employer. A Pennsylvania appeals court, for example, refused to award unemployment compensation to an employee fired for beginning a business in competition with his employer while still employed by him.[57] On the other hand, telling a coworker that he loved her was not deemed sufficient to justify denying compensation to an employee.[58] Using peyote as part of a American religious ceremony also was held not to be the kind of misconduct that justifies withholding such compensation.[59]

CONCLUSION

Courts differ widely on the issue of whether employees may be legally dismissed based on off-duty personal relationships or sexual conduct. In the public sector, employers must be cognizant of the "right to privacy" guarded by the U.S. Constitution as well as state laws and court decisions that may recognize the "wrongful discharge" and "breach of the implied covenant of good faith and fair dealing" theories of tort and contract law. Some courts have held that off-duty sexual behavior does not afford good cause for an employee's dismissal and is protected by the constitutional right of privacy; others have disagreed. In the private sector, federal constitutional rights are generally not involved, but the foregoing tort and contract law concepts may come into play, even when at-will employees are involved, as may state laws and perhaps local ordinances. The safest rule is this: unless there is a direct and demonstrable relationship between the alleged immoral conduct and the employee's job performance, employers should not attempt to discipline or discharge employees based on their private lifestyle and behavior choices.

Most public and private employers are prohibited from discriminating against applicants or employees on religious grounds, with *religion* defined broadly to include any "sincere and meaningful" religious belief. Employers must also attempt to "reasonably accommodate" their employees' religious beliefs and practices if this can be done without undue hardship to their business. In other areas involving lifestyle choices and behavior, employers have somewhat more latitude. Residency requirements, for example, may be imposed if employees are given a reasonable time to move into the area. Employers may also require employees to abide by rules on conflicts of interest and outside employment, and to respect their "duty of loyalty" to the company while employed there. Finally, dismissals for off-duty misconduct will usually be upheld, although this should be done only where the conduct actually affects the workplace negatively and is not the kind that would reasonably call for a warning instead.

NOTES

1. 208 Cal. Rptr. 524 (Cal. App. 1984).
2. Sears v. Ryder Truck Rental, Inc., 596 F. Supp. 1001 (E.D. Mich. 1984).
3. 436 F. Supp. 1328 (W.D. Pa. 1977), aff'd 578 F.2d 1374 (3rd Cir. 1978), cert. denied 439 U.S. 1052 (1978).
4. 539 F. Supp. 612 (W.D. Va. 1982).
5. 563 F. Supp. 585 (W.D. Mich. 1983), aff'd 746 F.2d 1475 (6th Cir. 1984), cert. denied 473 U.S. 909 (1985).
6. 726 F.2d 459 (9th Cir. 1983), cert. denied 469 U.S. 979 (1984).
7. Lile v. Hancock Place School Dist., 701 S.W.2d 500 (Mo. App. 1985).
8. Ponton v. Newport News School Bd., 632 F. Supp. 1056 (E.D. Va. 1986).
9. Fisher v. Snyder, 476 F.2d 375 (8th Cir. 1973).
10. E.g., Saal v. Middendorf, 427 F. Supp. 192 (N.D. Cal. 1977).
11. 106 S. Ct. 2841 (1986).
12. 822 F.2d 97 (D.C. Cir. 1987).
13. E.g., Kukla v. Village of Antioch, 647 F. Supp. 799 (N.D. Ill. 1986).
14. Staats v. Ohio National Life Ins. Co., 620 F. Supp. 118 (W.D. Pa. 1985).
15. 627 P.2d 1029 (Alaska 1981).
16. Wis. Stat. Ann. §111.321 and §111.36; D.C. Code Ann. §1–2501 et seq.
17. Only Alabama, Arkansas, Colorado, Georgia, Mississippi, New Jersey, New York, Virginia, Wisconsin and Wyoming are excluded.
18. Frazee v. Ill. Dept. Emp. Sec., 109 S. Ct. 1514 (1989); United States v. Seeger, 380 U.S. 163 (1965).
19. Theriault v. Carlson, 495 F.2d 390 (5th Cir. 1974); Young v. Southwestern Savings and Loan Ass'n., 509 F.2d 140 (5th Cir. 1978).
20. Trans World Airlines, Inc. v. Hardison, 432 U.S. 63 (1977); United States v. City of Albuquerque, 545 F.2d 110 (10th Cir. 1976).
21. E.E.O.C. v. Ithaca Industries, Inc., 849 F.2d 116 (4th Cir. 1988).
22. Ansonia Bd. of Educ. v. Philbrook, 107 S. Ct. 367 (1986).
23. New York and Mass. Motor Serv., Inc., v. Mass. Comm'n Against Discrimination, 517 N.E.2d 1270 (Mass. 1988).
24. South Wind Motel v. Ohio Civil Rights Comm'n., 494 N.E.2d 1158 (Ohio App. 1985).
25. E.E.O.C. v. Townley Engineering & Mfg. Co., 859 F.2d 610 (9th Cir. 1988).

26. The First Amendment to the U. S. Constitution provides in relevant part that "Congress shall make no law respecting an establishment of religion, or prohibiting the free exercise thereof...."

27. Cooper v. Eugene School Dist. No. 4J, 723 P.2d 298 (Or. 1986).

28. Rhodes v. Laurel Highlands School Dist., 544 A.2d 562 (Pa. Cmwlth. 1988).

29. Estate of Thornton v. Caldor, Inc., 105 S. Ct. 2914 (1985).

30. Corp. of Presiding Bishop v. Amos, 107 S. Ct. 2862 (1987).

31. Clark v. Rev. Bd. of Dept. of Emp., 534 N.E.2d 260 (Ind. App. 1989).

32. Smith v. Employment Div., 763 P.2d 146 (Or. 1988).

33. Austin v. Berryman, 862 F.2d 1050 (4th Cir. 1988).

34. Hicklin v. Orbeck, 437 U.S. 518 (1978); Shapiro v. Thompson, 394 U.S. 618 (1969).

35. Wardwell v. Bd. of Educ. of Cincinnati, 529 F.2d 625 (6th Cir. 1976).

36. Carofano v. City of Bridgeport, 495 A.2d 1011 (Conn. 1985).

37. Appeal of McNelly, 553 A.2d 472 (Pa. Cmwlth. 1989); Chester Uplands School Dist. v. Pennsylvania, 495 A.2d 981 (Pa. Cmwlth. 1985).

38. Cool County College Teachers' Union v. Taylor, 432 F. Supp. 270 (N.D. Ill. 1977).

39. Wisconsin Emp. Rel. Comm'n. v. Teamsters Local No. 563, 250 N.W.2d 696 (Wis. 1977).

40. Long Beach Police v. City of Long Beach, 250 Cal. Rptr. 869 (Cal. 1988).

41. Pa. Dept. of Comm. Affairs v. Colston, 521 A.2d 509 (Pa. Cmwlth. 1987).

42. Pa. Dept. of Comm. Affairs v. Averette, 521 A.2d 534 (Pa. Cmwlth. 1987).

43. Ferrier v. Wallingford Personnel and Pension App. Bd., 510 A.2d 1385 (Conn. App. 1986).

44. New York Post Corp., 62 Lab. Arb. (BNA) 227 (1973).

45. 208 Cal. Rptr. 524 (1984).

46. Arnold's Ice Cream Co. v. Carlson, 330 F. Supp. 1185 (E.D.N.Y. 1971).

47. Henderson v. Hassur, 594 P.2d 650 (Kan. 1979).

48. Barcheski v. Grand Rapids Public Schools, 412 N.W.2d 296 (Mich. App. 1987).

49. Perry v. Philadelphia Civ. Service Comm'n., 529 A.2d 616 (Pa. Cmwlth. 1987).

50. Baltimore Transit Co., 47 Lab. Arb. (BNA) 62 (1966).

51. *E.g.*, Air Cal., 63 Lab. Arb. (BNA) 350 (1974); South Central Bell, 80 Lab. Arb. (BNA) 891 (1983).

52. General Telephone Co. of Kentucky, 69 Lab. Arb. (BNA) 351 (1977); Murray Machinery, Inc., 75 Lab. Arb. (BNA) 284 (1980).

53. New York State Dept. of Corrections, 86 Lab. Arb. (BNA) 793 (1986).

54. Menzie Dairy Co., 45 Lab. Arb. (BNA) 283 (1965).

55. Chicago Bd. of Educ. v. Illinois Bd. of Educ., 513 N.E.2d 845 (Ill. App. 1987).

56. McBroom v. Bd. of Educ., Dist. No. 205, 494 N.E.2d 1191 (Ill. App. 1986); Matter of Shelton, 408 N.W.2d 594 (Minn. App. 1987).

57. Jorden v. Unemp. Comp. Bd. of Review, 547 A.2d 811 (Pa. App. 1988).

58. Gradine v. College of St. Scholastica, 426 N.W.2d 459 (Minn. App. 1988).

59. Smith v. Employment Div., 763 P.2d 146 (Or. 1988).

19

Suing and Being Sued

Because the words *lawsuit* and *court* appear so often in this book, it is natural for readers to assume that virtually anything that employers and supervisors do might land them in court. In most of the cases reviewed, however, only the most sympathetic observers would not agree that the defendant deserved to be sued, because he acted arbitrarily, assumed too much authority over his employees, ignored existing legal requirements, or failed to follow accepted management principles. Managers and employers who are alert to these pitfalls do not, for the most part, get sued, and when they do they typically prevail.

Following are some rules by which employers and managers should abide, both to fend off lawsuits and to win those that are filed:

1. *Keep a Record of Everything.* Many employers lose in court, in agency proceedings, or at the unemployment compensation office because they lack necessary documentation. The same is true of employees. The latter should keep a daily logbook or diary noting everything significant—who ordered them to do what, when, and why—including their accomplishments.

2. *Keep Your Mouth Shut.* This book has referred to numerous instances of supervisors being sued for defamation and employees dismissed for having a foul mouth. Combine this with the fact that everything people say really can be used against them in court, and the result is a good reason to keep quiet. One cannot be misquoted if he says nothing.

3. *Talk to an Attorney Early.* Many lawsuits could be avoided if employers get legal advice before acting. It is hard for attorneys to protect employers after they make a mistake—the best that one can hope for then is a sound clean-up operation. Similarly, many employees could avoid throwing away their cases if they would talk to legal counsel before acting precipitously, like resigning or admitting guilt.

4. *Ask Questions.* Don't expect your lawyer to anticipate all of your concerns. Pose your own questions—ask how to handle situations that might arise. Hopefully, this book will give employers and employees guidance as to what questions to ask of each other and of legal counsel if the need for such consultation arises.

5. *Keep Track of Deadlines.* The law is enamored of deadlines. An employer may have only a few days to decide whether to challenge an application for unemployment, and the same is true of an employee who believes that she may have been subjected to illegal discrimination. Appeals in workers' and unemployment compensation cases must be filed within days and civil rights complaints within months. The major cause of malpractice suits against attorneys is that they waited past the deadline to file a lawsuit. The client should take enough interest in his case to ask about deadlines and to make sure the suit is timely filed.

6. *Do Not Accept Legal Advice from Anyone Other than Your Attorney.* People mean well and are often eager to render aid in the form of advice, legal and otherwise. Legal advice from laymen, however, is usually worth what it costs—nothing—and can put people in a worse position than they would have been in otherwise. One should also not assume that because her cousin Fred is a lawyer, he is the person to consult about an employment matter. Just as one would not allow a foot doctor to do brain surgery, one should not retain for an employment case an attorney who is not a specialist in that field. Finally, be certain you are crystal clear on the attorney's fee structure. Too many clients who have not clarified this at the outset have had rude awakenings later on, when it is too late to do anything but pay what is owed.

7. *Tell Your Attorney Everything that Might be Relevant.* Too many people withhold important details when discussing problems with their attorneys, usually out of embarrassment or fear that the information might hurt their cases. Attorneys, however, have little chance of affording sound advice and preparing an effective case if they lack all of the facts. The courtroom is hardly the place for an attorney to be confronted with surprise disclosures.

8. *A Little Kindness Goes a Long Way.* Many of the cases in this book arose because management was stupid or mean. Some employers have the idea that they must support their supervisors regardless of what has occurred. While this may be a sound rule generally, exceptions exist. Many lawsuits come about because a supervisor was unreasonable and higher management failed to act. Firing people justified in complaining about their treatment by a supervisor is almost a failsafe way to end up in court.[1]

NOTE

1. McWhirter, Your Rights at Work, Chap. 19 (1989).

20

Conclusion

Early on this book noted that privacy as a legal concept is quite a recent phenomenon. But this is not to say that our forefathers were unconcerned with privacy. In a tour of the French Quarter, for example, visitors to New Orleans learn that after the Louisiana Purchase, people from the backwoods called "Kentucks" came down the Mississippi River to settle in New Orleans. At that moment that city's architecture changed forever. These supposedly unsophisticated Americans were appalled at the lack of concern for privacy in the basic house design, so they created hallways—no longer would visitors have to go through bedrooms to get to living rooms. And thereafter stairways were put inside houses if possible, not outside for all the world to see.

When America became a nation, privacy was not a concern for the legal system, because the means of invading it and the modern reasons for doing so did not exist. Two centuries ago, for example, it was accepted that life began at birth, so questions about abortion did not arise. There were no laws against "illegal substances," the control of which is perhaps the main cause of privacy invasions by police today. Electronic surveillance devices and computer data banks simply did not exist.

There were no lie detectors, drug or personality tests to administer to employees, and employees were not routinely put in control of machines capable of taking human life with the wrong push of a button.

When most Americans are asked if they believe in a "right of privacy" they answer "yes," but it is easy to be "pro-privacy" in the abstract. The law does not deal with abstractions, but rather with concrete situations where privacy interests have collided with some other cherished value. Of course a woman should be able to control her own body, but what of the right of a fetus to have a chance at life? Of course police should stay out of people's homes, but how else is the traffic in illegal drugs to be controlled? Of course the media should leave people alone, but the right of the free press to print the news must be protected. Of course employers have no business being concerned with what employees do on their off hours, but no one wants to ride a plane or bus being controlled by someone impaired by drugs.

In early 1990 the *National Law Journal* and LEXIS released a survey of 805 adults. A majority of the respondents said that they thought that the U.S. Constitution contains a right to personal privacy that shields people from, for example, governmental interference in the private, consensual sex acts of homosexuals and decisions about when to end life support for a hopelessly ill relative. The media made much of the erroneous nature of these beliefs. The Supreme Court, it was noted, has so far refused to interfere with states that want to control "abnormal sex" or to rule on the so-called "right-to-die." The survey went on to ask citizens about other issues and found that the "average person" has as much trouble weighing privacy rights against other social values in particular instances as the Supreme Court does. For instance, although 73 percent said that the Constitution guarantees a right to privacy, a majority felt that this right does not allow employees to refuse drug tests or teenage girls to get an abortion without parental consent.

The views of the "average citizen" reflected in the survey reveal a basic misunderstanding of how the Constitution works. In a very real sense, the Constitution means what society thinks it means, and that belief has changed dramatically over the years. The role of judges in our society, whether they are interpreting the unwritten common law or the Constitution, is to mirror what society holds dear. A decade or two from now the Supreme Court may decide, for instance, that the Bill of Rights does protect the right to engage in consensual sex. At a few points in our history the Court has been ahead of the populace in interpreting the Constitution in new ways to protect individual rights, but the general pattern over two centuries has been one of the Court following the change in social attitudes, not leading it.

At the same time, the Court does not have the last word on privacy. It decides what the Constitution protects. While this is the final word as far as federal law is concerned, it represents only a line that states may not cross. State courts remain free to construe state constitutions to give citizens even greater privacy protection than the federal Constitution affords. As this book notes, for example, several appeals courts in California have held that the privacy provision in the state Constitution controls both governmental and private individuals. Other states have similar provisions, and it will be up to each state's courts to decide how far its provision extends. And even if the courts hold that the state constitution does not protect a particular form of privacy, the common law may do so, or the legislature may pass a statute having this effect. Such is the nature of the American legal system.

It is also important to remember that while modern technology makes many privacy invasions possible, it may also help to render them obsolete. For example, the typical drug test involves taking a urine sample. From that specimen a chemist can tell if the subject is pregnant, her genetic makeup, what medications are being taken, and so on. But the test cannot assess how "impaired" the individual was at the time of the test. Is it fair to fire someone because they were around pot smokers over the weekend? A new device is being tested that simply measures impairment. If an employee cannot perform with the manual dexterity required by the machine, he has no business driving a train or operating a crane, regardless of the reason for the inability. Civil libertarians have few problems with such a test, unless of course it discriminates according to race or sex or is unreliable.

Finally, although we have sought to make this book as accurate and up-to-date as possible, court decisions and statutes are always changing and are always subject to reinterpretation. While this book traces the development of privacy law through the 1980's as it concerns the workplace, there are many cases pending as the 1990's begin. Any reader with a specific question should consult an attorney who can advise them on the state of the law at that moment and at that location. It is our hope that after reading this book, people will better appreciate what the law generally is and has been, so they can better comprehend the legal environment within which employers and employees operate and anticipate what the law will become in the future.

Appendix

Americans with Disabilities Act of 1990

SECTION 1. SHORT TITLE; TABLE OF CONTENTS.

(a) SHORT TITLE.—*This Act may be cited as the "Americans with Disabilities Act of 1990".*

(b) TABLE OF CONTENTS.—*The table of contents is as follows:*

39–006

SEC. 2. FINDINGS AND PURPOSES.

(a) FINDINGS.—*The Congress finds that—*

(1) some 43,000,000 Americans have one or more physical or mental disabilities, and this number is increasing as the population as a whole is growing older;

(2) historically, society has tended to isolate and segregate individuals with disabilities, and, despite some improvements, such forms of discrimination against individuals with disabilities continue to be a serious and pervasive social problem;

(3) discrimination against individuals with disabilities persists in such critical areas as employment, housing, public accommodations, education, transportation, communication, recreation, institutionalization, health services, voting, and access to public services;

(4) unlike individuals who have experienced discrimination on the basis of race, color, sex, national origin, religion, or age, individuals who have experienced discrimination on the basis of disability have often had no legal recourse to redress such discrimination;

(5) individuals with disabilities continually encounter various forms of discrimination, including outright intentional exclusion, the discriminatory effects of architectural, transportation, and communication barriers, overprotective rules and policies, failure to make modifications to existing facilities and practices, exclusionary qualification standards and criteria, segregation, and relegation to lesser services, programs, activities, benefits, jobs, or other opportunities;

(6) census data, national polls, and other studies have documented that people with disabilities, as a group, occupy an inferior status in our society, and are severely disadvantaged socially, vocationally, economically, and educationally;

(7) individuals with disabilities are a discrete and insular minority who have been faced with restrictions and limitations, subjected to a history of purposeful unequal treatment, and relegated to a position of political powerlessness in our society, based on characteristics that are beyond the control of such individuals and resulting from stereotypic assumptions not truly indicative of the individual ability of such individuals to participate in, and contribute to, society;

(8) the Nation's proper goals regarding individuals with disabilities are to assure equality of opportunity, full participation, independent living, and economic self-sufficiency for such individuals; and

(9) the continuing existence of unfair and unnecessary discrimination and prejudice denies people with disabilities the opportunity to compete on an equal basis and to pursue those opportunities for which our free society is justifiably famous, and costs the United States billions of dollars in unnecessary expenses resulting from dependency and nonproductivity.

(b) PURPOSE.—It is the purpose of this Act—
  (1) to provide a clear and comprehensive national mandate for the elimination of discrimination against individuals with disabilities;
  (2) to provide clear, strong, consistent, enforceable standards addressing discrimination against individuals with disabilities;
  (3) to ensure that the Federal Government plays a central role in enforcing the standards established in this Act on behalf of individuals with disabilities; and
  (4) to invoke the sweep of congressional authority, including the power to enforce the fourteenth amendment and to regulate commerce, in order to address the major areas of discrimination faced day-to-day by people with disabilities.

SEC. 3. DEFINITIONS.
As used in this Act:
  (1) AUXILIARY AIDS AND SERVICES.—The term "auxiliary aids and services" includes—
    (A) qualified interpreters or other effective methods of making aurally delivered materials available to individuals with hearing impairments;
    (B) qualified readers, taped texts, or other effective methods of making visually delivered materials available to individuals with visual impairments;
    (C) acquisition or modification of equipment or devices; and
    (D) other similar services and actions.
  (2) DISABILITY.—The term "disability" means, with respect to an individual—
    (A) a physical or mental impairment that substantially limits one or more of the major life activities of such individual;
    (B) a record of such an impairment; or
    (C) being regarded as having such an impairment.
  (3) STATE.—The term "State" means each of the several States, the District of Columbia, the Commonwealth of Puerto Rico, Guam, American Samoa, the Virgin Islands, the Trust Territory of the Pacific Islands, and the Commonwealth of the Northern Mariana Islands.

TITLE I—EMPLOYMENT

SEC. 101. DEFINITIONS.
As used in this title:
  (1) COMMISSION.—The term "Commission" means the Equal Employment Opportunity Commission established by section 705 of the Civil Rights Act of 1964 (42 U.S.C. 2000e-4).
  (2) COVERED ENTITY.—The term "covered entity" means an employer, employment agency, labor organization, or joint labor-management committee.
  (3) DIRECT THREAT.—The term "direct threat" means a significant risk to the health or safety of others that cannot be eliminated by reasonable accommodation.

(4) EMPLOYEE.—The term "employee" means an individual employed by an employer.

(5) EMPLOYER.—

(A) IN GENERAL.—The term "employer" means a person engaged in an industry affecting commerce who has 15 or more employees for each working day in each of 20 or more calendar weeks in the current or preceding calendar year, and any agent of such person, except that, for two years following the effective date of this title, an employer means a person engaged in an industry affecting commerce who has 25 or more employees for each working day in each of 20 or more calendar weeks in the current or preceding year, and any agent of such person.

(B) EXCEPTIONS.—The term "employer" does not include—

(i) the United States, a corporation wholly owned by the government of the United States, or an Indian tribe; or

(ii) a bona fide private membership club (other than a labor organization) that is exempt from taxation under section 501(c) of the Internal Revenue Code of 1986.

(6) ILLEGAL USE OF DRUGS.—

(A) IN GENERAL.—The term "illegal use of drugs" means the use of drugs, the possession or distribution of which is unlawful under the Controlled Substances Act (21 U.S.C. 812). Such term does not include the use of a drug taken under supervision by a licensed health care professional, or other uses authorized by the Controlled Substances Act or other provisions of Federal law.

(B) DRUGS.—The term "drug" means a controlled substance, as defined in schedules I through V of section 202 of the Controlled Substances Act.

(7) PERSON, ETC.—The terms "person", "labor organization", "employment agency", "commerce", and "industry affecting commerce", shall have the same meaning given such terms in section 701 of the Civil Rights Act of 1964 (42 U.S.C. 2000e).

(8) QUALIFIED INDIVIDUAL WITH A DISABILITY.—The term "qualified individual with a disability" means an individual with a disability who, with or without reasonable accommodation, can perform the essential functions of the employment position that such individual holds or desires. For the purposes of this title, consideration shall be given to the employer's judgment as to what functions of a job are essential, and if an employer has prepared a written description before advertising or interviewing applicants for the job, this description shall be considered evidence of the essential functions of the job.

(9) REASONABLE ACCOMMODATION.—The term "reasonable accommodation" may include—

(A) making existing facilities used by employees readily accessible to and usable by individuals with disabilities; and

(B) job restructuring, part-time or modified work schedules, reassignment to a vacant position, acquisition or

modification of equipment or devices, appropriate adjustment or modifications of examinations, training materials or policies, the provision of qualified readers or interpreters, and other similar accommodations for individuals with disabilities.

(10) UNDUE HARDSHIP.—

*(A) IN GENERAL.—*The term "undue hardship" means an action requiring significant difficulty or expense, when considered in light of the factors set forth in subparagraph (B).

*(B) FACTORS TO BE CONSIDERED.—*In determining whether an accommodation would impose an undue hardship on a covered entity, factors to be considered include—

(i) the nature and cost of the accommodation needed under this Act;

(ii) the overall financial resources of the facility or facilities involved in the provision of the reasonable accommodation; the number of persons employed at such facility; the effect on expenses and resources, or the impact otherwise of such accommodation upon the operation of the facility;

(iii) the overall financial resources of the covered entity; the overall size of the business of a covered entity with respect to the number of its employees; the number, type, and location of its facilities; and

(iv) the type of operation or operations of the covered entity, including the composition, structure, and functions of the workforce of such entity; the geographic separateness, administrative, or fiscal relationship of the facility or facilities in question to the covered entity.

SEC. 102. DISCRIMINATION.

*(a) GENERAL RULE.—*No covered entity shall discriminate against a qualified individual with a disability because of the disability of such individual in regard to job application procedures, the hiring, advancement, or discharge of employees, employee compensation, job training, and other terms, conditions, and privileges of employment.

*(b) CONSTRUCTION.—*As used in subsection (a), the term "discriminate" includes—

(1) limiting, segregating, or classifying a job applicant or employee in a way that adversely affects the opportunities or status of such applicant or employee because of the disability of such applicant or employee;

(2) participating in a contractual or other arrangement or relationship that has the effect of subjecting a covered entity's qualified applicant or employee with a disability to the discrimination prohibited by this title (such relationship includes a relationship with an employment or referral agency, labor union, an organization providing fringe benefits to an employee of the covered entity, or an organization providing training and apprenticeship programs);

(3) utilizing standards, criteria, or methods of administration—

(A) that have the effect of discrimination on the basis of disability; or
(B) that perpetuate the discrimination of others who are subject to common administrative control;
(4) excluding or otherwise denying equal jobs or benefits to a qualified individual because of the known disability of an individual with whom the qualified individual is known to have a relationship or association;
(5)(A) not making reasonable accommodations to the known physical or mental limitations of an otherwise qualified individual with a disability who is an applicant or employee, unless such covered entity can demonstrate that the accommodation would impose an undue hardship on the operation of the business of such covered entity; or
(B) denying employment opportunities to a job applicant or employee who is an otherwise qualified individual with a disability, if such denial is based on the need of such covered entity to make reasonable accommodation to the physical or mental impairments of the employee or applicant;
(6) using qualification standards, employment tests or other selection criteria that screen out or tend to screen out an individual with a disability or a class of individuals with disabilities unless the standard, test or other selection criteria, as used by the covered entity, is shown to be job-related for the position in question and is consistent with business necessity; and
(7) failing to select and administer tests concerning employment in the most effective manner to ensure that, when such test is administered to a job applicant or employee who has a disability that impairs sensory, manual, or speaking skills, such test results accurately reflect the skills, aptitude, or whatever other factor of such applicant or employee that such test purports to measure, rather than reflecting the impaired sensory, manual, or speaking skills of such employee or applicant (except where such skills are the factors that the test purports to measure).

(c) MEDICAL EXAMINATIONS AND INQUIRIES.—
(1) IN GENERAL.—The prohibition against discrimination as referred to in subsection (a) shall include medical examinations and inquiries.
(2) PREEMPLOYMENT.—
(A) PROHIBITED EXAMINATION OR INQUIRY.—Except as provided in paragraph (3), a covered entity shall not conduct a medical examination or make inquiries of a job applicant as to whether such applicant is an individual with a disability or as to the nature or severity of such disability.
(B) ACCEPTABLE INQUIRY.—A covered entity may make preemployment inquiries into the ability of an applicant to perform job-related functions.
(3) EMPLOYMENT ENTRANCE EXAMINATION.—A covered entity may require a medical examination after an offer of employment has been made to a job applicant and prior to the commencement of the employment duties of such applicant, and

may condition an offer of employment on the results of such examination, if—

    (A) all entering employees are subjected to such an examination regardless of disability;

    (B) information obtained regarding the medical condition or history of the applicant is collected and maintained on separate forms and in separate medical files and is treated as a confidential medical record, except that—

        (i) supervisors and managers may be informed regarding necessary restrictions on the work or duties of the employee and necessary accommodations;

        (ii) first aid and safety personnel may be informed, when appropriate, if the disability might require emergency treatment; and

        (iii) government officials investigating compliance with this Act shall be provided relevant information on request; and

    (C) the results of such examination are used only in accordance with this title.

(4) EXAMINATION AND INQUIRY.—

    (A) PROHIBITED EXAMINATIONS AND INQUIRIES.—A covered entity shall not require a medical examination and shall not make inquiries of an employee as to whether such employee is an individual with a disability or as to the nature or severity of the disability, unless such examination or inquiry is shown to be job-related and consistent with business necessity.

    (B) ACCEPTABLE EXAMINATIONS AND INQUIRIES.—A covered entity may conduct voluntary medical examinations, including voluntary medical histories, which are part of an employee health program available to employees at that work site. A covered entity may make inquiries into the ability of an employee to perform job-related functions.

    (C) REQUIREMENT.—Information obtained under subparagraph (B) regarding the medical condition or history of any employee are subject to the requirements of subparagraphs (B) and (C) of paragraph (3).

SEC. 103. DEFENSES.

(a) IN GENERAL.—It may be a defense to a charge of discrimination under this Act that an alleged application of qualification standards, tests, or selection criteria that screen out or tend to screen out or otherwise deny a job or benefit to an individual with a disability has been shown to be job-related and consistent with business necessity, and such performance cannot be accomplished by reasonable accommodation, as required under this title.

(b) QUALIFICATION STANDARDS.—The term "qualification standards" may include a requirement that an individual shall not pose a direct threat to the health or safety of other individuals in the workplace.

(c) RELIGIOUS ENTITIES.—

    (1) IN GENERAL.—This title shall not prohibit a religious corporation, association, educational institution, or society from giving preference in employment to individuals of a particular

religion to perform work connected with the carrying on by such corporation, association, educational institution, or society of its activities.

(2) RELIGIOUS TENETS REQUIREMENT.—Under this title, a religious organization may require that all applicants and employees conform to the religious tenets of such organization.

(d) LIST OF INFECTIOUS AND COMMUNICABLE DISEASES.—

(1) IN GENERAL.—The Secretary of Health and Human Services, not later than 6 months after the date of enactment of this Act, shall—

(A) review all infectious and communicable diseases which may be transmitted through handling the food supply;

(B) publish a list of infectious and communicable diseases which are transmitted through handling the food supply;

(C) publish the methods by which such diseases are transmitted; and

(D) widely disseminate such information regarding the list of diseases and their modes of transmissability to the general public.

Such list shall be updated annually.

(2) APPLICATIONS.—In any case in which an individual has an infectious or communicable disease that is transmitted to others through the handling of food, that is included on the list developed by the Secretary of Health and Human Services under paragraph (1), and which cannot be eliminated by reasonable accommodation, a covered entity may refuse to assign or continue to assign such individual to a job involving food handling.

(3) CONSTRUCTION.—Nothing in this Act shall be construed to preempt, modify, or amend any State, county, or local law, ordinance, or regulation applicable to food handling which is designed to protect the public health from individuals who pose a significant risk to the health or safety of others, which cannot be eliminated by reasonable accommodation, pursuant to the list of infectious or communicable diseases and the modes of transmissability published by the Secretary of Health and Human Services.

SEC. 104. ILLEGAL USE OF DRUGS AND ALCOHOL.

(a) QUALIFIED INDIVIDUAL WITH A DISABILITY.—For purposes of this title, the term "qualified individual with a disability" shall not include any employee or applicant who is currently engaging in the illegal use of drugs, when the covered entity acts on the basis of such use.

(b) RULES OF CONSTRUCTION.—Nothing in subsection (a) shall be construed to exclude as a qualified individual with a disability an individual who—

(1) has successfully completed a supervised drug rehabilitation program and is no longer engaging in the illegal use of drugs, or has otherwise been rehabilitated successfully and is no longer engaging in such use;

(2) is participating in a supervised rehabilitation program and is no longer engaging in such use; or

(3) is erroneously regarded as engaging in such use, but is not engaging in such use;

except that it shall not be a violation of this Act for a covered entity to adopt or administer reasonable policies or procedures, including but not limited to drug testing, designed to ensure that an individual described in paragraph (1) or (2) is no longer engaging in the illegal use of drugs.

(c) AUTHORITY OF COVERED ENTITY.—A covered entity—

(1) may prohibit the illegal use of drugs and the use alcohol at the workplace by all employees;

(2) may require that employees shall not be under the influence of alcohol or be engaging in the illegal use of drugs at the workplace;

(3) may require that employees behave in conformance with the requirements established under the Drug-Free Workplace Act of 1988 (41 U.S.C. 701 et seq.);

(4) may hold an employee who engages in the illegal use of drugs or who is an alcoholic to the same qualification standards for employment or job performance and behavior that such entity holds other employees, even if any unsatisfactory performance or behavior is related to the drug use or alcoholism of such employee; and

(5) may, with respect to Federal regulations regarding alcohol and the illegal use of drugs, require that—

(A) employees comply with the standards established in such regulations of the Department of Defense, if the employees of the covered entity are employed in an industry subject to such regulations, including complying with regulations (if any) that apply to employment in sensitive positions in such an industry, in the case of employees of the covered entity who are employed in such positions (as defined in the regulations of the Department of Defense);

(B) employees comply with the standards established in such regulations of the Nuclear Regulatory Commission, if the employees of the covered entity are employed in an industry subject to such regulations, including complying with regulations (if any) that apply to employment in sensitive positions in such an industry, in the case of employees of the covered entity who are employed in such positions (as defined in the regulations of the Nuclear Regulatory Commission); and

(C) employees comply with the standards established in such regulations of the Department of Transportation, if the employees of the covered entity are employed in a transportation industry subject to such regulations, including complying with such regulations (if any) that apply to employment in sensitive positions in such an industry, in the case of employees of the covered entity who are employed in such positions (as defined in the regulations of the Department of Transportation).

(d) DRUG TESTING.—

(1) IN GENERAL.—For purposes of this title, a test to determine the illegal use of drugs shall not be considered a medical examination.

(2) CONSTRUCTION.—Nothing in this title shall be construed to encourage, prohibit, or authorize the conducting of drug testing for the illegal use of drugs by job applicants or employees or making employment decisions based on such test results.

(e) TRANSPORTATION EMPLOYEES.—Nothing in this title shall be construed to encourage, prohibit, restrict, or authorize the otherwise lawful exercise by entities subject to the jurisdiction of the Department of Transportation of authority to—

(1) test employees of such entities in, and applicants for, positions involving safety-sensitive duties for the illegal use of drugs and for on-duty impairment by alcohol; and

(2) remove such persons who test positive for illegal use of drugs and on-duty impairment by alcohol pursuant to paragraph (1) from safety-sensitive duties in implementing subsection (c).

SEC. 105. POSTING NOTICES.

Every employer, employment agency, labor organization, or joint labor-management committee covered under this title shall post notices in an accessible format to applicants, employees, and members describing the applicable provisions of this Act, in the manner prescribed by section 711 of the Civil Rights Act of 1964 (42 U.S.C. 2000e-10).

SEC. 106. REGULATIONS.

Not later than 1 year after the date of enactment of this Act, the Commission shall issue regulations in an accessible format to carry out this title in accordance with subchapter II of chapter 5 of title 5, United States Code.

SEC. 107. ENFORCEMENT.

(a) POWERS, REMEDIES, AND PROCEDURES.—The powers, remedies, and procedures set forth in sections 705, 706, 707, 709, and 710 of the Civil Rights Act of 1964 (42 U.S.C. 2000e-4, 2000e-5, 2000e-6, 2000e-8, and 2000e-9) shall be the powers, remedies, and procedures this title provides to the Commission, to the Attorney General, or to any person alleging discrimination on the basis of disability in violation of any provision of this Act, or regulations promulgated under section 106, concerning employment.

(b) COORDINATION.—The agencies with enforcement authority for actions which allege employment discrimination under this title and under the Rehabilitation Act of 1973 shall develop procedures to ensure that administrative complaints filed under this title and under the Rehabilitation Act of 1973 are dealt with in a manner that avoids duplication of effort and prevents imposition of inconsistent or conflicting standards for the same requirements under this title and the Rehabilitation Act of 1973. The Commission, the Attorney General, and the Office of Federal Contract Compliance Programs shall establish such coordinating mechanisms (similar to provisions contained in the joint regulations promulgated by the Commission and the Attorney General at part 42 of title 28 and part 1691 of title 29, Code of Federal Regulations, and the Memorandum

of Understanding between the Commission and the Office of Federal Contract Compliance Programs dated January 16, 1981 (46 Fed. Reg. 7435, January 23, 1981)) in regulations implementing this title and the Rehabilitation Act of 1973 not later than 18 months after the date of enactment of this Act.

SEC. 108. EFFECTIVE DATE.

This title shall become effective 24 months after the date of enactment.

TITLE II—PUBLIC SERVICES

Subtitle A—Prohibition Against Discrimination and Other Generally Applicable Provisions

SEC. 201. DEFINITION.

As used in this title:

(1) PUBLIC ENTITY.—The term "public entity" means—

(A) any State or local government;

(B) any department, agency, special purpose district, or other instrumentality of a State or States or local government; and

(C) the National Railroad Passenger Corporation, and any commuter authority (as defined in section 103(8) of the Rail Passenger Service Act).

(2) QUALIFIED INDIVIDUAL WITH A DISABILITY.—The term "qualified individual with a disability" means an individual with a disability who, with or without reasonable modifications to rules, policies, or practices, the removal of architectural, communication, or transportation barriers, or the provision of auxiliary aids and services, meets the essential eligibility requirements for the receipt of services or the participation in programs or activities provided by a public entity.

SEC. 202. DISCRIMINATION.

Subject to the provisions of this title, no qualified individual with a disability shall, by reason of such disability, be excluded from participation in or be denied the benefits of the services, programs, or activities of a public entity, or be subjected to discrimination by any such entity.

SEC. 203. ENFORCEMENT.

The remedies, procedures, and rights set forth in section 505 of the Rehabilitation Act of 1973 (29 U.S.C. 794a) shall be the remedies, procedures and rights this title provides to any person alleging discrimination on the basis of disability in violation of section 202.

SEC. 204. REGULATIONS.

(a) IN GENERAL.—Not later than 1 year after the date of enactment of this Act, the Attorney General shall promulgate regulations in an accessible format that implement this subtitle. Such regulations shall not include any matter within the scope of the authority of the Secretary of Transportation under section 223, 229, or 244.

(b) RELATIONSHIP TO OTHER REGULATIONS.—Except for "program accessibility, existing facilities", and "communications", regulations under subsection (a) shall be consistent with this Act and with the coordination regulations under part 41 of title 28, Code of Federal Regulations (as promulgated by the Department of Health, Education, and Welfare on January 13, 1978), applicable to recipients of Federal financial assistance under section 504 of the Rehabilitation Act of 1973 (29 U.S.C. 794). With respect to "program accessibility, existing facilities", and "communications", such regulations shall be consistent with regulations and analysis as in part 39 of title 28 of the Code of Federal Regulations, applicable to federally conducted activities under such section 504.

(c) STANDARDS.—Regulations under subsection (a) shall include standards applicable to facilities and vehicles covered by this subtitle, other than facilities, stations, rail passenger cars, and vehicles covered by subtitle B. Such standards shall be consistent with the minimum guidelines and requirements issued by the Architectural and Transportation Barriers Compliance Board in accordance with section 504(a) of this Act.

SEC. 205. EFFECTIVE DATE.

(a) GENERAL RULE.—Except as provided in subsection (b), this subtitle shall become effective 18 months after the date of enactment of this Act.

(b) EXCEPTION.—Section 204 shall become effective on the date of enactment of this Act.

Subtitle B—Actions Applicable to Public Transportation Provided by Public Entities Considered Discriminatory

PART I—PUBLIC TRANSPORTATION OTHER THAN BY AIRCRAFT OR CERTAIN RAIL OPERATIONS

SEC. 221. DEFINITIONS.

As used in this part:

(1) DEMAND RESPONSIVE SYSTEM.—The term "demand responsive system" means any system of providing designated public transportation which is not a fixed route system.

(2) DESIGNATED PUBLIC TRANSPORTATION.—The term "designated public transportation" means transportation (other than public school transportation) by bus, rail, or any other conveyance (other than transportation by aircraft or intercity or commuter rail transportation (as defined in section 241)) that provides the general public with general or special service (including charter service) on a regular and continuing basis.

(3) FIXED ROUTE SYSTEM.—The term "fixed route system" means a system of providing designated public transportation on which a vehicle is operated along a prescribed route according to a fixed schedule.

(4) OPERATES.—The term "operates", as used with respect to a fixed route system or demand responsive system, includes oper-

ation of such system by a person under a contractual or other arrangement or relationship with a public entity.

(5) Public school transportation.—The term "public school transportation" means transportation by schoolbus vehicles of schoolchildren, personnel, and equipment to and from a public elementary or secondary school and school-related activities.

(6) Secretary.—The term "Secretary" means the Secretary of Transportation.

SEC. 222. PUBLIC ENTITIES OPERATING FIXED ROUTE SYSTEMS.

(a) Purchase and Lease of New Vehicles.—It shall be considered discrimination for purposes of section 202 of this Act and section 504 of the Rehabilitation Act of 1973 (29 U.S.C. 794) for a public entity which operates a fixed route system to purchase or lease a new bus, a new rapid rail vehicle, a new light rail vehicle, or any other new vehicle to be used on such system, if the solicitation for such purchase or lease is made after the 30th day following the effective date of this subsection and if such bus, rail vehicle, or other vehicle is not readily accessible to and usable by individuals with disabilities, including individuals who use wheelchairs.

(b) Purchase and Lease of Used Vehicles.—Subject to subsection (c)(1), it shall be considered discrimination for purposes of section 202 of this Act and section 504 of the Rehabilitation Act of 1973 (29 U.S.C. 794) for a public entity which operates a fixed route system to purchase or lease, after the 30th day following the effective date of this subsection, a used vehicle for use on such system unless such entity makes demonstrated good faith efforts to purchase or lease a used vehicle for use on such system that is readily accessible to and usable by individuals with disabilities, including individuals who use wheelchairs.

(c) Remanufactured Vehicles.—

(1) General rule.—Except as provided in paragraph (2), it shall be considered discrimination for purposes of section 202 of this Act and section 504 of the Rehabilitation Act of 1973 (29 U.S.C. 794) for a public entity which operates a fixed route system—

(A) to remanufacture a vehicle for use on such system so as to extend its usable life for 5 years or more, which remanufacture begins (or for which the solicitation is made) after the 30th day following the effective date of this subsection; or

(B) to purchase or lease for use on such system a remanufactured vehicle which has been remanufactured so as to extend its usable life for 5 years or more, which purchase or lease occurs after such 30th day and during the period in which the usable life is extended;

unless, after remanufacture, the vehicle is, to the maximum extent feasible, readily accessible to and usable by individuals with disabilities, including individuals who use wheelchairs.

(2) Exception for historic vehicles.—

(A) General rule.—If a public entity operates a fixed route system any segment of which is included on the National Register of Historic Places and if making a vehicle

of historic character to be used solely on such segment readily accessible to and usable by individuals with disabilities would significantly alter the historic character of such vehicle, the public entity only has to make (or to purchase or lease a remanufactured vehicle with) those modifications which are necessary to meet the requirements of paragraph (1) and which do not significantly alter the historic character of such vehicle.

(B) VEHICLES OF HISTORIC CHARACTER DEFINED BY REGULATIONS.—For purposes of this paragraph and section 228(b), a vehicle of historic character shall be defined by the regulations issued by the Secretary to carry out this subsection.

SEC. 223. PARATRANSIT AS A COMPLEMENT TO FIXED ROUTE SERVICE.

(a) GENERAL RULE.—It shall be considered discrimination for purposes of section 202 of this Act and section 504 of the Rehabilitation Act of 1973 (29 U.S.C. 794) for a public entity which operates a fixed route system (other than a system which provides solely commuter bus service) to fail to provide with respect to the operations of its fixed route system, in accordance with this section, paratransit and other special transportation services to individuals with disabilities, including individuals who use wheelchairs, that are sufficient to provide to such individuals a level of service (1) which is comparable to the level of designated public transportation services provided to individuals without disabilities using such system; or (2) in the case of response time, which is comparable, to the extent practicable, to the level of designated public transportation services provided to individuals without disabilities using such system.

(b) ISSUANCE OF REGULATIONS.—Not later than 1 year after the effective date of this subsection, the Secretary shall issue final regulations to carry out this section.

(c) REQUIRED CONTENTS OF REGULATIONS.—

(1) ELIGIBLE RECIPIENTS OF SERVICE.—The regulations issued under this section shall require each public entity which operates a fixed route system to provide the paratransit and other special transportation services required under this section—

(A)(i) to any individual with a disability who is unable, as a result of a physical or mental impairment (including a vision impairment) and without the assistance of another individual (except an operator of a wheelchair lift or other boarding assistance device), to board, ride, or disembark from any vehicle on the system which is readily accessible to and usable by individuals with disabilities;

(ii) to any individual with a disability who needs the assistance of a wheelchair lift or other boarding assistance device (and is able with such assistance) to board, ride, and disembark from any vehicle which is readily accessible to and usable by individuals with disabilities if the individual wants to travel on a route on the system during the hours of operation of the system at a time (or within a reasonable period of such time) when such a vehicle is not being used to provide designated public transportation on the route; and

(iii) to any individual with a disability who has a specific impairment-related condition which prevents such individual from traveling to a boarding location or from a disembarking location on such system;

(B) to 1 other individual accompanying the individual with the disability; and

(C) to other individuals, in addition to the one individual described in subparagraph (B), accompanying the individual with a disability provided that space for these additional individuals is available on the paratransit vehicle carrying the individual with a disability and that the transportation of such additional individuals will not result in a denial of service to individuals with disabilities.

For purposes of clauses (i) and (ii) of subparagraph (A), boarding or disembarking from a vehicle does not include travel to the boarding location or from the disembarking location.

(2) SERVICE AREA.—The regulations issued under this section shall require the provision of paratransit and special transportation services required under this section in the service area of each public entity which operates a fixed route system, other than any portion of the service area in which the public entity solely provides commuter bus service.

(3) SERVICE CRITERIA.—Subject to paragraphs (1) and (2), the regulations issued under this section shall establish minimum service criteria for determining the level of services to be required under this section.

(4) UNDUE FINANCIAL BURDEN LIMITATION.—The regulations issued under this section shall provide that, if the public entity is able to demonstrate to the satisfaction of the Secretary that the provision of paratransit and other special transportation services otherwise required under this section would impose an undue financial burden on the public entity, notwithstanding any other provision of this section (other than paragraph (5)), shall only be required to provide such services to the extent that providing such services would not impose such a burden.

(5) ADDITIONAL SERVICES.—The regulations issued under this section shall establish circumstances under which the Secretary may require a public entity to provide, notwithstanding paragraph (4), paratransit and other special transportation services under this section beyond the level of paratransit and other special transportation services which would otherwise be required under paragraph (4).

(6) PUBLIC PARTICIPATION.—The regulations issued under this section shall require that each public entity which operates a fixed route system hold a public hearing, provide an opportunity for public comment, and consult with individuals with disabilities in preparing its plan under paragraph (7).

(7) PLANS.—The regulations issued under this section shall require that each public entity which operates a fixed route system—

(A) within 18 months after the effective date of this subsection, submit to the Secretary, and commence implementation of, a plan for providing paratransit and other spe-

cial *transportation services which meets the requirements of this section; and*

(B) on an annual basis thereafter, submit to the Secretary, and commence implementation of, a plan for providing such services.

(8) PROVISION OF SERVICES BY OTHERS.—*The regulations issued under this section shall—*

(A) require that a public entity submitting a plan to the Secretary under this section identify in the plan any person or other public entity which is providing a paratransit or other special transportation service for individuals with disabilities in the service area to which the plan applies; and

(B) provide that the public entity submitting the plan does not have to provide under the plan such service for individuals with disabilities.

(9) OTHER PROVISIONS.—*The regulations issued under this section shall include such other provisions and requirements as the Secretary determines are necessary to carry out the objectives of this section.*

(d) REVIEW OF PLAN.—

(1) GENERAL RULE.—*The Secretary shall review a plan submitted under this section for the purpose of determining whether or not such plan meets the requirements of this section, including the regulations issued under this section.*

(2) DISAPPROVAL.—*If the Secretary determines that a plan reviewed under this subsection fails to meet the requirements of this section, the Secretary shall disapprove the plan and notify the public entity which submitted the plan of such disapproval and the reasons therefor.*

(3) MODIFICATION OF DISAPPROVED PLAN.—*Not later than 90 days after the date of disapproval of a plan under this subsection, the public entity which submitted the plan shall modify the plan to meet the requirements of this section and shall submit to the Secretary, and commence implementation of, such modified plan.*

(e) DISCRIMINATION DEFINED.—*As used in subsection (a), the term "discrimination" includes—*

(1) a failure of a public entity to which the regulations issued under this section apply to submit, or commence implementation of, a plan in accordance with subsections (c)(6) and (c)(7);

(2) a failure of such entity to submit, or commence implementation of, a modified plan in accordance with subsection (d)(3);

(3) submission to the Secretary of a modified plan under subsection (d)(3) which does not meet the requirements of this section; or

(4) a failure of such entity to provide paratransit or other special transportation services in accordance with the plan or modified plan the public entity submitted to the Secretary under this section.

(f) STATUTORY CONSTRUCTION.—*Nothing in this section shall be construed as preventing a public entity—*

(1) from providing paratransit or other special transportation services at a level which is greater than the level of such services which are required by this section,

(2) from providing paratransit or other special transportation services in addition to those paratransit and special transportation services required by this section, or

(3) from providing such services to individuals in addition to those individuals to whom such services are required to be provided by this section.

SEC. 224. PUBLIC ENTITY OPERATING A DEMAND RESPONSIVE SYSTEM.

If a public entity operates a demand responsive system, it shall be considered discrimination, for purposes of section 202 of this Act and section 504 of the Rehabilitation Act of 1973 (29 U.S.C. 794), for such entity to purchase or lease a new vehicle for use on such system, for which a solicitation is made after the 30th day following the effective date of this section, that is not readily accessible to and usable by individuals with disabilities, including individuals who use wheelchairs, unless such system, when viewed in its entirety, provides a level of service to such individuals equivalent to the level of service such system provides to individuals without disabilities.

SEC. 225. TEMPORARY RELIEF WHERE LIFTS ARE UNAVAILABLE.

(a) GRANTING.—With respect to the purchase of new buses, a public entity may apply for, and the Secretary may temporarily relieve such public entity from the obligation under section 222(a) or 224 to purchase new buses that are readily accessible to and usable by individuals with disabilities if such public entity demonstrates to the satisfaction of the Secretary—

(1) that the initial solicitation for new buses made by the public entity specified that all new buses were to be lift-equipped and were to be otherwise accessible to and usable by individuals with disabilities;

(2) the unavailability from any qualified manufacturer of hydraulic, electromechanical, or other lifts for such new buses;

(3) that the public entity seeking temporary relief has made good faith efforts to locate a qualified manufacturer to supply the lifts to the manufacturer of such buses in sufficient time to comply with such solicitation; and

(4) that any further delay in purchasing new buses necessary to obtain such lifts would significantly impair transportation services in the community served by the public entity.

(b) DURATION AND NOTICE TO CONGRESS.—Any relief granted under subsection (a) shall be limited in duration by a specified date, and the appropriate committees of Congress shall be notified of any such relief granted.

(c) FRAUDULENT APPLICATION.—If, at any time, the Secretary has reasonable cause to believe that any relief granted under subsection (a) was fraudulently applied for, the Secretary shall—

(1) cancel such relief if such relief is still in effect; and

(2) take such other action as the Secretary considers appropriate.

SEC. 226. NEW FACILITIES.

For purposes of section 202 of this Act and section 504 of the Rehabilitation Act of 1973 (29 U.S.C. 794), it shall be considered discrimination for a public entity to construct a new facility to be used in the provision of designated public transportation services unless such facility is readily accessible to and usable by individuals with disabilities, including individuals who use wheelchairs.

SEC. 227. ALTERATIONS OF EXISTING FACILITIES.

(a) GENERAL RULE.—With respect to alterations of an existing facility or part thereof used in the provision of designated public transportation services that affect or could affect the usability of the facility or part thereof, it shall be considered discrimination, for purposes of section 202 of this Act and section 504 of the Rehabilitation Act of 1973 (29 U.S.C. 794), for a public entity to fail to make such alterations (or to ensure that the alterations are made) in such a manner that, to the maximum extent feasible, the altered portions of the facility are readily accessible to and usable by individuals with disabilities, including individuals who use wheelchairs, upon the completion of such alterations. Where the public entity is undertaking an alteration that affects or could affect usability of or access to an area of the facility containing a primary function, the entity shall also make the alterations in such a manner that, to the maximum extent feasible, the path of travel to the altered area and the bathrooms, telephones, and drinking fountains serving the altered area, are readily accessible to and usable by individuals with disabilities, including individuals who use wheelchairs, upon completion of such alterations, where such alterations to the path of travel or the bathrooms, telephones, and drinking fountains serving the altered area are not disproportionate to the overall alterations in terms of cost and scope (as determined under criteria established by the Attorney General).

(b) SPECIAL RULE FOR STATIONS.—

(1) GENERAL RULE.—For purposes of section 202 of this Act and section 504 of the Rehabilitation Act of 1973 (29 U.S.C. 794), it shall be considered discrimination for a public entity that provides designated public transportation to fail, in accordance with the provisions of this subsection, to make key stations (as determined under criteria established by the Secretary by regulation) in rapid rail and light rail systems readily accessible to and usable by individuals with disabilities, including individuals who use wheelchairs.

(2) RAPID RAIL AND LIGHT RAIL KEY STATIONS.—

(A) ACCESSIBILITY.—Except as otherwise provided in this paragraph, all key stations (as determined under criteria established by the Secretary by regulation) in rapid rail and light rail systems shall be made readily accessible to and usable by individuals with disabilities, including individuals who use wheelchairs, as soon as practicable but in no event later than the last day of the 3-year period beginning on the effective date of this paragraph.

(B) EXTENSION FOR EXTRAORDINARILY EXPENSIVE STRUCTURAL CHANGES.—The Secretary may extend the 3-year period under subparagraph (A) up to a 30-year period for *key stations in a rapid rail or light rail system which stations need extraordinarily expensive structural changes to, or replacement of, existing facilities; except that by the last day of the 20th year following the date of the enactment of this Act at least ⅔ of such key stations must be readily accessible to and usable by individuals with disabilities.*

(3) PLANS AND MILESTONES.—The Secretary shall require the appropriate public entity to develop and submit to the Secretary a plan for compliance with this subsection—

(A) that reflects consultation with individuals with disabilities affected by such plan and the results of a public hearing and public comments on such plan, and

(B) that establishes milestones for achievement of the requirements of this subsection.

SEC. 228. PUBLIC TRANSPORTATION PROGRAMS AND ACTIVITIES IN EXISTING FACILITIES AND ONE CAR PER TRAIN RULE.

(a) PUBLIC TRANSPORTATION PROGRAMS AND ACTIVITIES IN EXISTING FACILITIES.—

(1) IN GENERAL.—With respect to existing facilities used in the provision of designated public transportation services, it shall be considered discrimination, for purposes of section 202 of this Act and section 504 of the Rehabilitation Act of 1973 (29 U.S.C. 794), for a public entity to fail to operate a designated public transportation program or activity conducted in such facilities so that, when viewed in the entirety, the program or activity is readily accessible to and usable by individuals with disabilities.

(2) EXCEPTION.—Paragraph (1) shall not require a public entity to make structural changes to existing facilities in order to make such facilities accessible to individuals who use wheelchairs, unless and to the extent required by section 227(a) (relating to alterations) or section 227(b) (relating to key stations).

(3) UTILIZATION.—Paragraph (1) shall not require a public entity to which paragraph (2) applies, to provide to individuals who use wheelchairs services made available to the general public at such facilities when such individuals could not utilize or benefit from such services provided at such facilities.

(b) ONE CAR PER TRAIN RULE.—

(1) GENERAL RULE.—Subject to paragraph (2), with respect to 2 or more vehicles operated as a train by a light or rapid rail system, for purposes of section 202 of this Act and section 504 of the Rehabilitation Act of 1973 (29 U.S.C. 794), it shall be considered discrimination for a public entity to fail to have at least 1 vehicle per train that is accessible to individuals with disabilities, including individuals who use wheelchairs, as soon as practicable but in no event later than the last day of the 5-year period beginning on the effective date of this section.

(2) HISTORIC TRAINS.—In order to comply with paragraph (1) with respect to the remanufacture of a vehicle of historic character which is to be used on a segment of a light or rapid rail system which is included on the National Register of Historic Places, if making such vehicle readily accessible to and usable by individuals with disabilities would significantly alter the

historic character of such vehicle, the public entity which operates such system only has to make (or to purchase or lease a remanufactured vehicle with) those modifications which are necessary to meet the requirements of section 222(c)(1) and which do not significantly alter the historic character of such vehicle.

SEC. 229. REGULATIONS.

(a) IN GENERAL.—*Not later than 1 year after the date of enactment of this Act, the Secretary of Transportation shall issue regulations, in an accessible format, necessary for carrying out this part (other than section 223).*

(b) STANDARDS.—*The regulations issued under this section and section 223 shall include standards applicable to facilities and vehicles covered by this subtitle. The standards shall be consistent with the minimum guidelines and requirements issued by the Architectural and Transportation Barriers Compliance Board in accordance with section 504 of this Act.*

SEC. 230. INTERIM ACCESSIBILITY REQUIREMENTS.

If final regulations have not been issued pursuant to section 229, for new construction or alterations for which a valid and appropriate State or local building permit is obtained prior to the issuance of final regulations under such section, and for which the construction or alteration authorized by such permit begins within one year of the receipt of such permit and is completed under the terms of such permit, compliance with the Uniform Federal Accessibility Standards in effect at the time the building permit is issued shall suffice to satisfy the requirement that facilities be readily accessible to and usable by persons with disabilities as required under sections 226 and 227, except that, if such final regulations have not been issued one year after the Architectural and Transportation Barriers Compliance Board has issued the supplemental minimum guidelines required under section 504(a) of this Act, compliance with such supplemental minimum guidelines shall be necessary to satisfy the requirement that facilities be readily accessible to and usable by persons with disabilities prior to issuance of the final regulations.

SEC. 231. EFFECTIVE DATE.

(a) GENERAL RULE.—*Except as provided in subsection (b), this part shall become effective 18 months after the date of enactment of this Act.*

(b) EXCEPTION.—*Sections 222, 223 (other than subsection (a)), 224, 225, 227(b), 228(b), and 229 shall become effective on the date of enactment of this Act.*

PART II—PUBLIC TRANSPORTATION BY INTERCITY AND COMMUTER RAIL

SEC. 241. DEFINITIONS.

As used in this part:

(1) COMMUTER AUTHORITY.—*The term "commuter authority" has the meaning given such term in section 103(8) of the Rail Passenger Service Act (45 U.S.C. 502(8)).*

(2) COMMUTER RAIL TRANSPORTATION.—*The term "commuter rail transportation" has the meaning given the term "commuter*

service" in section 103(9) of the Rail Passenger Service Act (45 U.S.C. 502(9)).

(3) INTERCITY RAIL TRANSPORTATION.—The term "intercity rail transportation" means transportation provided by the National Railroad Passenger Corporation.

(4) RAIL PASSENGER CAR.—The term "rail passenger car" means, with respect to intercity rail transportation, single-level and bi-level coach cars, single-level and bi-level dining cars, single-level and bi-level sleeping cars, single-level and bi-level lounge cars, and food service cars.

(5) RESPONSIBLE PERSON.—The term "responsible person" means—

> *(A) in the case of a station more than 50 percent of which is owned by a public entity, such public entity;*

> *(B) in the case of a station more than 50 percent of which is owned by a private party, the persons providing intercity or commuter rail transportation to such station, as allocated on an equitable basis by regulation by the Secretary of Transportation; and*

> *(C) in a case where no party owns more than 50 percent of a station, the persons providing intercity or commuter rail transportation to such station and the owners of the station, other than private party owners, as allocated on an equitable basis by regulation by the Secretary of Transportation.*

(6) STATION.—The term "station" means the portion of a property located appurtenant to a right-of-way on which intercity or commuter rail transportation is operated, where such portion is used by the general public and is related to the provision of such transportation, including passenger platforms, designated waiting areas, ticketing areas, restrooms, and, where a public entity providing rail transportation owns the property, concession areas, to the extent that such public entity exercises control over the selection, design, construction, or alteration of the property, but such term does not include flag stops.

SEC. 242. INTERCITY AND COMMUTER RAIL ACTIONS CONSIDERED DISCRIMINATORY.

(a) INTERCITY RAIL TRANSPORTATION.—

> *(1) ONE CAR PER TRAIN RULE.—It shall be considered discrimination for purposes of section 202 of this Act and section 504 of the Rehabilitation Act of 1973 (29 U.S.C. 794) for a person who provides intercity rail transportation to fail to have at least one passenger car per train that is readily accessible to and usable by individuals with disabilities, including individuals who use wheelchairs, in accordance with regulations issued under section 244, as soon as practicable, but in no event later than 5 years after the date of enactment of this Act.*

> *(2) NEW INTERCITY CARS.—*

>> *(A) GENERAL RULE.—Except as otherwise provided in this subsection with respect to individuals who use wheelchairs, it shall be considered discrimination for purposes of section 202 of this Act and section 504 of the Rehabilitation Act of 1973 (29 U.S.C. 794) for a person to purchase or lease any*

new rail passenger cars for use in intercity rail transportation, and for which a solicitation is made later than 30 days after the effective date of this section, unless all such rail cars are readily accessible to and usable by individuals with disabilities, including individuals who use wheelchairs, as prescribed by the Secretary of Transportation in regulations issued under section 244.

(B) SPECIAL RULE FOR SINGLE-LEVEL PASSENGER COACHES FOR INDIVIDUALS WHO USE WHEELCHAIRS.—*Single-level passenger coaches shall be required to—*

(i) *be able to be entered by an individual who uses a wheelchair;*

(ii) *have space to park and secure a wheelchair;*

(iii) *have a seat to which a passenger in a wheelchair can transfer, and a space to fold and store such passenger's wheelchair; and*

(iv) *have a restroom usable by an individual who uses a wheelchair,*

only to the extent provided in paragraph (3).

(C) SPECIAL RULE FOR SINGLE-LEVEL DINING CARS FOR INDIVIDUALS WHO USE WHEELCHAIRS.—*Single-level dining cars shall not be required to—*

(i) *be able to be entered from the station platform by an individual who uses a wheelchair; or*

(ii) *have a restroom usable by an individual who uses a wheelchair if no restroom is provided in such car for any passenger.*

(D) SPECIAL RULE FOR BI-LEVEL DINING CARS FOR INDIVIDUALS WHO USE WHEELCHAIRS.—*Bi-level dining cars shall not be required to—*

(i) *be able to be entered by an individual who uses a wheelchair;*

(ii) *have space to park and secure a wheelchair;*

(iii) *have a seat to which a passenger in a wheelchair can transfer, or a space to fold and store such passenger's wheelchair; or*

(iv) *have a restroom usable by an individual who uses a wheelchair.*

(3) ACCESSIBILITY OF SINGLE-LEVEL COACHES.—

(A) GENERAL RULE.—*It shall be considered discrimination for purposes of section 202 of this Act and section 504 of the Rehabilitation Act of 1973 (29 U.S.C. 794) for a person who provides intercity rail transportation to fail to have on each train which includes one or more single-level rail passenger coaches—*

(i) *a number of spaces—*

(I) *to park and secure wheelchairs (to accommodate individuals who wish to remain in their wheelchairs) equal to not less than one-half of the number of single-level rail passenger coaches in such train; and*

(II) *to fold and store wheelchairs (to accommodate individuals who wish to transfer to coach*

seats) equal to not less than one-half of the
number of single-level rail passenger coaches in
such train,
as soon as practicable, but in no event later than 5
years after the date of enactment of this Act; and
    (ii) a number of spaces—
        (I) to park and secure wheelchairs (to accommo-
date individuals who wish to remain in their
wheelchairs) equal to not less than the total
number of single-level rail passenger coaches in
such train; and
        (II) to fold and store wheelchairs (to accommo-
date individuals who wish to transfer to coach
seats) equal to not less than the total number of
single-level rail passenger coaches in such train,
as soon as practicable, but in no event later than 10 years
after the date of enactment of this Act.
    (B) LOCATION.—Spaces required by subparagraph (A)
shall be located in single-level rail passenger coaches or
food service cars.
    (C) LIMITATION.—Of the number of spaces required on a
train by subparagraph (A), not more than two spaces to
park and secure wheelchairs nor more than two spaces to
fold and store wheelchairs shall be located in any one
coach or food service car.
    (D) OTHER ACCESSIBILITY FEATURES.—Single-level rail
passenger coaches and food service cars on which the spaces
required by subparagraph (A) are located shall have a restroom usable by an individual who uses a wheelchair and
shall be able to be entered from the station platform by an
individual who uses a wheelchair.
(4) FOOD SERVICE.—
  , (A) SINGLE-LEVEL DINING CARS.—On any train in which a
single-level dining car is used to provide food service—
    (i) if such single-level dining car was purchased after
the date of enactment of this Act, table service in such
car shall be provided to a passenger who uses a wheelchair if—
        (I) the car adjacent to the end of the dining car
through which a wheelchair may enter is itself accessible to a wheelchair;
        (II) such passenger can exit to the platform from
the car such passenger occupies, move down the
platform, and enter the adjacent accessible car described in subclause (I) without the necessity of the
train being moved within the station; and
        (III) space to park and secure a wheelchair is
available in the dining car at the time such passenger wishes to eat (if such passenger wishes to
remain in a wheelchair), or space to store and fold
a wheelchair is available in the dining car at the
time such passenger wishes to eat (if such passenger wishes to transfer to a dining car seat); and

(ii) appropriate auxiliary aids and services, including a hard surface on which to eat, shall be provided to ensure that other equivalent food service is available to individuals with disabilities, including individuals who use wheelchairs, and to passengers traveling with such individuals.

Unless not practicable, a person providing intercity rail transportation shall place an accessible car adjacent to the end of a dining car described in clause (i) through which an individual who uses a wheelchair may enter.

(B) BI-LEVEL DINING CARS.—On any train in which a bi-level dining car is used to provide food service—

(i) if such train includes a bi-level lounge car purchased after the date of enactment of this Act, table service in such lounge car shall be provided to individuals who use wheelchairs and to other passengers; and

(ii) appropriate auxiliary aids and services, including a hard surface on which to eat, shall be provided to ensure that other equivalent food service is available to individuals with disabilities, including individuals who use wheelchairs, and to passengers traveling with such individuals.

(b) COMMUTER RAIL TRANSPORTATION.—

(1) ONE CAR PER TRAIN RULE.—It shall be considered discrimination for purposes of section 202 of this Act and section 504 of the Rehabilitation Act of 1973 (29 U.S.C. 794) for a person who provides commuter rail transportation to fail to have at least one passenger car per train that is readily accessible to and usable by individuals with disabilities, including individuals who use wheelchairs, in accordance with regulations issued under section 244, as soon as practicable, but in no event later than 5 years after the date of enactment of this Act.

(2) NEW COMMUTER RAIL CARS.—

(A) GENERAL RULE.—It shall be considered discrimination for purposes of section 202 of this Act and section 504 of the Rehabilitation Act of 1973 (29 U.S.C. 794) for a person to purchase or lease any new rail passenger cars for use in commuter rail transportation, and for which a solicitation is made later than 30 days after the effective date of this section, unless all such rail cars are readily accessible to and usable by individuals with disabilities, including individuals who use wheelchairs, as prescribed by the Secretary of Transportation in regulations issued under section 244.

(B) ACCESSIBILITY.—For purposes of section 202 of this Act and section 504 of the Rehabilitation Act of 1973 (29 U.S.C. 794), a requirement that a rail passenger car used in commuter rail transportation be accessible to or readily accessible to and usable by individuals with disabilities, including individuals who use wheelchairs, shall not be construed to require—

(i) a restroom usable by an individual who uses a wheelchair if no restroom is provided in such car for any passenger;

      (ii) space to fold and store a wheelchair; or

      (iii) a seat to which a passenger who uses a wheelchair can transfer.

  (c) USED RAIL CARS.—*It shall be considered discrimination for purposes of section 202 of this Act and section 504 of the Rehabilitation Act of 1973 (29 U.S.C. 794) for a person to purchase or lease a used rail passenger car for use in intercity or commuter rail transportation, unless such person makes demonstrated good faith efforts to purchase or lease a used rail car that is readily accessible to and usable by individuals with disabilities, including individuals who use wheelchairs, as prescribed by the Secretary of Transportation in regulations issued under section 244.*

  (d) REMANUFACTURED RAIL CARS.—

    (1) REMANUFACTURING.—*It shall be considered discrimination for purposes of section 202 of this Act and section 504 of the Rehabilitation Act of 1973 (29 U.S.C. 794) for a person to remanufacture a rail passenger car for use in intercity or commuter rail transportation so as to extend its usable life for 10 years or more, unless the rail car, to the maximum extent feasible, is made readily accessible to and usable by individuals with disabilities, including individuals who use wheelchairs, as prescribed by the Secretary of Transportation in regulations issued under section 244.*

    (2) PURCHASE OR LEASE.—*It shall be considered discrimination for purposes of section 202 of this Act and section 504 of the Rehabilitation Act of 1973 (29 U.S.C. 794) for a person to purchase or lease a remanufactured rail passenger car for use in intercity or commuter rail transportation unless such car was remanufactured in accordance with paragraph (1).*

  (e) STATIONS.—

    (1) NEW STATIONS.—*It shall be considered discrimination for purposes of section 202 of this Act and section 504 of the Rehabilitation Act of 1973 (29 U.S.C. 794) for a person to build a new station for use in intercity or commuter rail transportation that is not readily accessible to and usable by individuals with disabilities, including individuals who use wheelchairs, as prescribed by the Secretary of Transportation in regulations issued under section 244.*

    (2) EXISTING STATIONS.—

      (A) FAILURE TO MAKE READILY ACCESSIBLE.—

        (i) GENERAL RULE.—*It shall be considered discrimination for purposes of section 202 of this Act and section 504 of the Rehabilitation Act of 1973 (29 U.S.C. 794) for a responsible person to fail to make existing stations in the intercity rail transportation system, and existing key stations in commuter rail transportation systems, readily accessible to and usable by individuals with disabilities, including individuals who use wheelchairs, as prescribed by the Secretary of Transportation in regulations issued under section 244.*

        (ii) PERIOD FOR COMPLIANCE.—

          (I) INTERCITY RAIL.—*All stations in the intercity rail transportation system shall be made readily accessible to and usable by individuals with dis-*

abilities, including individuals who use wheelchairs, as soon as practicable, but in no event later than 20 years after the date of enactment of this Act.

(II) COMMUTER RAIL.—Key stations in commuter rail transportation systems shall be made readily accessible to and usable by individuals with disabilities, including individuals who use wheelchairs, as soon as practicable but in no event later than 3 years after the date of enactment of this Act, except that the time limit may be extended by the Secretary of Transportation up to 20 years after the date of enactment of this Act in a case where the raising of the entire passenger platform is the only means available of attaining accessibility or where other extraordinarily expensive structural changes are necessary to attain accessibility.

(iii) DESIGNATION OF KEY STATIONS.—Each commuter authority shall designate the key stations in its commuter rail transportation system, in consultation with individuals with disabilities and organizations representing such individuals, taking into consideration such factors as high ridership and whether such station serves as a transfer or feeder station. Before the final designation of key stations under this clause, a commuter authority shall hold a public hearing.

(iv) PLANS AND MILESTONES.—The Secretary of Transportation shall require the appropriate person to develop a plan for carrying out this subparagraph that reflects consultation with individuals with disabilities affected by such plan and that establishes milestones for achievement of the requirements of this subparagraph.

(B) REQUIREMENT WHEN MAKING ALTERATIONS.—

(i) GENERAL RULE.—It shall be considered discrimination, for purposes of section 202 of this Act and section 504 of the Rehabilitation Act of 1973 (29 U.S.C. 794), with respect to alterations of an existing station or part thereof in the intercity or commuter rail transportation systems that affect or could affect the usability of the station or part thereof, for the responsible person, owner, or person in control of the station to fail to make the alterations in such a manner that, to the maximum extent feasible, the altered portions of the station are readily accessible to and usable by individuals with disabilities, including individuals who use wheelchairs, upon completion of such alterations.

(ii) ALTERATIONS TO A PRIMARY FUNCTION AREA.—It shall be considered discrimination, for purposes of section 202 of this Act and section 504 of the Rehabilitation Act of 1973 (29 U.S.C. 794), with respect to alterations that affect or could affect the usability of or access to an area of the station containing a primary function, for the responsible person, owner, or person in

control of the station to fail to make the alterations in such a manner that, to the maximum extent feasible, the path of travel to the altered area, and the bathrooms, telephones, and drinking fountains serving the altered area, are readily accessible to and usable by individuals with disabilities, including individuals who use wheelchairs, upon completion of such alterations, where such alterations to the path of travel or the bathrooms, telephones, and drinking fountains serving the altered area are not disproportionate to the overall alterations in terms of cost and scope (as determined under criteria established by the Attorney General).

(C) REQUIRED COOPERATION.—It shall be considered discrimination for purposes of section 202 of this Act and section 504 of the Rehabilitation Act of 1973 (29 U.S.C. 794) for an owner, or person in control, of a station governed by subparagraph (A) or (B) to fail to provide reasonable cooperation to a responsible person with respect to such station in that responsible person's efforts to comply with such subparagraph. An owner, or person in control, of a station shall be liable to a responsible person for any failure to provide reasonable cooperation as required by this subparagraph. Failure to receive reasonable cooperation required by this subparagraph shall not be a defense to a claim of discrimination under this Act.

SEC. 243. CONFORMANCE OF ACCESSIBILITY STANDARDS.

Accessibility standards included in regulations issued under this part shall be consistent with the minimum guidelines issued by the Architectural and Transportation Barriers Compliance Board under section 504(a) of this Act.

SEC. 244. REGULATIONS.

Not later than 1 year after the date of enactment of this Act, the Secretary of Transportation shall issue regulations, in an accessible format, necessary for carrying out this part.

SEC. 245. INTERIM ACCESSIBILITY REQUIREMENTS.

(a) STATIONS.—If final regulations have not been issued pursuant to section 244, for new construction or alterations for which a valid and appropriate State or local building permit is obtained prior to the issuance of final regulations under such section, and for which the construction or alteration authorized by such permit begins within one year of the receipt of such permit and is completed under the terms of such permit, compliance with the Uniform Federal Accessibility Standards in effect at the time the building permit is issued shall suffice to satisfy the requirement that stations be readily accessible to and usable by persons with disabilities as required under section 242(e), except that, if final regulations have not been issued one year after the Architectural and Transportation Barriers Compliance Board has issued the supplemental minimum guidelines required under section 504(a) of this Act, compliance with such supplemental minimum guidelines shall be necessary to satisfy the requirement that stations be readily accessible to and *usable by persons with disabilities prior to issuance of the final regulations.*

(b) RAIL PASSENGER CARS.—*If final regulations have not been issued pursuant to section 244, a person shall be considered to have complied with the requirements of section 242(a) through (d) that a rail passenger car be readily accessible to and usable by individuals with disabilities, if the design for such car complies with the laws and regulations (including the Minimum Guidelines and Requirements for Accessible Design and such supplemental minimum guidelines as are issued under section 504(a) of this Act) governing accessibility of such cars, to the extent that such laws and regulations are not inconsistent with this part and are in effect at the time such design is substantially completed.*

SEC. 246. EFFECTIVE DATE.

(a) GENERAL RULE.—*Except as provided in subsection (b), this part shall become effective 18 months after the date of enactment of this Act.*

(b) EXCEPTION.—*Sections 242 and 244 shall become effective on the date of enactment of this Act.*

TITLE III—PUBLIC ACCOMMODATIONS AND SERVICES OPERATED BY PRIVATE ENTITIES

SEC. 301. DEFINITIONS.

As used in this title:

(1) COMMERCE.—*The term "commerce" means travel, trade, traffic, commerce, transportation, or communication—*

(A) *among the several States;*

(B) *between any foreign country or any territory or possession and any State; or*

(C) *between points in the same State but through another State or foreign country.*

(2) COMMERCIAL FACILITIES.—*The term "commercial facilities" means facilities—*

(A) *that are intended for nonresidential use; and*

(B) *whose operations will affect commerce.*

Such term shall not include railroad locomotives, railroad freight cars, railroad cabooses, railroad cars described in section 242 or covered under this title, railroad rights-of-way, or facilities that are covered or expressly exempted from coverage under the Fair Housing Act of 1968 (42 U.S.C. 3601 et seq.).

(3) DEMAND RESPONSIVE SYSTEM.—*The term "demand responsive system" means any system of providing transportation of individuals by a vehicle, other than a system which is a fixed route system.*

(4) FIXED ROUTE SYSTEM.—*The term "fixed route system" means a system of providing transportation of individuals (other than by aircraft) on which a vehicle is operated along a prescribed route according to a fixed schedule.*

(5) OVER-THE-ROAD BUS.—The term "over-the-road bus" means a bus characterized by an elevated passenger deck located over a baggage compartment.

(6) PRIVATE ENTITY.—The term "private entity" means any entity other than a public entity (as defined in section 201(1)).

(7) PUBLIC ACCOMMODATION.—The following private entities are considered public accommodations for purposes of this title, if the operations of such entities affect commerce—

(A) an inn, hotel, motel, or other place of lodging, except for an establishment located within a building that contains not more than five rooms for rent or hire and that is actually occupied by the proprietor of such establishment as the residence of such proprietor;

(B) a restaurant, bar, or other establishment serving food or drink;

(C) a motion picture house, theater, concert hall, stadium, or other place of exhibition or entertainment;

(D) an auditorium, convention center, lecture hall, or other place of public gathering;

(E) a bakery, grocery store, clothing store, hardware store, shopping center, or other sales or rental establishment;

(F) a laundromat, dry-cleaner, bank, barber shop, beauty shop, travel service, shoe repair service, funeral parlor, gas station, office of an accountant or lawyer, pharmacy, insurance office, professional office of a health care provider, hospital, or other service establishment;

(G) a terminal, depot, or other station used for specified public transportation;

(H) a museum, library, gallery, or other place of public display or collection;

(I) a park, zoo, amusement park, or other place of recreation;

(J) a nursery, elementary, secondary, undergraduate, or postgraduate private school, or other place of education;

(K) a day care center, senior citizen center, homeless shelter, food bank, adoption agency, or other social service center establishment; and

(L) a gymnasium, health spa, bowling alley, golf course, or other place of exercise or recreation.

(8) RAIL AND RAILROAD.—The terms "rail" and "railroad" have the meaning given the term "railroad" in section 202(e) of the Federal Railroad Safety Act of 1970 (45 U.S.C. 431(e)).

(9) READILY ACHIEVABLE.—The term "readily achievable" means easily accomplishable and able to be carried out without much difficulty or expense. In determining whether an action is readily achievable, factors to be considered include—

(A) the nature and cost of the action needed under this Act;

(B) the overall financial resources of the facility or facilities involved in the action; the number of persons employed at such facility; the effect on expenses and resources, or the impact otherwise of such action upon the operation of the facility;

(C) *the overall financial resources of the covered entity; the overall size of the business of a covered entity with respect to the number of its employees; the number, type, and location of its facilities; and*

(D) *the type of operation or operations of the covered entity, including the composition, structure, and functions of the workforce of such entity; the geographic separateness, administrative or fiscal relationship of the facility or facilities in question to the covered entity.*

(10) SPECIFIED PUBLIC TRANSPORTATION.—*The term "specified public transportation" means transportation by bus, rail, or any other conveyance (other than by aircraft) that provides the general public with general or special service (including charter service) on a regular and continuing basis.*

(11) VEHICLE.—*The term "vehicle" does not include a rail passenger car, railroad locomotive, railroad freight car, railroad caboose, or a railroad car described in section 242 or covered under this title.*

SEC. 302. PROHIBITION OF DISCRIMINATION BY PUBLIC ACCOMMODATIONS.

(a) GENERAL RULE.—*No individual shall be discriminated against on the basis of disability in the full and equal enjoyment of the goods, services, facilities, privileges, advantages, or accommodations of any place of public accommodation by any person who owns, leases (or leases to), or operates a place of public accommodation.*

(b) CONSTRUCTION.—
   (1) GENERAL PROHIBITION.—
       (A) ACTIVITIES.—
           (i) DENIAL OF PARTICIPATION.—*It shall be discriminatory to subject an individual or class of individuals on the basis of a disability or disabilities of such individual or class, directly, or through contractual, licensing, or other arrangements, to a denial of the opportunity of the individual or class to participate in or benefit from the goods, services, facilities, privileges, advantages, or accommodations of an entity.*
           (ii) PARTICIPATION IN UNEQUAL BENEFIT.—*It shall be discriminatory to afford an individual or class of individuals, on the basis of a disability or disabilities of such individual or class, directly, or through contractual, licensing, or other arrangements with the opportunity to participate in or benefit from a good, service, facility, privilege, advantage, or accommodation that is not equal to that afforded to other individuals.*
           (iii) SEPARATE BENEFIT.—*It shall be discriminatory to provide an individual or class of individuals, on the basis of a disability or disabilities of such individual or class, directly, or through contractual, licensing, or other arrangements with a good, service, facility, privilege, advantage, or accommodation that is different or separate from that provided to other individuals, unless such action is necessary to provide the individual or class of individuals with a good, service, facili-*

ty, privilege, advantage, or accommodation, or other opportunity that is as effective as that provided to others.

(iv) INDIVIDUAL OR CLASS OF INDIVIDUALS.—For purposes of clauses (i) through (iii) of this subparagraph, the term "individual or class of individuals" refers to the clients or customers of the covered public accommodation that enters into the contractual, licensing or other arrangement.

(B) INTEGRATED SETTINGS.—Goods, services, facilities, privileges, advantages, and accommodations shall be afforded to an individual with a disability in the most integrated setting appropriate to the needs of the individual.

(C) OPPORTUNITY TO PARTICIPATE.—Notwithstanding the existence of separate or different programs or activities provided in accordance with this section, an individual with a disability shall not be denied the opportunity to participate in such programs or activities that are not separate or different.

(D) ADMINISTRATIVE METHODS.—An individual or entity shall not, directly or through contractual or other arrangements, utilize standards or criteria or methods of administration—

(i) that have the effect of discriminating on the basis of disability; or

(ii) that perpetuate the discrimination of others who are subject to common administrative control.

(E) ASSOCIATION.—It shall be discriminatory to exclude or otherwise deny equal goods, services, facilities, privileges, advantages, accommodations, or other opportunities to an individual or entity because of the known disability of an individual with whom the individual or entity is known to have a relationship or association.

(2) SPECIFIC PROHIBITIONS.—

(A) DISCRIMINATION.—For purposes of subsection (a), discrimination includes—

(i) the imposition or application of eligibility criteria that screen out or tend to screen out an individual with a disability or any class of individuals with disabilities from fully and equally enjoying any goods, services, facilities, privileges, advantages, or accommodations, unless such criteria can be shown to be necessary for the provision of the goods, services, facilities, privileges, advantages, or accommodations being offered;

(ii) a failure to make reasonable modifications in policies, practices, or procedures, when such modifications are necessary to afford such goods, services, facilities, privileges, advantages, or accommodations to individuals with disabilities, unless the entity can demonstrate that making such modifications would fundamentally alter the nature of such goods, services, facilities, privileges, advantages, or accommodations;

(iii) a failure to take such steps as may be necessary to ensure that no individual with a disability is ex-

cluded, denied services, segregated or otherwise treated differently than other individuals because of the absence of auxiliary aids and services, unless the entity can demonstrate that taking such steps would fundamentally alter the nature of the good, service, facility, privilege, advantage, or accommodation being offered or would result in an undue burden;

(iv) a failure to remove architectural barriers, and communication barriers that are structural in nature, in existing facilities, and transportation barriers in existing vehicles and rail passenger cars used by an establishment for transporting individuals (not including barriers that can only be removed through the retrofitting of vehicles or rail passenger cars by the installation of a hydraulic or other lift), where such removal is readily achievable; and

(v) where an entity can demonstrate that the removal of a barrier under clause (iv) is not readily achievable, a failure to make such goods, services, facilities, privileges, advantages, or accommodations available through alternative methods if such methods are readily achievable.

(B) FIXED ROUTE SYSTEM.—

(i) ACCESSIBILITY.—It shall be considered discrimination for a private entity which operates a fixed route system and which is not subject to section 304 to purchase or lease a vehicle with a seating capacity in excess of 16 passengers (including the driver) for use on such system, for which a solicitation is made after the 30th day following the effective date of this subparagraph, that is not readily accessible to and usable by individuals with disabilities, including individuals who use wheelchairs.

(ii) EQUIVALENT SERVICE.—If a private entity which operates a fixed route system and which is not subject to section 304 purchases or leases a vehicle with a seating capacity of 16 passengers or less (including the driver) for use on such system after the effective date of this subparagraph that is not readily accessible to or usable by individuals with disabilities, it shall be considered discrimination for such entity to fail to operate such system so that, when viewed in its entirety, such system ensures a level of service to individuals with disabilities, including individuals who use wheelchairs, equivalent to the level of service provided to individuals without disabilities.

(C) DEMAND RESPONSIVE SYSTEM.—For purposes of subsection (a), discrimination includes—

(i) a failure of a private entity which operates a demand responsive system and which is not subject to section 304 to operate such system so that, when viewed in its entirety, such system ensures a level of service to individuals with disabilities, including individuals

who use wheelchairs, equivalent to the level of service
provided to individuals without disabilities; and

(ii) the purchase or lease by such entity for use on
such system of a vehicle with a seating capacity in
excess of 16 passengers (including the driver), for which
solicitations are made after the 30th day following the
effective date of this subparagraph, that is not readily
accessible to and usable by individuals with disabilities (including individuals who use wheelchairs)
unless such entity can demonstrate that such system,
when viewed in its entirety, provides a level of service
to individuals with disabilities equivalent to that provided to individuals without disabilities.

(D) OVER-THE-ROAD BUSES.—

*(i) LIMITATION ON APPLICABILITY.—Subparagraphs
(B) and (C) do not apply to over-the-road buses.*

*(ii) ACCESSIBILITY REQUIREMENTS.—For purposes of
subsection (a), discrimination includes (I) the purchase
or lease of an over-the-road bus which does not comply
with the regulations issued under section 306(a)(2) by a
private entity which provides transportation of individuals and which is not primarily engaged in the business of transporting people, and (II) any other failure
of such entity to comply with such regulations.*

*(3) SPECIFIC CONSTRUCTION.—Nothing in this title shall re-
quire an entity to permit an individual to participate in or benefit from the goods, services, facilities, privileges, advantages
and accommodations of such entity where such individual poses
a direct threat to the health or safety of others. The term
"direct threat" means a significant risk to the health or safety
of others that cannot be eliminated by a modification of policies, practices, or procedures or by the provision of auxiliary
aids or services.*

**SEC. 303. NEW CONSTRUCTION AND ALTERATIONS IN PUBLIC ACCOMMODA-
TIONS AND COMMERCIAL FACILITIES.**

*(a) APPLICATION OF TERM.—Except as provided in subsection (b),
as applied to public accommodations and commercial facilities, discrimination for purposes of section 302(a) includes—*

*(1) a failure to design and construct facilities for first occu-
pancy later than 30 months after the date of enactment of this
Act that are readily accessible to and usable by individuals
with disabilities, except where an entity can demonstrate that it
is structurally impracticable to meet the requirements of such
subsection in accordance with standards set forth or incorporated by reference in regulations issued under this title; and*

*(2) with respect to a facility or part thereof that is altered by,
on behalf of, or for the use of an establishment in a manner
that affects or could affect the usability of the facility or part
thereof, a failure to make alterations in such a manner that, to
the maximum extent feasible, the altered portions of the facility
are readily accessible to and usable by individuals with disabilities, including individuals who use wheelchairs. Where the
entity is undertaking an alteration that affects or could affect*

usability of or access to an area of the facility containing a primary function, the entity shall also make the alterations in such a manner that, to the maximum extent feasible, the path of travel to the altered area and the bathrooms, telephones, and drinking fountains serving the altered area, are readily accessible to and usable by individuals with disabilities where such alterations to the path of travel or the bathrooms, telephones, and drinking fountains serving the altered area are not disproportionate to the overall alterations in terms of cost and scope (as determined under criteria established by the Attorney General).

(b) ELEVATOR.—Subsection (a) shall not be construed to require the installation of an elevator for facilities that are less than three stories or have less than 3,000 square feet per story unless the building is a shopping center, a shopping mall, or the professional office of a health care provider or unless the Attorney General determines that a particular category of such facilities requires the installation of elevators based on the usage of such facilities.

SEC. 304. PROHIBITION OF DISCRIMINATION IN SPECIFIED PUBLIC TRANSPORTATION SERVICES PROVIDED BY PRIVATE ENTITIES.

(a) GENERAL RULE.—No individual shall be discriminated against on the basis of disability in the full and equal enjoyment of specified public transportation services provided by a private entity that is primarily engaged in the business of transporting people and whose operations affect commerce.

(b) CONSTRUCTION.—For purposes of subsection (a), discrimination includes—

(1) the imposition or application by a entity described in subsection (a) of eligibility criteria that screen out or tend to screen out an individual with a disability or any class of individuals with disabilities from fully enjoying the specified public transportation services provided by the entity, unless such criteria can be shown to be necessary for the provision of the services being offered;

(2) the failure of such entity to—

(A) make reasonable modifications consistent with those required under section 302(b)(2)(A)(ii);

(B) provide auxiliary aids and services consistent with the requirements of section 302(b)(2)(A)(iii); and

(C) remove barriers consistent with the requirements of section 302(b)(2)(A) and with the requirements of section 303(a)(2);

(3) the purchase or lease by such entity of a new vehicle (other than an automobile, a van with a seating capacity of less than 8 passengers, including the driver, or an over-the-road bus) which is to be used to provide specified public transportation and for which a solicitation is made after the 30th day following the effective date of this section, that is not readily accessible to and usable by individuals with disabilities, including individuals who use wheelchairs; except that the new vehicle need not be readily accessible to and usable by such individuals if the new vehicle is to be used solely in a demand responsive system and if the entity can demonstrate that such system,

when viewed in its entirety, provides a level of service to such individuals equivalent to the level of service provided to the general public;

(4)(A) the purchase or lease by such entity of an over-the-road bus which does not comply with the regulations issued under section 306(a)(2); and

(B) any other failure of such entity to comply with such regulations; and

(5) the purchase or lease by such entity of a new van with a seating capacity of less than 8 passengers, including the driver, which is to be used to provide specified public transportation and for which a solicitation is made after the 30th day following the effective date of this section that is not readily accessible to or usable by individuals with disabilities, including individuals who use wheelchairs; except that the new van need not be readily accessible to and usable by such individuals if the entity can demonstrate that the system for which the van is being purchased or leased, when viewed in its entirety, provides a level of service to such individuals equivalent to the level of service provided to the general public;

(6) the purchase or lease by such entity of a new rail passenger car that is to be used to provide specified public transportation, and for which a solicitation is made later than 30 days after the effective date of this paragraph, that is not readily accessible to and usable by individuals with disabilities, including individuals who use wheelchairs; and

(7) the remanufacture by such entity of a rail passenger car that is to be used to provide specified public transportation so as to extend its usable life for 10 years or more, or the purchase or lease by such entity of such a rail car, unless the rail car, to the maximum extent feasible, is made readily accessible to and usable by individuals with disabilities, including individuals who use wheelchairs.

(c) HISTORICAL OR ANTIQUATED CARS.—

(1) EXCEPTION.—To the extent that compliance with subsection (b)(2)(C) or (b)(7) would significantly alter the historic or antiquated character of a historical or antiquated rail passenger car, or a rail station served exclusively by such cars, or would result in violation of any rule, regulation, standard, or order issued by the Secretary of Transportation under the Federal Railroad Safety Act of 1970, such compliance shall not be required.

(2) DEFINITION.—As used in this subsection, the term "historical or antiquated rail passenger car" means a rail passenger car—

(A) which is not less than 30 years old at the time of its use for transporting individuals;

(B) the manufacturer of which is no longer in the business of manufacturing rail passenger cars; and

(C) which—

(i) has a consequential association with events or persons significant to the past; or

(ii) embodies, or is being restored to embody, the distinctive characteristics of a type of rail passenger car

used in the past, or to represent a time period which has passed.

SEC. 305. STUDY.

(a) PURPOSES.—The Office of Technology Assessment shall undertake a study to determine—

(1) the access needs of individuals with disabilities to over-the-road buses and over-the-road bus service; and

(2) the most cost-effective methods for providing access to over-the-road buses and over-the-road bus service to individuals with disabilities, particularly individuals who use wheelchairs, through all forms of boarding options.

(b) CONTENTS.—The study shall include, at a minimum, an analysis of the following:

(1) The anticipated demand by individuals with disabilities for accessible over-the-road buses and over-the-road bus service.

(2) The degree to which such buses and service, including any service required under sections 304(b)(4) and 306(a)(2), are readily accessible to and usable by individuals with disabilities.

(3) The effectiveness of various methods of providing accessibility to such buses and service to individuals with disabilities.

(4) The cost of providing accessible over-the-road buses and bus service to individuals with disabilities, including consideration of recent technological and cost saving developments in equipment and devices.

(5) Possible design changes in over-the-road buses that could enhance accessibility, including the installation of accessible restrooms which do not result in a loss of seating capacity.

(6) The impact of accessibility requirements on the continuation of over-the-road bus service, with particular consideration of the impact of such requirements on such service to rural communities.

(c) ADVISORY COMMITTEE.—In conducting the study required by subsection (a), the Office of Technology Assessment shall establish an advisory committee, which shall consist of—

(1) members selected from among private operators and manufacturers of over-the-road buses;

(2) members selected from among individuals with disabilities, particularly individuals who use wheelchairs, who are potential riders of such buses; and

(3) members selected for their technical expertise on issues included in the study, including manufacturers of boarding assistance equipment and devices.

The number of members selected under each of paragraphs (1) and (2) shall be equal, and the total number of members selected under paragraphs (1) and (2) shall exceed the number of members selected under paragraph (3).

(d) DEADLINE.—The study required by subsection (a), along with recommendations by the Office of Technology Assessment, including any policy options for legislative action, shall be submitted to the President and Congress within 36 months after the date of the enactment of this Act. If the President determines that compliance with the regulations issued pursuant to section 306(a)(2)(B) on or before the applicable deadlines specified in section 306(a)(2)(B) will

result in a significant reduction in intercity over-the-road bus serv-ice, the President shall extend each such deadline by 1 year.

(e) REVIEW.—In developing the study required by subsection (a), the Office of Technology Assessment shall provide a preliminary draft of such study to the Architectural and Transportation Barriers Compliance Board established under section 502 of the Rehabilitation Act of 1973 (29 U.S.C. 792). The Board shall have an opportunity to comment on such draft study, and any such comments by the Board made in writing within 120 days after the Board's receipt of the draft study shall be incorporated as part of the final study required to be submitted under subsection (d).

SEC. 306. REGULATIONS.

(a) TRANSPORTATION PROVISIONS.—

(1) GENERAL RULE.—Not later than 1 year after the date of the enactment of this Act, the Secretary of Transportation shall issue regulations in an accessible format to carry out sections 302(b)(2)(B) and (C) and to carry out section 304 (other than subsection (b)(4)).

(2) SPECIAL RULES FOR PROVIDING ACCESS TO OVER-THE-ROAD BUSES.—

(A) INTERIM REQUIREMENTS—

(i) ISSUANCE.—Not later than 1 year after the date of the enactment of this Act, the Secretary of Transportation shall issue regulations in an accessible format to carry out sections 304(b)(4) and 302(b)(2)(D)(ii) that require each private entity which uses an over-the-road bus to provide transportation of individuals to provide accessibility to such bus; except that such regulations shall not require any structural changes in over-the-road buses in order to provide access to individuals who use wheelchairs during the effective period of such regulations and shall not require the purchase of boarding assistance devices to provide access to such individuals.

(ii) EFFECTIVE PERIOD.—The regulations issued pursuant to this subparagraph shall be effective until the effective date of the regulations issued under subparagraph (B).

(B) FINAL REQUIREMENT.—

(i) REVIEW OF STUDY AND INTERIM REQUIREMENTS.—The Secretary shall review the study submitted under section 305 and the regulations issued pursuant to subparagraph (A).

(ii) ISSUANCE.—Not later than 1 year after the date of the submission of the study under section 305, the Secretary shall issue in an accessible format new regulations to carry out sections 304(b)(4) and 302(b)(2)(D)(ii) that require, taking into account the purposes of the study under section 305 and any recommendations resulting from such study, each private entity which uses an over-the-road bus to provide transportation to individuals to provide accessibility to such bus to individ-

uals with disabilities, including individuals who use wheelchairs.

(iii) EFFECTIVE PERIOD.—Subject to section 305(d), the regulations issued pursuant to this subparagraph shall take effect—

(I) with respect to small providers of transportation (as defined by the Secretary), 7 years after the date of the enactment of this Act; and

(II) with respect to other providers of transportation, 6 years after such date of enactment.

(C) LIMITATION ON REQUIRING INSTALLATION OF ACCESSIBLE RESTROOMS.—The regulations issued pursuant to this paragraph shall not require the installation of accessible restrooms in over-the-road buses if such installation would result in a loss of seating capacity.

(3) STANDARDS.—The regulations issued pursuant to this subsection shall include standards applicable to facilities and vehicles covered by sections 302(b)(2) and 304.

(b) OTHER PROVISIONS.—Not later than 1 year after the date of the enactment of this Act, the Attorney General shall issue regulations in an accessible format to carry out the provisions of this title not referred to in subsection (a) that include standards applicable to facilities and vehicles covered under section 302.

(c) CONSISTENCY WITH ATBCB GUIDELINES.—Standards included in regulations issued under subsections (a) and (b) shall be consistent with the minimum guidelines and requirements issued by the Architectural and Transportation Barriers Compliance Board in accordance with section 504 of this Act.

(d) INTERIM ACCESSIBILITY STANDARDS.—

(1) FACILITIES.—If final regulations have not been issued pursuant to this section, for new construction or alterations for which a valid and appropriate State or local building permit is obtained prior to the issuance of final regulations under this section, and for which the construction or alteration authorized by such permit begins within one year of the receipt of such permit and is completed under the terms of such permit, compliance with the Uniform Federal Accessibility Standards in effect at the time the building permit is issued shall suffice to satisfy the requirement that facilities be readily accessible to and usable by persons with disabilities as required under section 303, except that, if such final regulations have not been issued one year after the Architectural and Transportation Barriers Compliance Board has issued the supplemental minimum guidelines required under section 504(a) of this Act, compliance with such supplemental minimum guidelines shall be necessary to satisfy the requirement that facilities be readily accessible to and usable by persons with disabilities prior to issuance of the final regulations.

(2) VEHICLES AND RAIL PASSENGER CARS.—If final regulations have not been issued pursuant to this section, a private entity shall be considered to have complied with the requirements of this title, if any, that a vehicle or rail passenger car be readily accessible to and usable by individuals with disabilities, if the design for such vehicle or car complies with the laws and regu-

lations (including the Minimum Guidelines and Requirements for Accessible Design and such supplemental minimum guidelines as are issued under section 504(a) of this Act) governing accessibility of such vehicles or cars, to the extent that such laws and regulations are not inconsistent with this title and are in effect at the time such design is substantially completed.

SEC. 307. EXEMPTIONS FOR PRIVATE CLUBS AND RELIGIOUS ORGANIZATIONS.

The provisions of this title shall not apply to private clubs or establishments exempted from coverage under title II of the Civil Rights Act of 1964 (42 U.S.C. 2000-a(e)) or to religious organizations or entities controlled by religious organizations, including places of worship.

SEC. 308. ENFORCEMENT.

(a) IN GENERAL.—

(1) AVAILABILITY OF REMEDIES AND PROCEDURES.—The remedies and procedures set forth in section 204(a) of the Civil Rights Act of 1964 (42 U.S.C. 2000a-3(a)) are the remedies and procedures this title provides to any person who is being subjected to discrimination on the basis of disability in violation of this title or who has reasonable grounds for believing that such person is about to be subjected to discrimination in violation of section 303. Nothing in this section shall require a person with a disability to engage in a futile gesture if such person has actual notice that a person or organization covered by this title does not intend to comply with its provisions.

(2) INJUNCTIVE RELIEF.—In the case of violations of section 302(b)(2)(A)(iv) and section 303(a), injunctive relief shall include an order to alter facilities to make such facilities readily accessible to and usable by individuals with disabilities to the extent required by this title. Where appropriate, injunctive relief shall also include requiring the provision of an auxiliary aid or service, modification of a policy, or provision of alternative methods, to the extent required by this title.

(b) ENFORCEMENT BY THE ATTORNEY GENERAL.—

(1) DENIAL OF RIGHTS.—

(A) DUTY TO INVESTIGATE.—

(i) IN GENERAL.—The Attorney General shall investigate alleged violations of this title, and shall undertake periodic reviews of compliance of covered entities under this title.

(ii) ATTORNEY GENERAL CERTIFICATION.—On the application of a State or local government, the Attorney General may, in consultation with the Architectural and Transportation Barriers Compliance Board, and after prior notice and a public hearing at which persons, including individuals with disabilities, are provided an opportunity to testify against such certification, certify that a State law or local building code or similar ordinance that establishes accessibility requirements meets or exceeds the minimum requirements of this Act for the accessibility and usability of covered facilities under this title. At any enforcement proceed-

ing under this section, such certification by the Attorney General shall be rebuttable evidence that such State law or local ordinance does meet or exceed the minimum requirements of this Act.

(B) POTENTIAL VIOLATION.—If the Attorney General has reasonable cause to believe that—

(i) any person or group of persons is engaged in a pattern or practice of discrimination under this title; or

(ii) any person or group of persons has been discriminated against under this title and such discrimination raises an issue of general public importance,

the Attorney General may commence a civil action in any appropriate United States district court.

(2) AUTHORITY OF COURT.—In a civil action under paragraph (1)(B), the court—

(A) may grant any equitable relief that such court considers to be appropriate, including, to the extent required by this title—

(i) granting temporary, preliminary, or permanent relief;

(ii) providing an auxiliary aid or service, modification of policy, practice, or procedure, or alternative method; and

(iii) making facilities readily accessible to and usable by individuals with disabilities;

(B) may award such other relief as the court considers to be appropriate, including monetary damages to persons aggrieved when requested by the Attorney General; and

(C) may, to vindicate the public interest, assess a civil penalty against the entity in an amount—

(i) not exceeding $50,000 for a first violation; and

(ii) not exceeding $100,000 for any subsequent violation.

(3) SINGLE VIOLATION.—For purposes of paragraph (2)(C), in determining whether a first or subsequent violation has occurred, a determination in a single action, by judgment or settlement, that the covered entity has engaged in more than one discriminatory act shall be counted as a single violation.

(4) PUNITIVE DAMAGES.—For purposes of subsection (b)(2)(B), the term "monetary damages" and "such other relief" does not include punitive damages.

(5) JUDICIAL CONSIDERATION.—In a civil action under paragraph (1)(B), the court, when considering what amount of civil penalty, if any, is appropriate, shall give consideration to any good faith effort or attempt to comply with this Act by the entity. In evaluating good faith, the court shall consider, among other factors it deems relevant, whether the entity could have reasonably anticipated the need for an appropriate type of auxiliary aid needed to accommodate the unique needs of a particular individual with a disability.

SEC. 309. EXAMINATIONS AND COURSES.

Any person that offers examinations or courses related to applications, licensing, certification, or credentialing for secondary or post-

secondary education, professional, or trade purposes shall offer such examinations or courses in a place and manner accessible to persons with disabilities or offer alternative accessible arrangements for such individuals.

SEC. 310. EFFECTIVE DATE.

(a) GENERAL RULE.—Except as provided in subsections (b) and (c), this title shall become effective 18 months after the date of the enactment of this Act.

(b) CIVIL ACTIONS.—Except for any civil action brought for a violation of section 303, no civil action shall be brought for any act or omission described in section 302 which occurs—

(1) during the first 6 months after the effective date, against businesses that employ 25 or fewer employees and have gross receipts of $1,000,000 or less; and

(2) during the first year after the effective date, against businesses that employ 10 or fewer employees and have gross receipts of $500,000 or less.

(c) EXCEPTION.—Sections 302(a) for purposes of section 302(b)(2)(B) and (C) only, 304(a) for purposes of section 304(b)(3) only, 304(b)(3), 305, and 306 shall take effect on the date of the enactment of this Act.

TITLE IV—TELECOMMUNICATIONS

SEC. 401. TELECOMMUNICATIONS RELAY SERVICES FOR HEARING-IMPAIRED AND SPEECH-IMPAIRED INDIVIDUALS.

(a) TELECOMMUNICATIONS.—Title II of the Communications Act of 1934 (47 U.S.C. 201 et seq.) is amended by adding at the end thereof the following new section:

"SEC. 225. TELECOMMUNICATIONS SERVICES FOR HEARING-IMPAIRED AND SPEECH-IMPAIRED INDIVIDUALS.

"(a) DEFINITIONS.—As used in this section—

"(1) COMMON CARRIER OR CARRIER.—The term 'common carrier' or 'carrier' includes any common carrier engaged in interstate communication by wire or radio as defined in section 3(h) and any common carrier engaged in intrastate communication by wire or radio, notwithstanding sections 2(b) and 221(b).

"(2) TDD.—The term 'TDD' means a Telecommunications Device for the Deaf, which is a machine that employs graphic communication in the transmission of coded signals through a wire or radio communication system.

"(3) TELECOMMUNICATIONS RELAY SERVICES.—The term 'telecommunications relay services' means telephone transmission services that provide the ability for an individual who has a hearing impairment or speech impairment to engage in communication by wire or radio with a hearing individual in a manner that is functionally equivalent to the ability of an individual who does not have a hearing impairment or speech impairment to communicate using voice communication services by wire or radio. Such term includes services that enable two-way communication between an individual who uses a TDD or

other nonvoice terminal device and an individual who does not use such a device.

"*(b) AVAILABILITY OF TELECOMMUNICATIONS RELAY SERVICES.—*

"*(1) IN GENERAL.—In order to carry out the purposes established under section 1, to make available to all individuals in the United States a rapid, efficient nationwide communication service, and to increase the utility of the telephone system of the Nation, the Commission shall ensure that interstate and intrastate telecommunications relay services are available, to the extent possible and in the most efficient manner, to hearing-impaired and speech-impaired individuals in the United States.*

"*(2) USE OF GENERAL AUTHORITY AND REMEDIES.—For the purposes of administering and enforcing the provisions of this section and the regulations prescribed thereunder, the Commission shall have the same authority, power, and functions with respect to common carriers engaged in intrastate communication as the Commission has in administering and enforcing the provisions of this title with respect to any common carrier engaged in interstate communication. Any violation of this section by any common carrier engaged in intrastate communication shall be subject to the same remedies, penalties, and procedures as are applicable to a violation of this Act by a common carrier engaged in interstate communication.*

"*(c) PROVISION OF SERVICES.—Each common carrier providing telephone voice transmission services shall, not later than 3 years after the date of enactment of this section, provide in compliance with the regulations prescribed under this section, throughout the area in which it offers service, telecommunications relay services, individually, through designees, through a competitively selected vendor, or in concert with other carriers. A common carrier shall be considered to be in compliance with such regulations—*

"*(1) with respect to intrastate telecommunications relay services in any State that does not have a certified program under subsection (f) and with respect to interstate telecommunications relay services, if such common carrier (or other entity through which the carrier is providing such relay services) is in compliance with the Commission's regulations under subsection (d); or*

"*(2) with respect to intrastate telecommunications relay services in any State that has a certified program under subsection (f) for such State, if such common carrier (or other entity through which the carrier is providing such relay services) is in compliance with the program certified under subsection (f) for such State.*

"*(d) REGULATIONS.—*

"*(1) IN GENERAL.—The Commission shall, not later than 1 year after the date of enactment of this section, prescribe regulations to implement this section, including regulations that—*

"*(A) establish functional requirements, guidelines, and operations procedures for telecommunications relay services;*

"*(B) establish minimum standards that shall be met in carrying out subsection (c);*

"*(C) require that telecommunications relay services operate every day for 24 hours per day;*

"*(D) require that users of telecommunications relay services pay rates no greater than the rates paid for functionally equivalent voice communication services with respect to such factors as the duration of the call, the time of day, and the distance from point of origination to point of termination;*

"*(E) prohibit relay operators from failing to fulfill the obligations of common carriers by refusing calls or limiting the length of calls that use telecommunications relay services;*

"*(F) prohibit relay operators from disclosing the content of any relayed conversation and from keeping records of the content of any such conversation beyond the duration of the call; and*

"*(G) prohibit relay operators from intentionally altering a relayed conversation.*

"*(2) TECHNOLOGY.—The Commission shall ensure that regulations prescribed to implement this section encourage, consistent with section 7(a) of this Act, the use of existing technology and do not discourage or impair the development of improved technology.*

"*(3) JURISDICTIONAL SEPARATION OF COSTS.—*

"*(A) IN GENERAL.—Consistent with the provisions of section 410 of this Act, the Commission shall prescribe regulations governing the jurisdictional separation of costs for the services provided pursuant to this section.*

"*(B) RECOVERING COSTS.—Such regulations shall generally provide that costs caused by interstate telecommunications relay services shall be recovered from all subscribers for every interstate service and costs caused by intrastate telecommunications relay services shall be recovered from the intrastate jurisdiction. In a State that has a certified program under subsection (f), a State commission shall permit a common carrier to recover the costs incurred in providing intrastate telecommunications relay services by a method consistent with the requirements of this section.*

"*(e) ENFORCEMENT.—*

"*(1) IN GENERAL.—Subject to subsections (f) and (g), the Commission shall enforce this section.*

"*(2) COMPLAINT.—The Commission shall resolve, by final order, a complaint alleging a violation of this section within 180 days after the date such complaint is filed.*

"*(f) CERTIFICATION.—*

"*(1) STATE DOCUMENTATION.—Any State desiring to establish a State program under this section shall submit documentation to the Commission that describes the program of such State for implementing intrastate telecommunications relay services and the procedures and remedies available for enforcing any requirements imposed by the State program.*

"*(2) REQUIREMENTS FOR CERTIFICATION.—After review of such documentation, the Commission shall certify the State program if the Commission determines that—*

"*(A) the program makes available to hearing-impaired and speech-impaired individuals, either directly, through designees, through a competitively selected vendor, or through regulation of intrastate common carriers, intrastate telecommunications relay services in such State in a manner that meets or exceeds the requirements of regulations prescribed by the Commission under subsection (d); and*

"(B) the program makes available adequate procedures and remedies for enforcing the requirements of the State program.

"(3) METHOD OF FUNDING.—Except as provided in subsection (d), the Commission shall not refuse to certify a State program based solely on the method such State will implement for funding intrastate telecommunication relay services.

"(4) SUSPENSION OR REVOCATION OF CERTIFICATION.—The Commission may suspend or revoke such certification if, after notice and opportunity for hearing, the Commission determines that such certification is no longer warranted. In a State whose program has been suspended or revoked, the Commission shall take such steps as may be necessary, consistent with this section, to ensure continuity of telecommunications relay services.

"(g) COMPLAINT.—

"(1) REFERRAL OF COMPLAINT.—If a complaint to the Commission alleges a violation of this section with respect to intrastate telecommunications relay services within a State and certification of the program of such State under subsection (f) is in effect, the Commission shall refer such complaint to such State.

"(2) JURISDICTION OF COMMISSION.—After referring a complaint to a State under paragraph (1), the Commission shall exercise jurisdiction over such complaint only if—

"(A) final action under such State program has not been taken on such complaint by such State—

"(i) within 180 days after the complaint is filed with such State; or

"(ii) within a shorter period as prescribed by the regulations of such State; or

"(B) the Commission determines that such State program is no longer qualified for certification under subsection (f).".

(b) CONFORMING AMENDMENTS.—The Communications Act of 1934 (47 U.S.C. 151 et seq.) is amended—

(1) in section 2(b) (47 U.S.C. 152(b)), by striking "section 224" and inserting "sections 224 and 225"; and

(2) in section 221(b) (47 U.S.C. 221(b)), by striking "section 301" and inserting "sections 225 and 301".

SEC. 402. CLOSED-CAPTIONING OF PUBLIC SERVICE ANNOUNCEMENTS.

Section 711 of the Communications Act of 1934 is amended to read as follows:

"SEC. 711. CLOSED-CAPTIONING OF PUBLIC SERVICE ANNOUNCEMENTS.

"Any television public service announcement that is produced or funded in whole or in part by any agency or instrumentality of Federal government shall include closed captioning of the verbal content of such announcement. A television broadcast station licensee—

"*(1) shall not be required to supply closed captioning for any such announcement that fails to include it; and*

"*(2) shall not be liable for broadcasting any such announcement without transmitting a closed caption unless the licensee intentionally fails to transmit the closed caption that was included with the announcement.*".

TITLE V—MISCELLANEOUS PROVISIONS

SEC. 501. CONSTRUCTION.

(a) IN GENERAL.—Except as otherwise provided in this Act, nothing in this Act shall be construed to apply a lesser standard than the standards applied under title V of the Rehabilitation Act of 1973 (29 U.S.C. 790 et seq.) or the regulations issued by Federal agencies pursuant to such title.

(b) RELATIONSHIP TO OTHER LAWS.—Nothing in this Act shall be construed to invalidate or limit the remedies, rights, and procedures of any Federal law or law of any State or political subdivision of any State or jurisdiction that provides greater or equal protection for the rights of individuals with disabilities than are afforded by this Act. Nothing in this Act shall be construed to preclude the prohibition of, or the imposition of restrictions on, smoking in places of employment covered by title I, in transportation covered by title II or III, or in places of public accommodation covered by title III.

(c) INSURANCE.—Titles I through IV of this Act shall not be construed to prohibit or restrict—

(1) an insurer, hospital or medical service company, health maintenance organization, or any agent, or entity that administers benefit plans, or similar organizations from underwriting risks, classifying risks, or administering such risks that are based on or not inconsistent with State law; or

(2) a person or organization covered by this Act from establishing, sponsoring, observing or administering the terms of a bona fide benefit plan that are based on underwriting risks, classifying risks, or administering such risks that are based on or not inconsistent with State law; or

(3) a person or organization covered by this Act from establishing, sponsoring, observing or administering the terms of a bona fide benefit plan that is not subject to State laws that regulate insurance.

Paragraphs (1), (2), and (3) shall not be used as a subterfuge to evade the purposes of title I and III.

(d) ACCOMMODATIONS AND SERVICES.—Nothing in this Act shall be construed to require an individual with a disability to accept an accommodation, aid, service, opportunity, or benefit which such individual chooses not to accept.

SEC. 502. STATE IMMUNITY.

A State shall not be immune under the eleventh amendment to the Constitution of the United States from an action in Federal or State court of competent jurisdiction for a violation of this Act. In any action against a State for a violation of the requirements of this Act, remedies (including remedies both at law and in equity) are available for such a violation to the same extent as such remedies are available for such a violation in an action against any public or private entity other than a State.

SEC. 503. PROHIBITION AGAINST RETALIATION AND COERCION.

(a) RETALIATION.—*No person shall discriminate against any individual because such individual has opposed any act or practice made unlawful by this Act or because such individual made a charge, testified, assisted, or participated in any manner in an investigation, proceeding, or hearing under this Act.*

(b) INTERFERENCE, COERCION, OR INTIMIDATION.—*It shall be unlawful to coerce, intimidate, threaten, or interfere with any individual in the exercise or enjoyment of, or on account of his or her having exercised or enjoyed, or on account of his or her having aided or encouraged any other individual in the exercise or enjoyment of, any right granted or protected by this Act.*

(c) REMEDIES AND PROCEDURES.—*The remedies and procedures available under sections 107, 203, and 308 of this Act shall be available to aggrieved persons for violations of subsections (a) and (b), with respect to title I, title II and title III, respectively.*

SEC. 504. REGULATIONS BY THE ARCHITECTURAL AND TRANSPORTATION BARRIERS COMPLIANCE BOARD.

(a) ISSUANCE OF GUIDELINES.—*Not later than 9 months after the date of enactment of this Act, the Architectural and Transportation Barriers Compliance Board shall issue minimum guidelines that shall supplement the existing Minimum Guidelines and Requirements for Accessible Design for purposes of titles II and III of this Act.*

(b) CONTENTS OF GUIDELINES.—*The supplemental guidelines issued under subsection (a) shall establish additional requirements, consistent with this Act, to ensure that buildings, facilities, rail passenger cars, and vehicles are accessible, in terms of architecture and design, transportation, and communication, to individuals with disabilities.*

(c) QUALIFIED HISTORIC PROPERTIES.—

(1) IN GENERAL.—*The supplemental guidelines issued under subsection (a) shall include procedures and requirements for alterations that will threaten or destroy the historic significance of qualified historic buildings and facilities as defined in 4.1.7 (1)(a) of the Uniform Federal Accessibility Standards.*

(2) SITES ELIGIBLE FOR LISTING IN NATIONAL REGISTER.—*With respect to alterations of buildings or facilities that are eligible for listing in the National Register of Historic Places under the National Historic Preservation Act (16 U.S.C. 470 et seq.), the guidelines described in paragraph (1) shall, at a minimum, maintain the procedures and requirements established in 4.1.7 (1) and (2) of the Uniform Federal Accessibility Standards.*

(3) OTHER SITES.—*With respect to alterations of buildings or facilities designated as historic under State or local law, the guidelines described in paragraph (1) shall establish procedures equivalent to those established by 4.1.7(1) (b) and (c) of the Uniform Federal Accessibility Standards, and shall require, at a minimum, compliance with the requirements established in 4.1.7(2) of such standards.*

SEC. 505. ATTORNEY'S FEES.

In any action or administrative proceeding commenced pursuant to this Act, the court or agency, in its discretion, may allow the prevailing party, other than the United States, a reasonable attorney's fee, including litigation expenses, and costs, and the United States shall be liable for the foregoing the same as a private individual.

SEC. 506. TECHNICAL ASSISTANCE.

(a) PLAN FOR ASSISTANCE.—

(1) IN GENERAL.—Not later than 180 days after the date of enactment of this Act, the Attorney General, in consultation with the Chair of the Equal Employment Opportunity Commission, the Secretary of Transportation, the Chair of the Architectural and Transportation Barriers Compliance Board, and the Chairman of the Federal Communications Commission, shall develop a plan to assist entities covered under this Act, and other Federal agencies, in understanding the responsibility of such entities and agencies under this Act.

(2) PUBLICATION OF PLAN.—The Attorney General shall publish the plan referred to in paragraph (1) for public comment in accordance with subchapter II of chapter 5 of title 5, United States Code (commonly known as the Administrative Procedure Act).

(b) AGENCY AND PUBLIC ASSISTANCE.—The Attorney General may obtain the assistance of other Federal agencies in carrying out subsection (a), including the National Council on Disability, the President's Committee on Employment of People with Disabilities, the Small Business Administration, and the Department of Commerce.

(c) IMPLEMENTATION.—

(1) RENDERING ASSISTANCE.—Each Federal agency that has responsibility under paragraph (2) for implementing this Act may render technical assistance to individuals and institutions that have rights or duties under the respective title or titles for which such agency has responsibility.

(2) IMPLEMENTATION OF TITLES.—

(A) TITLE I.—The Equal Employment Opportunity Commission and the Attorney General shall implement the plan for assistance developed under subsection (a), for title I.

(B) TITLE II.—

(i) SUBTITLE A.—The Attorney General shall implement such plan for assistance for subtitle A of title II.

(ii) SUBTITLE B.—The Secretary of Transportation shall implement such plan for assistance for subtitle B of title II.

(C) TITLE III.—The Attorney General, in coordination with the Secretary of Transportation and the Chair of the Architectural Transportation Barriers Compliance Board, shall implement such plan for assistance for title III, except for section 304, the plan for assistance for which shall be implemented by the Secretary of Transportation.

(D) TITLE IV.—The Chairman of the Federal Communications Commission, in coordination with the Attorney General, shall implement such plan for assistance for title IV.

(3) TECHNICAL ASSISTANCE MANUALS.—*Each Federal agency that has responsibility under paragraph (2) for implementing this Act shall, as part of its implementation responsibilities, ensure the availability and provision of appropriate technical assistance manuals to individuals or entities with rights or duties under this Act no later than six months after applicable final regulations are published under titles I, II, III, and IV.*

(d) GRANTS AND CONTRACTS.—

(1) IN GENERAL.—*Each Federal agency that has responsibility under subsection (c)(2) for implementing this Act may make grants or award contracts to effectuate the purposes of this section, subject to the availability of appropriations. Such grants and contracts may be awarded to individuals, institutions not organized for profit and no part of the net earnings of which inures to the benefit of any private shareholder or individual (including educational institutions), and associations representing individuals who have rights or duties under this Act. Contracts may be awarded to entities organized for profit, but such entities may not be the recipients or grants described in this paragraph.*

(2) DISSEMINATION OF INFORMATION.—*Such grants and contracts, among other uses, may be designed to ensure wide dissemination of information about the rights and duties established by this Act and to provide information and technical assistance about techniques for effective compliance with this Act.*

(e) FAILURE TO RECEIVE ASSISTANCE.—*An employer, public accommodation, or other entity covered under this Act shall not be excused from compliance with the requirements of this Act because of any failure to receive technical assistance under this section, including any failure in the development or dissemination of any technical assistance manual authorized by this section.*

SEC. 507. FEDERAL WILDERNESS AREAS.

(a) STUDY.—*The National Council on Disability shall conduct a study and report on the effect that wilderness designations and wilderness land management practices have on the ability of individuals with disabilities to use and enjoy the National Wilderness Preservation System as established under the Wilderness Act (16 U.S.C. 1131 et seq.).*

(b) SUBMISSION OF REPORT.—*Not later than 1 year after the enactment of this Act, the National Council on Disability shall submit the report required under subsection (a) to Congress.*

(c) SPECIFIC WILDERNESS ACCESS.—

(1) IN GENERAL.—*Congress reaffirms that nothing in the Wilderness Act is to be construed as prohibiting the use of a wheelchair in a wilderness area by an individual whose disability requires use of a wheelchair, and consistent with the Wilderness Act no agency is required to provide any form of special treatment or accommodation, or to construct any facilities or modify any conditions of lands within a wilderness area in order to facilitate such use.*

(2) DEFINITION.—*For purposes of paragraph (1), the term "wheelchair" means a device designed solely for use by a mobil-*

ity-impaired person for locomotion, that is suitable for use in an indoor pedestrian area.

SEC. 508. TRANSVESTITES.

For the purposes of this Act, the term "disabled" or "disability" shall not apply to an individual solely because that individual is a transvestite.

SEC. 509. COVERAGE OF CONGRESS AND THE AGENCIES OF THE LEGISLA-TIVE BRANCH.

(a) COVERAGE OF THE SENATE.—

(1) COMMITMENT TO RULE XLII.—The Senate reaffirms its commitment to Rule XLII of the Standing Rules of the Senate which provides as follows:

"No member, officer, or employee of the Senate shall, with respect to employment by the Senate or any office thereof—

"(a) fail or refuse to hire an individual;

"(b) discharge an individual; or

"(c) otherwise discriminate against an individual with respect to promotion, compensation, or terms, conditions, or privileges of employment

on the basis of such individual's race, color, religion, sex, national origin, age, or state of physical handicap.".

(2) APPLICATION TO SENATE EMPLOYMENT.—The rights and protections provided pursuant to this Act, the Civil Rights Act of 1990 (S. 2104, 101st Congress), the Civil Rights Act of 1964, the Age Discrimination in Employment Act of 1967, and the Rehabilitation Act of 1973 shall apply with respect to employment by the United States Senate.

(3) INVESTIGATION AND ADJUDICATION OF CLAIMS.—All claims raised by any individual with respect to Senate employment, pursuant to the Acts referred to in paragraph (2), shall be investigated and adjudicated by the Select Committee on Ethics, pursuant to S. Res. 338, 88th Congress, as amended, or such other entity as the Senate may designate.

(4) RIGHTS OF EMPLOYEES.—The Committee on Rules and Administration shall ensure that Senate employees are informed of their rights under the Acts referred to in paragraph (2).

(5) APPLICABLE REMEDIES.—When assigning remedies to individuals found to have a valid claim under the Acts referred to in paragraph (2), the Select Committee on Ethics, or such other entity as the Senate may designate, should to the extent practicable apply the same remedies applicable to all other employees covered by the Acts referred to in paragraph (2). Such remedies shall apply exclusively.

(6) MATTERS OTHER THAN EMPLOYMENT.—

(A) IN GENERAL.—The rights and protections under this Act shall, subject to subparagraph (B), apply with respect to the conduct of the Senate regarding matters other than employment.

(B) REMEDIES.—The Architect of the Capitol shall establish remedies and procedures to be utilized with respect to the rights and protections provided pursuant to subparagraph (A). Such remedies and procedures shall apply exclusively, after approval in accordance with subparagraph (C).

(C) PROPOSED REMEDIES AND PROCEDURES.—For purposes of subparagraph (B), the Architect of the Capitol shall submit proposed remedies and procedures to the Senate Committee on Rules and Administration. The remedies and procedures shall be effective upon the approval of the Committee on Rules and Administration.

(7) EXERCISE OF RULEMAKING POWER.—Notwithstanding any other provision of law, enforcement and adjudication of the rights and protections referred to in paragraphs (2) and (6)(A) shall be within the exclusive jurisdiction of the United States Senate. The provisions of paragraphs (1), (3), (4), (5), (6)(B), and (6)(C) are enacted by the Senate as an exercise of the rulemaking power of the Senate, with full recognition of the right of the Senate to change its rules, in the same manner, and to the same extent, as in the case of any other rule of the Senate.

(b) COVERAGE OF THE HOUSE OF REPRESENTATIVES.—

(1) IN GENERAL.—Notwithstanding any other provision of this Act or of law, the purposes of this Act shall, subject to paragraphs (2) and (3), apply in their entirety to the House of Representatives.

(2) EMPLOYMENT IN THE HOUSE.—

(A) APPLICATION.—The rights and protections under this Act shall, subject to subparagraph (B), apply with respect to any employee in an employment position in the House of Representatives and any employing authority of the House of Representatives.

(B) ADMINISTRATION.—

(i) IN GENERAL.—In the administration of this paragraph, the remedies and procedures made applicable pursuant to the resolution described in clause (ii) shall apply exclusively.

(ii) RESOLUTION.—The resolution referred to in clause (i) is House Resolution 15 of the One Hundredth First Congress, as agreed to January 3, 1989, or any other provision that continues in effect the provisions of, or is a successor to, the Fair Employment Practices Resolution (House Resolution 558 of the One Hundredth Congress, as agreed to October 4, 1988).

(C) EXERCISE OF RULEMAKING POWER.—The provisions of subparagraph (B) are enacted by the House of Representatives as an exercise of the rulemaking power of the House of Representatives, with full recognition of the right of the House to change its rules, in the same manner, and to the same extent as in the case of any other rule of the House.

(3) MATTERS OTHER THAN EMPLOYMENT.—

(A) IN GENERAL.—The rights and protections under this Act shall, subject to subparagraph (B), apply with respect to the conduct of the House of Representatives regarding matters other than employment.

(B) REMEDIES.—The Architect of the Capitol shall establish remedies and procedures to be utilized with respect to the rights and protections provided pursuant to subparagraph (A). Such remedies and procedures shall apply exclusively, after approval in accordance with subparagraph (C).

(C) APPROVAL.—For purposes of subparagraph (B), the Architect of the Capitol shall submit proposed remedies and procedures to the Speaker of the House of Representatives. The remedies and procedures shall be effective upon the approval of the Speaker, after consultation with the House Office Building Commission.

(c) INSTRUMENTALITIES OF CONGRESS.—

(1) IN GENERAL.—The rights and protections under this Act shall, subject to paragraph (2), apply with respect to the conduct of each instrumentality of the Congress.

(2) ESTABLISHMENT OF REMEDIES AND PROCEDURES BY INSTRUMENTALITIES.—The chief official of each instrumentality of the Congress shall establish remedies and procedures to be utilized with respect to the rights and protections provided pursuant to paragraph (1). Such remedies and procedures shall apply exclusively.

(3) REPORT TO CONGRESS.—The chief official of each instrumentality of the Congress shall, after establishing remedies and procedures for purposes of paragraph (2), submit to the Congress a report describing the remedies and procedures.

(4) DEFINITION OF INSTRUMENTALITIES.—For purposes of this section, instrumentalities of the Congress include the following: the Architect of the Capitol, the Congressional Budget Office, the General Accounting Office, the Government Printing Office, the Library of Congress, the Office of Technology Assessment, and the United States Botanic Garden.

(5) CONSTRUCTION.—Nothing in this section shall alter the enforcement procedures for individuals with disabilities provided in the General Accounting Office Personnel Act of 1980 and regulations promulgated pursuant to that Act.

SEC. 510. ILLEGAL USE OF DRUGS.

(a) IN GENERAL.—For purposes of this Act, the term "individual with a disability" does not include an individual who is currently engaging in the illegal use of drugs, when the covered entity acts on the basis of such use.

(b) RULES OF CONSTRUCTION.—Nothing in subsection (a) shall be construed to exclude as an individual with a disability an individual who—

(1) has successfully completed a supervised drug rehabilitation program and is no longer engaging in the illegal use of drugs, or has otherwise been rehabilitated successfully and is no longer engaging in such use;

(2) is participating in a supervised rehabilitation program and is no longer engaging in such use; or

(3) is erroneously regarded as engaging in such use, but is not engaging in such use;

except that it shall not be a violation of this Act for a covered entity to adopt or administer reasonable policies or procedures, including but not limited to drug testing, designed to ensure that an individual described in paragraph (1) or (2) is no longer engaging in the illegal use of drugs; however, nothing in this section shall be construed to encourage, prohibit, restrict, or authorize the conducting of testing for the illegal use of drugs.

(c) HEALTH AND OTHER SERVICES.—Notwithstanding subsection (a) and section 511(b)(3), an individual shall not be denied health services, or services provided in connection with drug rehabilitation, on the basis of the current illegal use of drugs if the individual is otherwise entitled to such services.

(d) DEFINITION OF ILLEGAL USE OF DRUGS.—

(1) IN GENERAL.—The term "illegal use of drugs" means the use of drugs, the possession or distribution of which is unlawful under the Controlled Substances Act (21 U.S.C. 812). Such term does not include the use of a drug taken under supervision by a licensed health care professional, or other uses authorized by the Controlled Substances Act or other provisions of Federal law.

(2) DRUGS.—The term "drug" means a controlled substance, as defined in schedules I through V of section 202 of the Controlled Substances Act.

SEC. 511. DEFINITIONS.

(a) HOMOSEXUALITY AND BISEXUALITY.—For purposes of the definition of "disability" in section 3(2), homosexuality and bisexuality are not impairments and as such are not disabilities under this Act.

(b) CERTAIN CONDITIONS.—Under this Act, the term "disability" shall not include—

(1) transvestism, transsexualism, pedophilia, exhibitionism, voyeurism, gender identity disorders not resulting from physical impairments, or other sexual behavior disorders;

(2) compulsive gambling, kleptomania, or pyromania; or

(3) psychoactive substance use disorders resulting from current illegal use of drugs.

SEC. 512. AMENDMENTS TO THE REHABILITATION ACT.

(a) DEFINITION OF HANDICAPPED INDIVIDUAL.—Section 7(8) of the Rehabilitation Act of 1973 (29 U.S.C. 706(8)) is amended by redesignating subparagraph (C) as subparagraph (D), and by inserting after subparagraph (B) the following subparagraph:

"(C)(i) For purposes of title V, the term 'individual with handicaps' does not include an individual who is currently engaging in the illegal use of drugs, when a covered entity acts on the basis of such use.

"(ii) Nothing in clause (i) shall be construed to exclude as an individual with handicaps an individual who—

"(I) has successfully completed a supervised drug rehabilitation program and is no longer engaging in the illegal use of drugs, or has otherwise been rehabilitated successfully and is no longer engaging in such use;

"(II) is participating in a supervised rehabilitation program and is no longer engaging in such use; or

"(III) is erroneously regarded as engaging in such use, but is not engaging in such use;

except that it shall not be a violation of this Act for a covered entity to adopt or administer reasonable policies or procedures, including but not limited to drug testing, designed to ensure that an individual described in subclause (I) or (II) is no longer engaging in the illegal use of drugs.

"(iii) Notwithstanding clause (i), for purposes of programs and activities providing health services and services provided under titles I, II, and III, an individual shall not be excluded from the benefits of such programs or activities on the basis of his or her current illegal use of drugs if he or she is otherwise entitled to such services.

"(iv) For purposes of programs and activities providing educational services, local educational agencies may take disciplinary action pertaining to the use or possession of illegal drugs or alcohol against any handicapped student who currently is engaging in the illegal use of drugs or in the use of alcohol to the same extent that such disciplinary action is taken against nonhandicapped students. Furthermore, the due process procedures at 34 CFR 104.36 shall not apply to such disciplinary actions.

"(v) For purposes of sections 503 and 504 as such sections relate to employment, the term 'individual with handicaps' does not include any individual who is an alcoholic whose current use of alcohol prevents such individual from performing the duties of the job in question or whose employment, by reason of such current alcohol abuse, would constitute a direct threat to property or the safety of others.".

(b) DEFINITION OF ILLEGAL DRUGS.—Section 7 of the Rehabilitation Act of 1973 (29 U.S.C. 706) is amended by adding at the end the following new paragraph:

"(22)(A) The term 'drug' means a controlled substance, as defined in schedules I through V of section 202 of the Controlled Substances Act (21 U.S.C. 812).

"(B) The term 'illegal use of drugs' means the use of drugs, the possession or distribution of which is unlawful under the Controlled Substances Act. Such term does not include the use of a drug taken under supervision by a licensed health care professional, or other uses authorized by the Controlled Substances Act or other provisions of Federal law.".

(c) CONFORMING AMENDMENTS.—Section 7(8)(B) of the Rehabilitation Act of 1973 (29 U.S.C. 706(8)(B)) is amended—

(1) in the first sentence, by striking "Subject to the second sentence of this subparagraph," and inserting "Subject to subparagraphs (C) and (D),"; and

(2) by striking the second sentence.

SEC. 513. ALTERNATIVE MEANS OF DISPUTE RESOLUTION.

Where appropriate and to the extent authorized by law, the use of alternative means of dispute resolution, including settlement negotiations, conciliation, facilitation, mediation, factfinding, minitrials, and arbitration, is encouraged to resolve disputes arising under this Act.

SEC. 514. SEVERABILITY.

Should any provision in this Act be found to be unconstitutional by a court of law, such provision shall be severed from the remainder of the Act, and such action shall not affect the enforceability of the remaining provisions of the Act.

And the House agree to the same.

Index

About the Authors

JON D. BIBLE is Assistant Professor of Business Law at Southwest Texas State University. Prior to that he was Assistant
Attorney General of Texas.

DARIEN A. MCWHIRTER is general counsel at the National
Center for Employee Ownership in Oakland, CA. He has taught
public management at Miami University of Ohio and Southwest Texas State University.